By the Editors of Consumer Guide

Food Processor BREAD Book

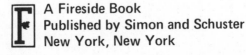

A Fireside Book
Published by Simon and Schuster
New York, New York

CONTENTS

White Bread • Cinnamon Swirl Loaf • Refrigerator White Bread • Butter Crust Bread • Old-Fashioned Oatmeal Bread • Sesame Oat Bread • Refrigerator Molasses Oat Bread • Old-Fashioned Cinnamon Braid • Old-Fashioned Cinnamon Raisin Braid • Buttermilk Bread • Poppy Seed Braid • Whole Wheat Bread • Old-Fashioned 100% Whole Wheat Bread • Rosemary Whole Wheat Bread • Honey Wheat Bread • Three Wheat Bread • Cracked Wheat Bread • Cornmeal Bread • Farmer-Style Sour Cream Bread • Modern Potato Bread • Egg Braid • Refrigerator Egg Braid • Raisin Bread • Poppy Seed Pull-Apart Loaf • Crusty Rye Bread • Golden Honey Braid • Italian Rosemary Bread • Cheddar Anadama Bread • Pioneer Bread • Cottage Cheese Dill Bread • Whole Wheat Zucchini Yeast Bread • Old-Fashioned Hearth Bread • Mini Herb Breads • Three Colored Party Braid

Light Rye Rolls • Light Rye Bread • Raised Buttermilk Biscuits • Saffron Raisin Buns • Parkerhouse Rolls • Herbed Cloverleaf Rolls • Italian Pan Rolls • Easy Croissants • Whole Grain Caraway Onion Buns • Hamburger Buns • Hot Dog Buns • Onion Rolls • Rye Pull-Apart Rolls • Wheat Germ Pan Rolls • Cottage Cheese Pan Rolls • Crusty Water Rolls • Bolillos • Buttery Pan Rolls • Whole Wheat Sesame Burger Buns

Basic Sweet Dough • Refrigerator Sweet Dough • Danish Coffee Pretzel • Orange Sugar Twists • Cinnamon Breakfast Braid • Poppy Seed Coffee Bread • Cinnamon Doughnut Twists • Fried Cinnamon Puffs • Caramel Sticky Buns • Cardamom Buns • Kolaches • Pulla • Date Tea Ring • Lemon Raisin Bread • Cream Dream Rolls • Sunday Breakfast Rolls • Brown Sugar Sticky Rolls • Cinnamon Rolls • Kuchen • Elephant Ears • Sweet Egg Braid

A Fireside Book
Published by Simon and Schuster
A Division of Gulf + Western Corporation
New York, New York 10020

Manufactured in the United States of America
1 2 3 4 5 6 7 8 9 10

Library of Congress Catalog Card Number: 80-65634
ISBN 0-671-25201-1
ISBN 0-671-25138-4 pbk.

Author: Beatrice Ojakangas
Recipe Testing: Gail Klatt
Food Styling for Photography: Gail Klatt
Cover and Color Photography: Dave Jordano Photography Inc.
Cover and Book Design: Frank Peiler

About the author: Beatrice Ojakangas is the author of several cookbooks including *The Finnish Cookbook, Gourmet Cooking for Two* and *Complete Fondue Menu and Party Book* and a frequent contributor to various women's interest magazines. She specializes in recipe development and teaches cooking classes, when time permits, in her rural Minnesota home.

CONTENTS

INTRODUCTION

Savoring the warm, rich aroma of homemade bread fresh from the oven has to be one of life's finer experiences. The yeasty fragrance of spicy cinnamon rolls, buttery croissants, chewy French bread, or a hearty round of rye can tempt even the crustiest appetite. Many people miss out on this unparalleled sensation because they have never ventured into the kitchen to attempt what is really a simple operation—making bread from scratch. Some may fear they can't unlock the secret of mixing and kneading a few ingredients into a successful dough. Others think they are too busy to take the time to do home bread-baking.

Actually, both of these viewpoints are unfounded. First, there is nothing mysterious or difficult about bread-making. It is one culinary accomplishment easily within the grasp of anyone, whether an experienced or novice cook. Second, the amount of time needed to make bread is minimal, thanks to one of the handiest kitchen helpers yet—the food processor. Imagine mixing the dough for an old-fashioned white bread in less than 5 minutes, a batch of flaky French croissants in about 3 minutes, fresh cinnamon-spiced breakfast rolls in 2½ minutes, or a sweet holiday braid in less than 2 minutes. All that and much more is possible when you turn the mixing and kneading tasks over to your food processor. This little electric workhorse can open the door to a world of bread-baking that our ancestors never dreamed possible.

The art of bread-making has come a long way since its beginnings in ancient Egypt. The first bread dough was simply pounded grain that was mixed with a little water; it was then pressed into cakes and dried in the sun. Later, one of our crafty ancestors discovered that bread could be baked in an oven. Next, people found that dough could be leavened and thus originated sourdoughs. Through the centuries, advancements were made in the milling of grain, development of leavening agents, mixing of doughs, baking of bread and storage of the finished loaves. All of this eventually led to mass production of the white bread that is so typically a part of life and eating in this country. Old-fashioned home bread-baking seemed doomed.

However, during the past two decades, there has been a resurgence of interest in the older, more basic methods of doing and making things. One reflection of this trend is the current enthusiasm for making breads at home. There are a variety of reasons why people favor homemade bread. Many are concerned about the freshness and wholesomeness of foods and have decided they can make bread that is better than many of the commercial varieties. They prefer bread prepared from natural ingredients without artificial flavorings and preservatives. Some home bakers want to increase natural fiber in their diets and incorporate whole grains into their breads. Others have developed an interest in bread-baking as a means of returning to a simpler, more independent life style. For some, bread-making is an expression of creativity. For others, it is a labor of love, a way of showing family and friends they care enough to do something special for them.

Whatever your reasons for baking bread, you'll find an abundance of tantalizing recipes in this book. A myriad of delectable breads are awaiting you: basic loaf breads, sweet rolls, dinner rolls, coffee cakes, holiday favorites, ethnic treasures, fun and novelty breads, sourdough standbys and a collection of quick breads. Every one of them can be prepared easily and quickly with your food processor.

Note: Before you select the tempting loaf that will star at tonight's dinner table or the luscious coffee cake for tomorrow's breakfast, take time to read **Food Processor Techniques** and **The Inside Story: Ingredients** on the next few pages. Becoming familiar with this information will save you time, make bread-making easier, and clear up any confusion or questions you might have about doughs and how to process them. Also take special note of **Solving Problems**. Detailed there are specific problems that might arise in the bread-making process, what may have caused them and what you can do to correct them.

Before you begin mixing any doughs, we strongly advise that you read the use and care manual that accompanied your food processor. Be sure you clearly understand what the manufacturer instructs regarding processing dough in your machine. There may be some special precautions of which you should be aware, or perhaps one or two steps in the method of making dough that differ slightly from the procedures we have included in this book.

When mixing and kneading bread doughs, some processors work better than others. Generally, those with strong, direct-drive motors are a bit more efficient at handling doughs than are the belt-driven machines that may have smaller motors. The recipes in this book have been tested with different food processors, both direct- and belt-drive. In most cases, the techniques we use work efficiently in both types of machine. As much as possible, we have tried to standardize the techniques so any processor can handle the recipes with relatively few problems.

At least one manufacturer is now marketing a larger capacity food processor that can handle 6-cup (1.5 L) batches of flour. If desired, any recipe in this book may be doubled for use in that processor.

FOOD PROCESSOR TECHNIQUES

Mixing Methods

Several methods of preparing bread are presented in this book. *Yeast doughs* that are smooth, pliable and hold their shape are prepared primarily in two different ways:

• *Liquid Sponge Method:* Dry yeast is dissolved in part of the warm liquid—usually ¼ cup (60 mL) of water. The temperature of the liquid should be 105° to 115°F. (41° to 46°C.). The yeast mixture is then added to the dry ingredients in the food processor's work bowl. While the machine is running, the remaining liquids are slowly drizzled through the feed tube into the dough forming in the work bowl.

• *Dry Mix Method:* Dry yeast is mixed with part of the flour and with other dry ingredients in the work bowl. Warm liquid at a temperature of 120° to 130°F. (49° to 54°C.) is then added. The remaining flour is gradually added through the feed tube while the machine is processing the dough.

Each method is effective in producing a dough that is soft, smooth and satiny but not sticky. When making dough with the food processor, it is important to avoid the formation of a sticky dough. That can be a particular problem with a less powerful food processor because sticky dough will slow down the revolving blade and strain the motor. A machine with automatic braking (a circuit breaker) will stop running completely. For a discussion of this and other less serious problems you might encounter, along with suggested solutions, see **Solving Problems**.

Yeast batter breads, also called casserole breads, are ideally suited to any food processor. Like their yeast dough counterparts, they can be prepared using either the Liquid Sponge Method or the Dry Mix Method. Both produce a batter that is smooth and thick.

Quick breads are a snap to prepare in the food processor. Anything from muffins and biscuits to popovers, scones or loaf breads can be mixed literally in seconds. The main precaution here is to avoid overprocessing the batter or dough. Most are completely processed with just a few on/off bursts of power.

Proofing the Dough or Letting It Rise

Quick breads do not need proofing, but yeast breads do. Proofing allows the yeast to ferment, thus producing the gas that leavens the bread and makes it light. The optimal temperature for proofing is about 85°F. (30°C.). There are several easy ways to provide a place at this temperature:

• If you have a gas range with a pilot light, set the dough inside the unheated oven.

• If you have a range without a pilot light, place the dough in the unheated oven with a large pan of hot tap water beneath it.

• If you have an electric range, turn the heat to

200°F. (94°C.) for 1 to 2 minutes. Then turn off the heat and set the dough inside the oven.

• Place a wire rack over a large pan or bowl that is half-filled with hot tap water. Set the dough on the rack, and cover the dough and pan with a towel.

• Set the dough on top of a radiator or near (not on) a range in which the oven is heated.

Recipes usually specify to let dough stand in a warm place until doubled. To test dough, dent it with one or two fingers or the handle of a wooden spoon. If the indentation remains, the dough has doubled. If the indentation fills in, the dough is not yet ready. This test does not work with a yeast batter because it cannot be dented. For a batter, lightness must be judged entirely by an increase in volume.

After a dough is shaped, it generally has a second rising time. To determine if it has risen sufficiently, lightly press the side of the bread (or some other spot that will not be conspicuous after baking) with one finger. If the fingerprint remains, the dough has doubled.

Two rising periods are desirable to give bread a fine, even texture, good volume and an attractive shape. Some recipes specify only one rising period. In that case, expect the bread to have a slightly coarse, but still acceptable texture. If a finer texture is desired, you may let the dough rise twice (once after processing and again after shaping).

Sometimes a dough can partially rise in the refrigerator. In this method, a dough is usually shaped, wrapped tightly in plastic and refrigerated until thoroughly chilled—6 to 24 hours. Before baking, it should stand at room temperature about 30 minutes to give the yeast a chance to reactivate.

Shaping

In most of the recipes in this book, specific directions are given for shaping the bread. In addition, photographs that demonstrate various shaping techniques are presented on pages 16 to 21.

Baking

Each recipe specifies exact baking temperatures required to achieve the best results. To complete baking in the time indicated, the oven must be preheated to the given temperature.

Color of the bread's crust is not always a true indication of doneness. When the baking time has elapsed—this should be measured with an accurate timer—remove the bread from the oven and gently tap it with the handle of a wooden spoon or a knuckle of one finger. If it sounds hollow, you can be sure that it is done.

Cooling

Most of the time bread should be removed from its baking pan as soon as it comes out of the oven. This will prevent the sides and/or bottom of the bread from becoming soggy. Cool the bread on a wire rack. One ex-

ception to the general rule is a quick loaf bread. It should be allowed to cool 15 minutes in its pan before removing it to a wire rack.

THE INSIDE STORY: INGREDIENTS

Yeast

Yeast is the leavening in breads and rolls that makes them rise and gives them a light, airy texture. Yeast is actually a living plant. When combined with moisture and carbohydrates, it converts them into alcohol and carbon dioxide. This process is known as fermentation.

Yeast is available in two forms: active dry and compressed fresh (moist). Dry yeast is packaged in a premeasured, airtight envelope that contains ¼ ounce (7 g) of yeast. This is equal to a scant tablespoon (15 mL) of yeast. Though the yeast is dehydrated, the cells are still alive; they are just dormant. When rehydrated, they become active. Dry yeast need not be refrigerated and will keep for months in a cool, dry place. It should be used before the expiration date stamped on the package.

Compressed yeast is moist, active yeast that is perishable. It must be refrigerated and even then it will keep only one to two weeks. For home use, it is packaged in cakes weighing ⅗ ounce (17 g), 1 ounce (30 g) or 2 ounces (60 g). It is interchangeable with dry yeast: one cake of compressed yeast equals one envelope of dry yeast; one large cake equals two envelopes of dry yeast. (However, we do not recommend using compressed yeast for the recipes in this book because active dry yeast was used in developing and testing these recipes.)

Yeast is heat sensitive because it is a living organism. Too little heat will inhibit its growth, and too much heat will kill it. Compressed yeast is usually combined with the liquid before adding to the dry ingredients. The temperature of the liquids should be about 95°F. (35°C.). Dry yeast can tolerate higher temperatures. In the Liquid Sponge Method, dry yeast is combined with liquid that is warmed to 105° to 115°F. (41° to 46°C.). When rehydrating the yeast by this method, be sure to use a measuring cup or bowl large enough to allow for expansion of the yeast which usually doubles in volume. If the yeast does not bubble and become foamy, dispose of it and start over with other yeast. In the Dry Mix Method, the flour acts as a buffer to the yeast; the liquid should be warmed to 120° to 130°F. (49° to 54°C.). Both methods of rehydrating yeast are used in this book.

Note: In every yeast recipe in this book, the optimal temperature for the liquids is specified. Do not attempt to guess the temperature of the liquid. Measure it with an accurate thermometer. Either a candy or a deep fat thermometer works well.

Some food processors generate a lot of heat when processing dough. If you consistently have trouble with doughs that do not rise or rise unevenly, it may be that your processor is overheating all or a portion of the dough. See **Solving Problems** for suggestions on handling this situation.

Sugar

Sugar is the food that yeast needs to ferment and form the gas that makes bread rise. A small amount of sugar is usually added to the liquid in which the yeast is dissolved to speed up the growth of the yeast. It also adds flavor, increases tenderness, improves crust color and aids in giving bread good grain and texture. Generally, granulated white sugar (sucrose) is used in bread-making. However, for variety in color and flavor, brown sugar, honey or molasses may also be used.

For nonsweet white doughs, the recipes in this book usually call for 1 or 2 tablespoons (15 or 30 mL) of sugar. For richer sweet doughs, about ¼ cup (60 mL) of sugar is used. (A larger quantity of sugar can cause mixing problems in a food processor because it increases the stickiness of the dough. As mentioned earlier, a sticky dough can strain the motor and cause it to slow down or stop completely.)

Flour

Grain that has been milled into flour is the common denominator of all breads, whether they are yeast or quick breads. Almost without exception, the flour used in bread-making is derived from wheat. It is the only grain which contains proteins that form—in the presence of liquid and manipulation (mixing and kneading)—an elastic substance called gluten. Gluten is what provides the cellular structure in breads which holds the trapped gas bubbles produced by the yeast.

Certain varieties of wheat contain more proteins than others. Hard wheat has a high protein level and, therefore, produces a strong gluten network. For this reason, it is better suited for bread-making than is soft wheat, which forms less gluten. Soft-wheat flours are more appropriate for fine textured cakes, biscuits and pastries.

For home bread-making, all-purpose flour is most commonly used. It is a fine flour that is milled from the inner part of the wheat kernel. It does not contain bran (the outer section of the kernel) or germ (the embryo or sprouting section of the kernel). All-purpose flour is usually made from a blend of hard and soft wheats. This makes it suitable for baking a complete range of products in addition to yeast breads, including cakes, cookies, biscuits, muffins and quick loaf breads.

Flour readily absorbs and retains moisture. The amount of moisture in flour depends on atmospheric and storage conditions. When humidity is high—during warm summer months, rain storms, and the like—flour tends to have increased moisture content. Under dry conditions—during cold winter months and in desert environs, for example—flour contains less moisture.

The flour-to-liquid ratio needed to make an acceptable dough that is soft, smooth and satiny but not sticky, may vary from one part of the country to another, from one season of the year to another and from one bread-making session to the next. For this reason, a recipe will give a range in the amount specified for one ingredient. Whether the adjustment is made in the liquid or the flour is determined by the mixing technique. In the Liquid Sponge Method, just enough liquid is used to make the dough the correct consistency. In the Dry Mix Method, the amount of flour is adjusted.

Note: How you measure all-purpose flour is critical in successfully preparing bread doughs with the food processor. For best results, follow this method of measurement: Spoon the flour from the bag or storage container into a dry measuring cup, then level off with a spatula or straight-edged knife. Do not shake, tap, press or pack the flour down into the cup before leveling. For the recipes in this book, it is not necessary to sift the flour.

In addition to all-purpose flour, other flours may be used for bread-making. Whole wheat flour—also called graham flour—is milled from the entire wheat kernel. It has a higher fat content than all-purpose flour because it contains the germ. Therefore, it also tends to spoil more quickly. Whole wheat flour should be purchased in small quantities and stored in the refrigerator in an airtight container. Bread containing whole wheat flour tends to be heavy and dense. Sharp particles of bran in this flour cut into and partially destroy the cell structure. Usually, bread made with whole wheat flour also contains all-purpose flour to provide a better gluten structure, higher volume and a finer texture.

Rye flour is used in rye breads and specialty items, such as Swedish Limpa and German Pumpernickel. Unlike wheat flour, it does not contain gluten. Thus, rye flour cannot form an elastic dough with cell walls that trap and hold the gas from the yeast. It is combined with all-purpose flour to yield a more satisfactory baked product.

Other types of flour are also available. Cake flour and instant blending or "instantized" flour are not recommended for use in any of the recipes in this book. However, self-rising flour may be substituted for all-purpose flour. If so, the salt should be eliminated in any of the yeast leavened bread recipes. In the chemically leavened quick bread recipes, both the salt and the baking powder should be omitted. Generally, self-rising flour contains more soft wheat than hard wheat. It will produce yeast breads of less volume and finer texture than those made with all-purpose flour.

Several millers now are marketing flour designed specifically for bread-making. Called "bread flour" or "high protein flour," it contains more protein than all-purpose flour and is capable of producing a stronger gluten structure. It also absorbs more liquid, necessitating some adjustment of the flour-to-liquid ratio.

Bread flour may be used in any of the recipes in this book. When substituting bread flour, be prepared to use more liquid or less flour than specified in a particular recipe. In the Liquid Sponge Method, more liquid than is indicated in the recipe may be required. In the Dry-Mix Method, less flour than is called for may be required.

INTRODUCTION

Liquid

Water or milk—or a combination of both—are the liquids most commonly used in making bread. In bread recipes for the food processor, any viscous ingredient should be considered as part of the liquid. For example, although they add other qualities to the dough, eggs should be considered a liquid. Many other ingredients, such as fruit juice, canned soup, oil, melted butter, honey, molasses, and even such unlikely items as sour cream and cottage cheese, also may contribute to the liquid content of a recipe.

Yeast breads made with water as the only liquid have a crisp crust and a wheaty flavor. They also tend to get stale rapidly. Breads made with milk have a creamy color, a more velvety texture, a softer, browner crust, and tend to stay fresh longer.

Controversy still exists concerning the necessity of scalding fresh milk for use in bread-making. The only milk that *must* be scalded is raw, unpasteurized milk because it contains an organism that breaks down the gluten structure. Unless you have your own cows and use their milk for baking, it is unlikely that you would have access to raw milk. All milk produced by commercial dairies in the United States has been pasteurized to destroy any harmful bacteria that may have been present in the milk. If you do prefer to scald your pasteurized milk, be sure to cool it to the temperature recommended in the recipe before combining it with the yeast and other ingredients.

Other forms of milk are handy for bread-making. Instant nonfat dry milk solids are particularly convenient because they can be added directly from the package to the flour—reconstituting is not necessary. Undiluted canned, evaporated milk is convenient, too. Both of these types of milk help produce a richer dough. If desired, evaporated milk may be diluted with an equal amount of water; the result will be a liquid similar to fresh milk.

The presence of milk in the dough—whatever its form—helps counteract some of the acidity caused by the fermentation of the yeast. As a result, bread dough made with milk may require slightly longer rising times than dough made solely with water.

Note: The way in which the liquids are added to the dry ingredients is very important when making bread doughs or batters in the food processor. When the liquid is to be added gradually to dry ingredients, it is crucial that it be added as slowly as possible. In the recipes in this book, directions indicate to "very slowly drizzle" in the liquid. This holds true whether the liquid is water, milk, eggs or a mixture of various ingredients. By adding the liquid in this manner, you reduce the chances of producing a dough that is too sticky. Remember the stickier a dough becomes, the greater the possibility of straining the motor of your food processor. (See **Solving Problems** for a detailed discussion of this problem.)

It is also important to remember that the exact amount of liquid required in a specific recipe depends upon the moisture content of the flour. During humid conditions, less liquid may be needed. During dry conditions, more liquid may be needed.

Eggs

Eggs add flavor, color, nutrients and richness to bread. They also contribute to the liquid content. For all recipes in this book, use Grade AA or Grade A "Large" eggs. One "Large" egg will account for ¼ cup (60 mL) liquid. "Medium" eggs will not add enough liquid; "Extra Large" or "Jumbo" eggs will add too much liquid.

Most of the recipes in this book were developed and tested using eggs directly from the refrigerator. If a recipe requires eggs to be at room temperature, specific instructions are given.

Fat

Fat or shortening lubricates the gluten strands in bread. This promotes elasticity of the strands and prevents them from becoming long and tough. Fat also adds flavor, increases tenderness and helps keep bread moist. Its effect is more noticeable in quick breads, such as muffins and biscuits, where it is used in larger proportions than in yeast breads.

Although most types of shortening are acceptable for making bread, each recipe in this book specifies the particular fat to be used. Most recipes also indicate whether it should be cold, cut into pieces, at room temperature, melted and cooled, or the like. Where this type of direction is not given—as in a recipe where the amount of fat is small—you can assume that the temperature of the fat or whether it is cut up is not crucial.

Salt

Salt adds flavor to bread and controls the yeast growth. Generally, ¼ to ½ teaspoon (1 to 2 mL) of salt is used for each cup of flour.

Nuts, Fruits, Herbs and Spices

Nuts and fruits add flavor and texture to bread. They should be kneaded into the dough after processing, unless the recipe directs otherwise. Herbs and spices are used for flavoring and, in most cases, are mixed into the dry ingredients before the liquid is added.

GALLERY OF TECHNIQUES

The comprehensive section of photographed techniques that follows deserves your careful scrutiny. It shows you step-by-step how to prepare yeast doughs, yeast batter breads and several different quick breads. It also illustrates how dough is proofed, what it should look like, how to shape bread in assorted ways, plus many other tips for making breads. This pictorial section will aid you in perfecting your bread-making skills with the food processor.

Mixing—Liquid Sponge Method:

Dissolve the dry yeast in part of the liquid, usually ¼ cup (60 mL) water. To activate yeast properly, the water must be between 105° and 115°F. (41° to 46°C.).

Add a small amount of sugar or other sweetener to yeast-water mixture and let stand until bubbly and foamy, about 5 minutes. If yeast doesn't bubble, discard and start over with new yeast.

To successfully prepare the recipes in this book, the flour must be measured properly. Spoon it from bowl, bag or cannister into a metal measure . . .

Then level it off with a metal spatula or straight-edged knife.

Fit processor with steel blade; then measure dry ingredients and butter (cut into pieces) into work bowl.

Process the dry ingredients until mixed, about 15 seconds. Mixture should look like coarse crumbs.

Add the foamy yeast mixture to the dry ingredients.

Process until the yeast-flour mixture is blended, about 10 seconds.

To help prevent formation of a sticky dough, drizzle the remaining liquid (whether it's water, milk or a combination) very slowly into the flour-yeast mixture while the processor is running.

If the recipe calls for beaten egg, it also should be drizzled very slowly into flour-yeast mixture while processor is running.

Add enough liquid to dough so it forms a ball that cleans sides of bowl; process so ball turns around bowl about 25 times. Let stand 1 to 2 minutes for flour to absorb the liquid (dough will be slightly sticky).

Turn on processor and very slowly drizzle in more liquid to make dough soft, smooth and satiny but not sticky. Process until ball turns around bowl about 15 times.

Mixing—Dry Mix Method:

Combine liquids in small saucepan. Heat just until 120° to 130°F. (49° to 54°C.).

Fit processor with steel blade. Add part of the flour, other dry ingredients and dry yeast to work bowl. Process on/off a few times to mix.

Add liquid mixture to flour mixture.

Process until smooth, about 20 seconds.

Turn on processor and add enough remaining flour through feed tube so dough forms a ball that cleans the sides of the bowl.

Process until ball turns around bowl about 25 times. Dough should be soft, smooth and satiny but not sticky.

GALLERY OF TECHNIQUES

Problem Doughs:

If too much water or too little flour has been added, dough will be very soft and sticky. It will probably cause processor to sound strained, slow down or stop completely.

If dough is too sticky, turn off processor and let stand 5 minutes. Scrape sides of work bowl with rubber spatula and pull dough up over center post. Sprinkle with 1 or 2 tablespoons (15 or 30 mL) of flour. Turn on processor. If dough is still too sticky, repeat.

If too little liquid or too much flour is added, dough will become dry and hard.

To correct dry dough, cut it into quarters; then sprinkle 1 tablespoon (15 mL) water over dough. Turn on processor and add more water very gradually, if necessary, to make dough soft, smooth and pliable.

If liquid is not evenly blended into dough, a hard ball or "topknot" of dry dough may form around top of center post. Dough in bottom of work bowl will be soft and moist around edges.

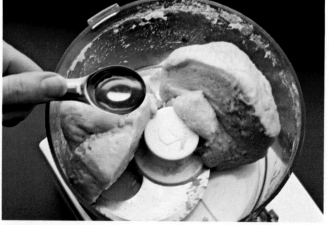

To correct topknot, scrape sides of work bowl and steel blade. Cut topknot in half and place it upside down in work bowl. Process, gradually adding 1 to 3 teaspoons (5 to 15 mL) water if necessary to form dough that is soft, smooth and satiny.

Proofing The Dough (Letting It Rise):

If the dough contains 2 tablespoons (30 mL) or more fat, after processing turn dough onto a lightly floured surface and shape it into a smooth ball (knead slightly by hand, if necessary).

If the dough contains less than 2 tablespoons (30 mL) fat, turn it onto lightly greased surface and shape it into a smooth ball.

Dough should be smooth and satiny with tiny bubbles barely visible below the surface.

If recipe calls for nuts and/or raisins, they are generally kneaded by hand into the dough before it rises.

Place dough in lightly greased bowl and turn dough to grease all sides.

Cover loosely with plastic wrap.

GALLERY OF TECHNIQUES

Proofing The Dough (Letting It Rise): (continued)

The optimal temperature for proofing is 85°F. (30°C.). If you have a gas range with a pilot light, the inside of the oven will be about that temperature.

If you have a range without a pilot light, place a large pan of hot tap water on the lowest rack of the oven; then place dough on rack above it.

If you have an electric range, turn the heat to 200°F. (94°C.) for 1 to 2 minutes. Then turn off the heat and set dough inside the oven.

If desired, a wire cooling rack may be placed on top of a pan or dish of hot tap water; then set the dough on the rack. Cover dough, rack and pan of water with a towel.

Dough may be left in processor work bowl to rise at room temperature if desired. This usually takes longer because room temperature is cooler than 85°F. (30°C.).

If letting dough stand in work bowl, be sure to cover dough with the top of work bowl and insert pusher in feed tube.

Proofing The Dough (Letting It Rise): *(continued)*

Dough is usually allowed to proof until it has doubled in volume. This can be judged visually, but the standard test is to insert two fingers into dough.

If the indentations remain, the dough has doubled.

If the indentations fill in, the dough is not ready yet.

If desired, you may test for doneness by poking the handle of a wooden spoon into dough instead of fingers.

When dough has doubled, it should be "punched down" lightly with a fist in the center of the dough.

Gently pull the outer edges of dough toward the center.

GALLERY OF TECHNIQUES

Shaping—Loaf:

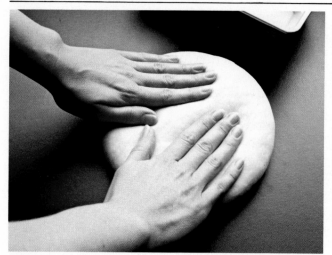

After punching down dough, flatten the dough with hands.

Roll dough evenly into rectangle wide enough to fit a loaf pan.

Roll up dough tightly jelly-roll fashion.

Pinch seam and ends of dough with fingers to seal well.

Dough also may be shaped into a loaf by shaping the ball of proofed dough into a smooth oval; then gently pulling top surface to underside.

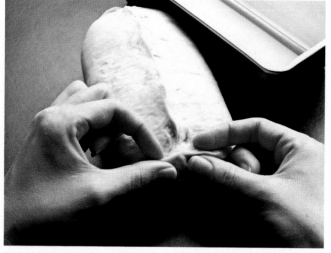

Turn dough over and pinch seam and ends with fingers to seal well.

Shaping — Loaf: (continued)

Fit shaped loaf into greased loaf pan.

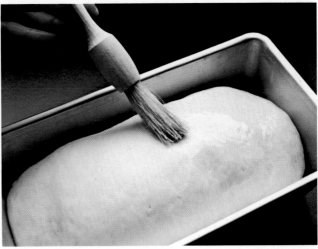

To prevent dough from drying out, brush top surface with vegetable oil or melted butter . . .

Or cover loaf loosely with plastic wrap.

Shaping—Round Bread:

Shape proofed dough into a smooth round ball and place on a greased cookie sheet.

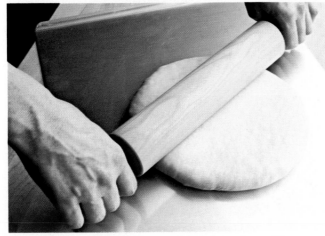

Dough may be flattened into desired size by rolling evenly with a rolling pin . . .

Or patting evenly with hands.

GALLERY OF TECHNIQUES

Shaping—Braid:

Shape proofed dough into a smooth oval. Cut into 3 equal parts.

Shape each part into a strand (see selected recipe for specific length) by rolling dough gently between palms of hands and work surface.

Braid strands by gently overlapping as illustrated.

Braid strands by gently overlapping as illustrated.

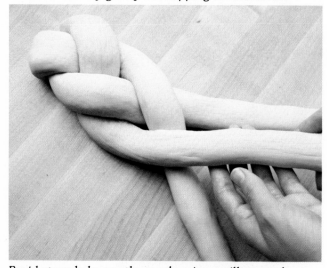

Braid strands by gently overlapping as illustrated.

Place braid on greased cookie sheet, tuck ends under and pinch to seal. (If baking braid in loaf pan, tuck ends under before fitting into pan.)

Shaping—French Bread (recipes on pages 87, 138 and 139):

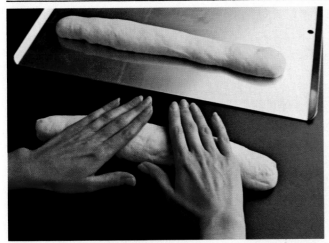

Shape proofed dough into one or two strands by gently rolling dough between palms of hands and work surface. Place on greased cookie sheet.

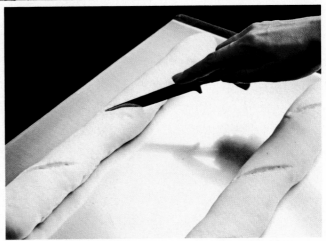

Make parallel cuts diagonally in top of bread using a sharp knife or a razor blade.

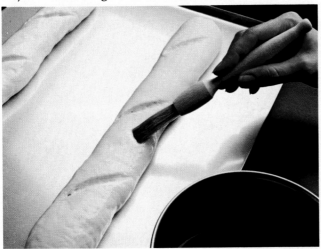

Brush loaf with water (or a water-cornstarch mixture) for a crisper crust.

Shaping—Croissants (recipe on page 50):
Divide chilled Croissant dough into quarters. Roll each quarter into a circle 17 inches (43 cm) in diameter on a lightly floured surface. Cut into wedges.

Roll up each wedge beginning at wide edge and rolling towards point.

Place dough on ungreased cookie sheet and gently curve ends to form a crescent shape.

Shaping—Rolls and Buns:

Parkerhouse Rolls (recipe on page 48): Cut dough with 3-inch (8 cm) round cutter. Make a crease just off center of each round and fold larger side over. Pinch center of edges slightly to seal.

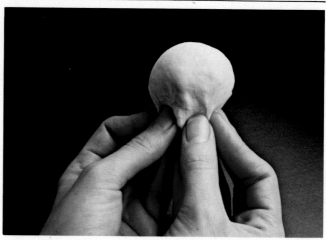

Crusty Water Rolls (recipe on page 54): Divide dough into 9 equal pieces. Shape each piece into a smooth ball by gently pulling top surface to underside. Pinch bottom to seal.

Hamburger Buns (recipe on page 51): Divide dough into 12 equal parts. Shape each into a smooth ball and place on greased cookie sheet. Flatten balls with hand.

Wheat Germ Pan Rolls (recipe on pages 52 and 53): Divide dough into 16 equal parts. Shape each part into a smooth ball and place in greased cake pan.

Cloverleaf Rolls (recipe on pages 48 and 49): Shape dough into small, smooth balls and arrange three in each greased muffin cup. (Balls may be dipped in oil and herbs, if desired, before placing in pan.)

Cinnamon Rolls (recipe on page 72): Roll dough jelly-roll fashion around cinnamon sugar mixture; then slice it into 1-inch (2.5 cm) thick slices and arrange on greased cookie sheet or in baking pan.

Shaping — Miscellaneous:

Date Tea Ring (recipe on pages 68 and 69): Shape filled dough into a ring and make cuts ⅔ of the way through dough at 1-inch (2.5 cm) intervals. Gently lay each section on its side, cut side up to show filling.

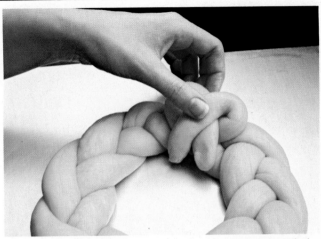

Saint Lucia Crown (recipe on page 82): Shape braided strands into ring. Shape small amount of remaining dough into a bow and place over seam of braid.

Bread Sticks (recipes on pages 122 and 124): Divide dough as directed in recipe. Shape each piece of dough into a strand by gently rolling dough between palms of hands and work surface.

Bagels (recipes on pages 118 and 120): Divide dough into 12 equal parts. Shape each part into a strand by gently rolling dough between palms of hands and work surface. Bring ends together and pinch to seal.

Kuchen (recipe on page 72): To make a fruit kuchen, arrange desired fruit over dough in pans before topping with cream mixture and cinnamon sugar.

English Muffins (recipe on page 103): Cut out dough using a floured 3-inch round cutter (or a glass or can) and place on cookie sheet sprinkled with corn meal.

GALLERY OF TECHNIQUES

Mixing—Casserole (Batter) Breads:

Measure part of the flour, other dry ingredients and the active dry yeast, into work bowl; process until mixed, about 5 seconds. Mixture should resemble corn meal.

Turn on processor and add liquid all at once through feed tube to flour mixture.

Process until smooth and blended, about 30 seconds.

Turn on processor and add remaining flour, ¼ cup (60 mL) at a time, processing about 5 to 10 seconds after each addition.

Pour batter into greased baking dish.

Let batter stand in warm place (85°F. or 30°C.) until almost doubled in volume (must be judged visually).

Mixing—Quick Breads:

To prepare the batter for most muffins, measure dry ingredients into work bowl. Process on/off 8 to 10 times until mixture resembles coarse crumbs.

Combine liquids (usually milk or other liquid and egg) and pour over flour-butter mixture.

Process on/off only 5 or 6 times, or just until flour is moistened. Do not overprocess. Batter should be lumpy.

If batter is smooth (as shown), it has been overprocessed and will result in a finished product of inferior quality (muffins will be filled with tunnels and have pointed tops).

Loaf quick breads are prepared using the same technique as for mufflins. The finished batter should be lumpy (as shown), not smooth.

Baking Powder Biscuits (recipe on page 158) are prepared using a similar technique except the end product will be a dough not a batter. Process only until flour is blended in and dough is soft. Do not overprocess.

Miscellaneous:

To test a baked bread for doneness, gently tap the crust with handle of a wooden spoon . . .

Or your knuckles. If the bread sounds hollow, it is done.

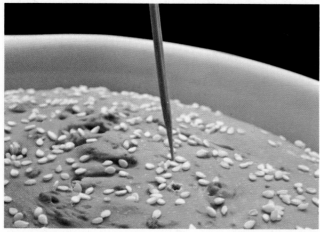

To test a casserole (batter) bread for doneness, insert a long bamboo shish-kabob skewer into bread. If skewer comes out clean (without crumbs), the bread is done.

To test a loaf of quick bread for doneness, insert a bamboo skewer or metal cake tester into center of loaf. If any batter or crumbs stick to skewer, the bread is not done; if it comes out clean, it is done.

If bread seems to be browning too quickly, cover it loosely with aluminum foil during the last 10 to 15 minutes of baking.

Almost all breads, rolls and coffeecakes should be removed from pan immediately after baking and placed on a wire rack to cool. This prevents bottom and sides from becoming soggy.

SOLVING PROBLEMS

Problem: Food processor slows down and sounds strained.

Probable Cause(s): Dough is too sticky because it contains too much liquid and/or sugar. May be also that food processor cannot handle yeast dough at all.

Solution(s): If dough is too sticky, turn off processor and let dough stand about 5 minutes. Scrape sides of work bowl and pull dough up and over the center post of the blade. Scrape blade edges clean. Sprinkle 1 or 2 tablespoons (15 or 30 mL) all-purpose flour over dough. Turn on processor; if blade still revolves slowly, turn off processor and let stand 15 minutes. Sprinkle with 1 or 2 tablespoons (15 or 30 mL) more flour and turn on processor. If processor still runs slowly, turn off processor, remove dough from work bowl and finish kneading by hand on lightly floured surface.

If machine consistently cannot handle yeast dough, complete as much mixing in the work bowl as the processor will easily handle. Turn dough out onto floured surface and knead by hand, working in as much flour as is necessary to make dough smooth and satiny.

Problem: Food processor becomes overloaded and automatically stops—circuit breaker cuts off.

Probable Cause: Motor overheats due to processing a dough that is too sticky because it contains too much liquid and/or sugar.

Solution: Turn off and unplug processor. Let stand 15 minutes. Scrape sides of bowl and blade and pull dough up and over the center post of the blade. Sprinkle 1 or 2 tablespoons (15 or 30 mL) all-purpose flour over dough. Plug in processor and turn it on. If machine runs very slowly or shuts off again, turn off processor, remove dough from work bowl and finish kneading by hand on lightly floured surface.

Problem: Dough is hard and dry.

Probable Cause(s): Not enough liquid or too much flour was added to dough, or flour is very dry.

Solution: Remove dough from work bowl, cut it into quarters and place it back in work bowl. Sprinkle 1 tablespoon (15 mL) water over dough. Turn on processor. Process 5 to 10 seconds. If dough still seems dry, add more water very gradually and process until dough is soft, smooth and pliable.

Problem: Dough has a hard ball or "topknot" that forms around top of center post of the blade, while dough in bottom of work bowl is quite moist around the edges.

Probable Cause: Liquid is not evenly blended into dough, either because it was added too quickly or too slowly.

Solution: Scrape sides of bowl and blade. Cut topknot in half and place it upside down in work bowl. Process again, slowly adding 1 to 3 teaspoons (5 to 15 mL) more water, if necessary, to form dough that is soft, smooth and satiny.

Problem: Doughs consistently do not rise or rise unevenly.

Probable Cause: Food processor generates too much heat during processing. Thus, dough becomes overheated and yeast is destroyed.

Solution: Keep dough cooler by adjusting temperature of liquids. When using Liquid Sponge Method, be sure water in which yeast is dissolved is 105° to 115°F. (41° to 46°C.). Lower temperature of remaining liquid to about 80°F. (27°C.). When using the Dry Mix Method, warm liquid only to 110° to 115°F. (43° to 46°C.).

Other problems, such as those that follow, may affect the quality of the dough or finished bread. In most of these cases, you will not be able to correct the dough or bread you have already made. However, identifying the problem should help to avoid making the same mistakes in the future.

SOLVING PROBLEMS

Problem: Occasionally, dough does not rise.
Probable Cause(s):
• Temperature of liquids may have been too low to activate yeast—below 105°F. (41°C.) if yeast was dissolved in liquid or below 120°F. (49°C.) if yeast was combined with dry ingredients.
• Temperature of liquids may have been too high—above 115°F. (46°C.) if yeast was dissolved in liquid or above 130°F. (54°C.) if yeast was combined with dry ingredients.
• Yeast may have been too old—check expiration date on the package.

Problem: Dough takes longer to double than the recipe instructs.
Probable Cause(s):
• Temperature of place where dough is rising is not warm enough.
• Yeast action may have been impaired by overprocessing the dough or adding liquids that were too warm.
• Dough may be very rich—with more than average amounts of fat, sugar and/or eggs—and, thus, will take longer to rise.

Problem: Bread is dry and tough.
Probable Cause(s):
• Not enough liquid and/or fat was added to dough.
• Too much flour was added to dough.
• Bread baked too long or oven temperature too low.

Problem: Bread is too compact and heavy.
Probable Cause(s):
• Too much flour or not enough liquid was added to dough.
• If it is a whole grain bread, an insufficient amount of all-purpose flour was used in proportion to the whole grain flour.
• Bread did not rise long enough.
• Baking pan was too large.
• Too much salt was added to dough.
• Oven temperature was too high.

Problem: Bread is shaped unevenly.
Probable Cause(s):
• Loaf was shaped improperly.
• Part of the dough may have been overheated by the processor's motor, thus killing the yeast action.
• There was too much or too little dough for the pan.
• Rising time was too short or too long.

Problem: Bread is too large and/or is full of large air bubbles.
Probable Cause(s):
• Dough was allowed to rise too long.
• Temperature where dough was rising was too high.
• Too much yeast was used in preparing dough.
• Oven temperature was too low.

HELPFUL HINTS FOR BETTER BREADS

• Organize your work area and assemble all required ingredients and measuring utensils before beginning to prepare a recipe.
• Use only fresh ingredients.
• Follow recipe directions exactly. Do not guess at measurements or temperatures.
• If your food processor slows down, sounds strained or stops processing, turn it off and check **Solving Problems** to see what to do.
• If you forget to add an ingredient to a dough, such as a seasoning, or the fat, cut the processed bread dough into 4 or 5 pieces. Place the pieces in the work bowl fitted with the steel blade. Add the missing ingredient; then process, allowing dough to spin around bowl about 15 times.
• Grease baking pans and cookie sheets with vegetable shortening instead of with oil or butter. Bread will be less likely to stick to the pan.
• As soon as bread has finished baking, remove it from the pan and place it on a wire rack to cool. This prevents the bottom and sides from becoming soggy.
• Be certain that your oven has reached recommended baking temperature before putting dough in the oven.
• If the top of bread, rolls or a coffee cake gets too brown, cover the top loosely with aluminum foil during the last 10 to 15 minutes of baking.
• Cool breads, rolls and coffee cakes completely before wrapping to store or freeze.
• For a pretty glaze on breads and rolls, mix 1 egg with 1 tablespoon (15 mL) water and brush mixture over dough before baking.
• If large air bubbles form just under the top surface of shaped dough during rising, gently puncture bubble with a wooden pick or straight pin before baking.
• For a pretty, more tender crust, brush butter, margarine or vegetable oil over the crust of a bread just after it comes out of the oven.
• For baking breads, place the oven rack in the lower ⅓ of the oven, but not on the bottom of the oven.
• For a crispy crust on white breads, French or Italian loaves, hard rolls and the like, spray or brush bread with water several times during baking. Also place a shallow pan of boiling water on the bottom of the oven to create steam.
• For tender, well shaped, tunnel-free muffins and quick loaf breads, process batter just until flour is moistened. Batter should be lumpy, not smooth.
• To quickly bring refrigerated eggs to room temperature, let them stand in a bowl of hot tap water for 5 minutes.
• When a recipe calls for baking a dough or batter in a baking pan, use a metal (not glass) pan.
• To test a yeast batter bread or quick bread for doneness, use a long bamboo shish kebob skewer or a metal cake tester.

BASIC BREADS

White Bread

¾ to 1 cup (180 to 250 mL)
    warm water (105° to
    115°F. or 41° to 46°C.)
1 package (¼ oz. or 7 g)
    active dry yeast
1 tablespoon (15 mL) sugar
2¾ cups (680 mL) all-purpose
    flour*
3 tablespoons (45 mL) instant
    nonfat dry milk solids
2 tablespoons (30 mL) cold
    butter or margarine, cut
    into 2 pieces
1 teaspoon (5 mL) salt
    Vegetable oil or melted
    butter or margarine

This basic white bread is so good and so easy to make with a food processor. Keep a loaf of it sliced in the freezer for homemade bread any time.

1. Combine ¼ cup (60 mL) of the water, yeast and sugar. Stir to dissolve yeast and let stand until bubbly, about 5 minutes.

2. Fit processor with steel blade. Measure flour, dry milk, butter and salt into work bowl. Process until mixed, about 15 seconds.

3. Add yeast mixture to flour mixture. Process until blended, about 10 seconds.

4. Turn on processor and very slowly drizzle just enough remaining water through feed tube into flour mixture so dough forms a ball that cleans the sides of the bowl. Process until ball turns around bowl about 25 times. Turn off processor and let dough stand 1 to 2 minutes.

5. Turn on processor and gradually drizzle in enough remaining water to make dough soft, smooth and satiny but not sticky.** Process until dough turns around bowl about 15 times.

6. Turn dough onto lightly floured surface. Shape into ball and place in lightly greased bowl, turning to grease all sides. Cover loosely with plastic wrap and let stand in warm place (85°F. or 30°C.) until doubled, about 1 hour.

7. Punch down dough. Shape into loaf (see Shaping in Index) and place in greased 8½x4½x2½-inch (21.5x11.5x6.5 cm) loaf pan. Brush with oil. Let stand in warm place until doubled, 45 to 60 minutes.

8. Heat oven to 375°F. (190°C.). Bake until golden and loaf sounds hollow when tapped, 25 to 30 minutes.

9. Remove immediately from pan. Brush crust with oil, if desired. Cool on wire rack.

Refrigerator White Bread Prepare dough as directed for White Bread. Eliminate first rising period. Shape dough and place in loaf pan as directed for White Bread. Brush vegetable oil over dough and cover tightly with plastic wrap. Let stand at room temperature 20 minutes, then refrigerate 4 to 24 hours. Uncover and let stand at room temperature 30 minutes. Bake as directed for White Bread.

Cinnamon Swirl Loaf Prepare dough as directed for White Bread through first rising. Punch down dough. Roll out dough into an 8x16-inch (20x40 cm) rectangle. Mix 1 tablespoon (15 mL) sugar and 2 teaspoons (10 mL) ground cinnamon and sprinkle over rectangle. Roll up dough jelly-roll fashion. Pinch seam to seal. Place in greased 8½x4½x2½ inch (21.5x11.5x6.5 cm) loaf pan. Let dough rise and bake as directed for White Bread.

Butter Crust Bread Prepare dough, let rise, shape and place in loaf pan as directed for White Bread. Cut a 7-inch (18 cm) slash in top of bread using processor's steel blade, sharp knife or razor blade. Drizzle 1 to 2 tablespoons (15 to 30 mL) melted butter all along the slash. Let dough rise and bake as directed for White Bread.

---

*Spoon flour into dry measuring cup and level off. Do not scoop.

**If dough is too dry and stiff, too soft and sticky, or if the processor shuts off, correct problem according to directions on page 25.

Old-Fashioned Oatmeal Bread

1   cup (250 mL) water
½   teaspoon (2 mL) salt
⅓   cup (80 mL) uncooked old fashioned oats
¼   to ½ cup (60 to 125 mL) warm water (105° to 115°F. or 41° to 46°C.)
3   tablespoons (45 mL) packed light brown sugar or light molasses
1   package (¼ oz. or 7 g) active dry yeast
2½   cups (625 mL) all-purpose flour*
2   tablespoons (30 mL) vegetable oil

Good, old-fashioned flavor is what you get with this loaf. Oats add a slightly nutty taste. Brown sugar gives a light sweetness, or choose molasses if you like a heartier flavor and a dark, moist crumb.

1. Combine 1 cup (250 mL) water and salt in small saucepan. Bring to a boil. Stir in oats. Cook, uncovered, over medium heat 5 minutes. Remove from heat and cool until 105° to 115°F. (41° to 46°C.).

2. Combine ¼ cup (60 mL) of the warm water, 1 tablespoon (15 mL) of the brown sugar and yeast. Stir to dissolve yeast and let stand until bubbly, about 5 minutes.

3. Measure flour, remaining 2 tablespoons (30 mL) of sugar and oil into work bowl. Process until mixed, about 15 seconds.

4. Add yeast mixture and cooled oat mixture to flour mixture. Turn on processor and very slowly drizzle just enough remaining water through feed tube into flour mixture so dough forms a ball that cleans the sides of the bowl. Process until ball turns around bowl about 25 times. Turn off processor and let dough stand 1 to 2 minutes.

5. Turn on processor and gradually drizzle in enough remaining water to make dough soft, smooth and satiny but not sticky.** Process until dough turns around bowl about 15 times.

6. Turn dough onto lightly floured surface. Shape into ball and place in lightly greased bowl, turning to grease all sides. Cover loosely with plastic wrap and let stand in warm place (85°F. or 30°C.) until doubled, about 1 hour.

7. Punch down dough. Shape into loaf (see Shaping in Index) and place in greased 8½x4½x2½-inch (21.5x11.5x6.5 cm) loaf pan. Let stand in warm place until almost doubled, about 45 minutes.

8. Heat oven to 375°F. (190°C.). Bake until golden and loaf sounds hollow when tapped, 25 to 30 minutes.

9. Remove immediately from pan. Cool on wire rack.

Sesame Oat Bread

¾   cup (180 mL) water
½   cup (125 mL) quick cooking oats
¼   cup (60 mL) sesame seeds
¼   cup (60 mL) warm water (105° to 115°F. or 41° to 46°C.)
4   tablespoons (60 mL) packed light brown sugar or light molasses
1   package (¼ oz. or 7 g) active dry yeast
2½   to 3 cups (625 to 750 mL) all-purpose flour*
2   tablespoons (30 mL) butter or margarine
1   teaspoon (5 mL) salt

The combination of oats and toasted sesame seeds lends a rich, nut-like flavor to this bread. Molasses can be used to sweeten the loaf, but brown sugar is better.

1. Measure ¾ cup (180 mL) water into a small saucepan. Cook over high heat just until water boils. Remove from heat and stir in oats. Cool until 105° to 115°F. (41° to 46°C.).

2. Place sesame seeds in small fry pan. Cook over medium heat, stirring frequently, until seeds are golden, 3 to 5 minutes. Stir seeds into oat mixture.

3. Combine ¼ cup (60 mL) of the warm water, 1 tablespoon (15 mL) of the brown sugar and yeast. Stir to dissolve yeast and let stand until bubbly, about 5 minutes.

4. Measure 1½ cups (375 mL) of the flour, remaining 3 tablespoons (45 mL) of the sugar, butter and salt into work bowl. Process until mixed, about 15 seconds.   *continued*

---

*Spoon flour into dry measuring cup and level off. Do not scoop.

**If dough is too dry and stiff, too soft and sticky, or if the processor shuts off, correct problem according to directions on page 25.

Sesame Oat Bread *(continued)*

5. Add yeast mixture to flour mixture. Process until blended, about 10 seconds.

6. Add oat mixture to flour mixture. Turn on processor and gradually add enough of the remaining flour through feed tube so dough forms a ball that cleans the sides of the bowl. Turn off processor and let dough stand 5 minutes.

7. Turn dough onto lightly floured surface. Shape into ball and place in lightly greased bowl, turning to grease all sides. Cover loosely with plastic wrap and let stand in warm place (85°F. or 30°C.) until doubled, about 1 hour.

8. Punch down dough. Shape into a loaf (see Shaping in Index) and place in greased 8½x4½x2½-inch (21.5x11.5x6.5 cm) loaf pan. Let stand in warm place until doubled, about 1 hour.

9. Heat oven to 375°F. (190°C.). Bake until golden and loaf sounds hollow when tapped, 30 to 35 minutes.

10. Remove immediately from pan. Cool on wire rack.

Refrigerator Molasses Oat Bread

Makes 1 loaf

½ to ¾ cup (125 to 180 mL) warm water (105° to 115°F. or 41° to 46°C.)

2 tablespoons (30 mL) light molasses

1 package (¼ oz. or 7 g) active dry yeast

2 cups (500 mL) all-purpose flour*

¾ cup (180 mL) uncooked old fashioned or quick-cooking oats

1 tablespoon (15 mL) butter or margarine

1 teaspoon (5 mL) salt

½ cup (125 mL) dark raisins

1 egg white
Uncooked oats

Oats, raisins and molasses flavor this crusty, moist bread that rises in the refrigerator. Shape it into a round loaf, then cut into wedges to serve. For a special treat, split the wedges in half, toast and spread with butter and honey.

1. Combine ¼ cup (60 mL) of the water, molasses and yeast. Stir to dissolve yeast and let stand until bubbly, about 5 minutes.

2. Fit processor with steel blade. Measure flour, the ¾ cup (180 mL) oats, butter and salt into work bowl. Process until mixed, about 15 seconds.

3. Add yeast mixture to flour mixture. Process until blended, about 10 seconds.

4. Turn on processor and very slowly drizzle just enough remaining water through feed tube into flour mixture so dough forms a ball that cleans the sides of the bowl. Process until ball turns around bowl about 25 times. Turn off processor and let dough stand 1 to 2 minutes.

5. Turn on processor and gradually drizzle in enough remaining water to make dough soft, smooth and satiny but not sticky.** Process until dough turns around bowl about 15 times.

6. Turn dough onto lightly greased surface. Knead raisins into dough. Shape dough into smooth ball and place on greased cookie sheet. Roll or pat with hands into a circle about 8 inches (20 cm) in diameter. Cover tightly with plastic wrap and let stand at room temperature about 20 minutes. Refrigerate until thoroughly chilled, 6 to 24 hours.

7. Uncover dough and let stand at room temperature 30 minutes.

8. Heat oven to 375°F. (190°C.). Beat egg white with fork until foamy. Spread egg white over bread and sprinkle with oats. Bake until evenly browned, 30 to 40 minutes.

9. Remove from cookie sheet. Cool on wire rack.

---

*Spoon flour into dry measuring cup and level off. Do not scoop.

**If dough is too dry and stiff, too soft and sticky, or if the processor shuts off, correct problem according to directions on page 25.

BASIC BREADS

Old Fashioned Cinnamon Braid

⅓ cup (80 mL) instant mashed potato flakes

⅓ cup (80 mL) boiling water

¼ to ½ cup (60 to 125 mL) warm water (105° to 115°F. or 41° to 46°C.)

4 tablespoons (60 mL) sugar

1 package (¼ oz. or 7 g) active dry yeast

3 cups (750 mL) all-purpose flour*

¼ cup (60 mL) instant nonfat dry milk solids

¼ cup (60 mL) cold butter or margarine, cut into 4 pieces

1 teaspoon (5 mL) salt

1 egg

Cinnamon Sugar (see Index for page number)

Not only is this bread extremely good looking, but it's one of the most delicious and popular that you'll find. The delicately flavored dough is generously coated with cinnamon sugar before shaping into a beautiful braid. Add raisins to the dough for another old-fashioned favorite.

1. Stir potato flakes into boiling water. Cool until 105° to 115°F. (41° to 46°C.). Reserve.

2. Combine ¼ cup (60 mL) of the warm water, 1 tablespoon (15 mL) of the sugar and yeast. Stir to dissolve yeast and let stand until bubbly, about 5 minutes.

3. Fit processor with steel blade. Measure flour, dry milk, butter, remaining 3 tablespoons (45 mL) of the sugar and salt into work bowl. Process until mixed, about 15 seconds.

4. Add potato mixture to flour mixture. Process until mixed, about 5 seconds.

5. Add yeast mixture and egg to flour mixture. Turn on processor and very slowly drizzle just enough remaining water through feed tube into flour mixture so dough forms a ball that cleans the sides of the bowl. Process until ball turns around bowl about 25 times. Turn off processor and let dough stand 1 to 2 minutes.

6. Turn on processor and gradually drizzle in enough remaining water to make dough soft, smooth and satiny but not sticky.** Process until dough turns around bowl about 15 times.

7. Turn dough onto lightly floured surface. Shape into ball and place in lightly greased bowl, turning to grease all sides. Cover loosely with plastic wrap and let stand in warm place (85°F. or 30°C.) until doubled, about 1 hour.

8. Punch down dough. Prepare Cinnamon Sugar. Divide dough into 3 equal parts. Shape each part into strand 20 inches (50 cm) long. Roll each strand in Cinnamon Sugar. Braid strands together and place in greased 9x5x3-inch (23x13x8 cm) loaf pan. Tuck ends under and pinch to seal. Let stand in warm place until almost doubled, about 45 minutes.

9. Heat oven to 350°F. (180°C.). Bake until evenly brown and loaf sounds hollow when tapped, 35 to 40 minutes.

10. Remove immediately from pan. Cool on wire rack.

Old-Fashioned Cinnamon Raisin Braid Prepare dough as directed for Old Fashioned Cinnamon Braid. Turn dough onto lightly floured surface and knead ½ cup (125 mL) dark raisins into the dough. Continue as directed for Old Fashioned Cinnamon Braid.

Buttermilk Bread

2 tablespoons (30 mL) warm water (105° to 115°F. or 41° to 46°C.)

1 package (¼ oz. or 7 g) active dry yeast

1 tablespoon (15 mL) sugar
continued

Buttermilk gives this light white bread just a touch of sour flavor.

1. Combine water, yeast and sugar. Stir to dissolve yeast and let stand until bubbly, about 5 minutes.

2. Fit processor with steel blade. Measure flour, butter and salt into work bowl. Process until mixed, about 15 seconds.

3. Add yeast mixture to flour mixture. Process until blended, about 10 seconds.

---

*Spoon flour into dry measuring cup and level off. Do not scoop.

**If dough is too dry and stiff, too soft and sticky, or if the processor shuts off, correct problem according to directions on page 25.

Buttermilk Bread (continued)

2¾ cups (680 mL) all-purpose flour*

3 tablespoons (45 mL) cold butter or margarine, cut into 3 pieces

2 teaspoons (10 mL) salt

¾ to 1 cup (180 to 250 mL) buttermilk
 Melted butter, optional

4. Turn on processor and very slowly drizzle just enough buttermilk through feed tube into flour mixture so dough forms a ball that cleans the sides of the bowl. Process until ball turns around bowl about 25 times. Turn off processor and let dough stand 1 to 2 minutes.

5. Turn on processor and gradually drizzle in enough remaining buttermilk to make dough soft, smooth and satiny but not sticky.** Process until dough turns around bowl about 15 times.

6. Turn dough onto lightly floured surface. Shape into ball and place in lightly greased bowl, turning to grease all sides. Cover loosely with plastic wrap and let stand in warm place (85°F. or 30°C.) until doubled, about 1 hour.

7. Punch down dough. Shape into loaf (see Shaping in Index) and fit into greased 8½x4½x2½-inch (21.5x11.5x6.5 cm) loaf pan. Cover loosely with plastic wrap and let stand in warm place until almost doubled, about 45 minutes.

8. Heat oven to 375°F. (190°C.). Bake until golden and loaf sounds hollow when tapped, 25 to 30 minutes.

9. Remove immediately from pan. Brush with butter, if desired. Cool on wire rack.

Makes 1 loaf

Poppy Seed Braid

¼ to ½ cup (60 to 125 mL) warm water (105° to 115°F. or 41° to 46°C.)

2 tablespoons (30 mL) sugar

1 package (¼ oz. or 7 g) active dry yeast

2¼ cups (560 mL) all-purpose flour*

2 tablespoons (30 mL) butter or margarine

1 teaspoon (5 mL) salt

2 eggs, beaten

1 egg white

1 tablespoon (15 mL) poppy seeds

This attractive bread, made of a simple, non-sweet dough, traces its roots back to Europe, where doughs shaped into beautiful braids are a mark of excellence.

1. Combine ¼ cup (60 mL) of the water, sugar and yeast. Stir to dissolve yeast and let stand until bubbly, about 5 minutes.

2. Fit processor with steel blade. Measure flour, butter and salt into work bowl. Process until mixed, about 15 seconds.

3. Add yeast mixture and the 2 beaten eggs to flour mixture. Process until blended, about 10 seconds.

4. Turn on processor and very slowly drizzle just enough remaining water through feed tube into flour mixture so dough forms a ball that cleans the sides of the bowl. Process until ball turns around bowl about 25 times. Turn off processor and let dough stand 1 to 2 minutes.

5. Turn on processor and gradually drizzle in enough remaining water to make dough soft, smooth and satiny but not sticky.** Process until dough turns around bowl about 15 times.

6. Turn dough onto lightly greased surface. Shape into ball. Cover with inverted bowl or plastic wrap and let stand 20 minutes.

7. Uncover dough and knead 2 or 3 times to remove air bubbles. Divide dough into 3 equal parts. Shape each part into a strand 20 inches (50 cm) long. Braid strands loosely together and place on greased cookie sheet. Cover loosely with plastic wrap and let stand in warm place (85°F. or 30°C.) until doubled, about 1½ hours.

8. Heat oven to 375°F. (190°C.). Beat egg white with a fork and brush over braid. Sprinkle poppy seeds over braid. Bake until golden and loaf sounds hollow when tapped, 25 to 30 minutes.

9. Remove braid from cookie sheet. Cool on wire rack.

---

*Spoon flour into dry measuring cup and level off. Do not scoop.

**If dough is too dry and stiff, too soft and sticky, or if the processor shuts off, correct problem according to directions on page 25.

BASIC BREADS

Whole Wheat Bread

Makes 1 loaf

½ to ¾ cup (125 to 180 mL) warm water (105° to 115°F. or 41° to 46°C.)

2 tablespoons (30 mL) sugar

1 package (¼ oz. or 7 g) active dry yeast

1½ cups (375 mL) all-purpose flour*

1 cup (250 mL) whole wheat flour

¼ cup (60 mL) instant nonfat dry milk solids

1 tablespoon (15 mL) vegetable oil

1 teaspoon (5 mL) salt

This bread is made with both all-purpose and whole wheat flours which give it a relatively light texture and good volume. The 100% Whole Wheat variation is smaller in volume and has a more compact texture.

1. Combine ¼ cup (60 mL) of the water, sugar and yeast. Stir to dissolve yeast and let stand until bubbly, about 5 minutes.

2. Fit processor with steel blade. Measure flours, dry milk, oil and salt into work bowl. Process until mixed, about 10 seconds.

3. Add yeast mixture to flour mixture. Process until blended, about 10 seconds.

4. Turn on processor and very slowly drizzle just enough remaining water through feed tube into flour mixture so dough forms a ball that cleans the sides of the bowl. Process until ball turns around bowl about 25 times. Turn off processor and let dough stand 1 to 2 minutes.

5. Turn on processor and gradually drizzle in enough remaining water to make dough soft and smooth but not sticky.** Process until dough turns around bowl about 15 times.

6. Turn dough onto lightly greased surface. Shape into ball and place in lightly greased bowl, turning to grease all sides. Cover loosely with plastic wrap and let stand in warm place (85°F. or 30°C.) until doubled, about 1 hour.

7. Punch down dough. Shape into loaf (see Shaping in Index) and place in greased 8½x4½x2½-inch (21.5x11.5x6.5 cm) loaf pan. Let stand in warm place until almost doubled, about 45 minutes.

8. Heat oven to 375°F. (190°C.). Bake until loaf sounds hollow when tapped, 25 to 30 minutes.

9. Remove immediately from pan. Cool on wire rack.

Old-Fashioned 100% Whole Wheat Bread Prepare dough as directed for Whole Wheat Bread, eliminating all-purpose flour and increasing whole wheat flour to 2 cups (500 mL). Shape and bake as directed for Whole Wheat Bread.

Rosemary Whole Wheat Bread

Makes 1 loaf

¾ to 1 cup (180 to 250 mL) warm water (105° to 115° or 41° to 46°C.)

1 package (¼ oz. or 7 g) active dry yeast

2 teaspoons (10 mL) dried rosemary leaves

½ teaspoon (2 mL) sugar

1½ cups (375 mL) all-purpose flour*

1 cup (250 mL) whole wheat flour

1 teaspoon (5 mL) salt

1 egg yolk

1 tablespoon (15 mL) cold water

This light wheat bread gets a slightly sweet, herb flavoring from dried rosemary leaves. For an attractive, shiny crust, the loaf is brushed with egg before baking.

1. Combine ¼ cup (60 mL) of the warm water, yeast, rosemary and sugar. Stir to dissolve yeast and let stand until bubbly, about 5 minutes.

2. Fit processor with steel blade. Measure flours and salt into work bowl. Process on/off to mix.

3. Add yeast mixture to flour mixture. Process until blended, about 10 seconds.

4. Turn on processor and very slowly drizzle just enough remaining warm water through feed tube into flour mixture so dough forms a ball that cleans the sides of the bowl. Process until ball turns around bowl about 25 times. Turn off processor and let dough stand 1 to 2 minutes.
continued

---

*Spoon flour into dry measuring cup and level off. Do not scoop.

**If dough is too dry and stiff, too soft and sticky, or if the processor shuts off, correct problem according to directions on page 25.

5. Turn on processor and gradually drizzle in enough remaining warm water to make dough soft and smooth but not sticky.** Process until dough turns around bowl about 15 times.

6. Turn dough onto lightly greased surface. Shape into ball and place in lightly greased bowl, turning to grease all sides. Cover loosely with plastic wrap and let stand in warm place (85°F. or 30°C.) until doubled, about 1 hour.

7. Punch down dough. Shape into loaf (see Shaping in Index) and place in greased 8½x4½x2½-inch (21.5x11.5x6.5 cm) loaf pan. Let stand in warm place until almost doubled, about 45 minutes.

8. Heat oven to 375°F. (190°C.). Mix egg yolk and cold water with a fork. Brush over loaf. Bake until loaf sounds hollow when tapped, 25 to 30 minutes.

9. Remove immediately from pan. Cool on wire rack.

Honey Wheat Bread

Makes 1 loaf

¼ to ½ cup (60 to 125 mL) warm water (105° to 115°F. or 41° to 46°C.)

3 tablespoons (45 mL) honey

1 package (¼ oz. or 7 g) active dry yeast

2 cups (500 mL) all-purpose flour*

¾ cup (180 mL) whole wheat flour

¼ cup (60 mL) instant nonfat dry milk solids

2 tablespoons (30 mL) lard, butter or margarine

1 teaspoon (5 mL) salt

1 egg

The flavors of whole wheat and honey and the added richness of lard give this bread special taste and a tender crust.

1. Combine ¼ cup (60 mL) of the water, 1 tablespoon (15 mL) of the honey and yeast. Stir to dissolve yeast and let stand until bubbly, about 5 minutes.

2. Fit processor with steel blade. Measure flours, dry milk, lard, remaining 2 tablespoons (30 mL) of the honey, and salt into work bowl. Process until mixed, about 10 seconds.

3. Add yeast mixture and egg to flour mixture. Process until blended, about 10 seconds.

4. Turn on processor and very slowly drizzle just enough remaining water through feed tube into flour mixture so dough forms a ball that cleans the sides of the bowl. Process until ball turns around bowl about 25 times. Turn off processor and let dough stand 1 to 2 minutes.

5. Turn on processor and gradually drizzle in enough remaining water to make dough soft and smooth but not sticky.** Process until dough turns around bowl about 15 times.

6. Turn dough onto lightly floured surface. Shape into ball and place in lightly greased bowl, turning to grease all sides. Cover loosely with plastic wrap and let stand in warm place (85°F. or 30°C.) until doubled, about 1 hour.

7. Punch down dough. Shape into loaf and place in greased 8½x4½x2½-inch (21.5x11.5x6.5 cm) loaf pan. Let stand in warm place until almost doubled, about 45 minutes.

8. Heat oven to 375°F. (190°C.). Bake until loaf sounds hollow when tapped, 25 to 30 minutes.

9. Remove immediately from pan. Cool on wire rack.

---

*Spoon flour into dry measuring cup and level off. Do not scoop.

**If dough is too dry and stiff, too soft and sticky, or if the processor shuts off, correct problem according to directions on page 25.

Three Wheat Bread

Makes 1 loaf

¾ to 1 cup (180 to 250 mL)
   warm water (105° to
   115°F. or 41° to 46°C.)
1 package (¼ oz. or 7 g)
   active dry yeast
1 tablespoon (15 mL) sugar
2 cups (500 mL) all-purpose
   flour*
½ cup (125 mL) whole wheat
   flour
½ cup (125 mL) instant nonfat
   dry milk solids
3 tablespoons (45 mL) wheat
   germ
2 tablespoons (30 mL)
   vegetable oil
1 teaspoon (5 mL) salt

This bread gets its name from the three different forms of wheat that go into the dough: all-purpose flour, whole wheat flour and wheat germ. Its hearty flavor makes it ideal for sandwich making and toasting.

1. Combine ¼ cup (60 mL) of the water, yeast and sugar. Stir to dissolve yeast and let stand until bubbly, about 5 minutes.

2. Fit processor with steel blade. Measure flours, dry milk, wheat germ, oil and salt into work bowl. Process until mixed, about 10 seconds.

3. Add yeast mixture to flour mixture. Process until blended, about 10 seconds.

4. Turn on processor and very slowly drizzle just enough remaining water through feed tube into flour mixture so dough forms a ball that cleans the sides of the bowl. Process until ball turns around bowl about 25 times. Turn off processor and let dough stand 1 to 2 minutes.

5. Turn on processor and gradually drizzle in enough remaining water to make dough soft and smooth but not sticky.** Process until dough turns around bowl about 15 times.

6. Turn dough onto lightly greased surface. Shape into ball and place in lightly greased bowl, turning to grease all sides. Cover loosely with plastic wrap and let stand in warm place (85°F. or 30°C.) until doubled, about 1 hour.

7. Punch down dough. Shape into loaf (see Shaping in Index) and place in greased 8½x4½x2½-inch (21.5x11.5x6.5 cm) loaf pan. Let stand in warm place until almost doubled, about 45 minutes.

8. Heat oven to 375°F. (190°C.). Bake until loaf sounds hollow when tapped, 25 to 30 minutes.

9. Remove immediately from pan. Cool on wire rack.

Cracked Wheat Bread

Makes 1 loaf

½ cup (125 mL) cracked
   wheat
½ cup (125 mL) water
½ cup (125 mL) milk
1 tablespoon (15 mL) sugar
1 tablespoon (15 mL) butter
   or margarine
1 teaspoon (5 mL) salt
½ cup (125 mL) whole wheat
   flour
1 package (¼ oz. or 7 g)
   active dry yeast
1½ to 1¾ cups (375 to 430
   mL) all-purpose flour*
   Vegetable oil or melted
   butter or margarine

Flecks of cracked wheat generously dot this light wheat bread for added flavor and a slightly crunchy texture.

1. Combine cracked wheat and water in small saucepan. Bring to a boil. Remove from heat and blend in milk, sugar, butter and salt. Cool until 120° to 130°F. (49° to 54°C.).

2. Fit processor with steel blade. Measure whole wheat flour and yeast into work bowl. Process on/off to mix.

3. Pour cooled cracked wheat mixture over flour in work bowl. Process until mixed, about 15 seconds.

4. Turn on processor and add enough of the all-purpose flour through feed tube so dough forms a ball that cleans the sides of the bowl. Process until ball turns around bowl about 25 times.

5. Turn dough onto lightly greased surface. Shape into ball and place in lightly greased bowl, turning to grease all sides. Cover loosely with plastic wrap and let stand in warm place (85°F. or 30°C.) until doubled, about 1 hour. *continued*

---

*Spoon flour into dry measuring cup and level off. Do not scoop.

**If dough is too dry and stiff, too soft and sticky, or if the processor shuts off, correct problem according to directions on page 25.

6. Punch down dough. Shape into loaf (see Shaping in Index) and place in greased 8½x4½x2½-inch (21.5x11.5x6.5 cm) loaf pan, or shape into ball, place on greased cookie sheet and roll or pat into circle about 6 inches (15 cm) in diameter. Brush with oil and let stand in warm place until almost doubled, about 45 minutes.

7. Heat oven to 375°F. (190°C.). Bake until golden and loaf sounds hollow when tapped, 25 to 30 minutes.

8. Remove immediately from pan or cookie sheet. Brush crust with oil. Cool on wire rack.

Cornmeal Bread

Makes 1 loaf

¼ cup (60 mL) cornmeal
½ cup (125 mL) boiling water
¼ to ½ cup (60 to 125 mL) warm water (105° to 115°F. or 41° to 46°C.)
3 tablespoons (45 mL) packed brown sugar
1 package (¼ oz. or 7 g) active dry yeast
2¼ cups (560 mL) all-purpose flour*
⅓ cup (80 mL) instant nonfat dry milk solids
1 tablespoon (15 mL) butter or margarine
1 teaspoon (5 mL) salt
Vegetable oil

There's just enough cornmeal in this pretty round loaf of bread to give it a pleasant, light corn flavor.

1. Stir cornmeal into boiling water. Cool until 105° to 115°F. (41° to 46°C.). Reserve.

2. Combine ¼ cup (60 mL) of the warm water, 1 tablespoon (15 mL) of the brown sugar and yeast. Stir to dissolve yeast and let stand until bubbly, about 5 minutes.

3. Fit processor with steel blade. Measure flour, dry milk, remaining 2 tablespoons (30 mL) of the sugar, butter and salt into work bowl. Process until mixed, about 15 seconds.

4. Add cornmeal mixture to flour mixture. Process until mixed, about 5 seconds.

5. Add yeast mixture to flour mixture. Turn on processor and very slowly drizzle just enough remaining water through feed tube into flour mixture so dough forms a ball that cleans the sides of the bowl. Process until ball turns around bowl about 25 times. Turn off processor and let dough stand 1 to 2 minutes.

6. Turn on processor and gradually drizzle in enough remaining water to make dough soft, smooth and satiny but not sticky.** Process until dough turns around bowl about 15 times.

7. Turn dough onto lightly floured surface. Shape into ball and place on greased cookie sheet. Roll or pat into a circle about 6 inches (15 cm) in diameter. Brush with oil and let stand in warm place (85°F. or 30°C.) until doubled, about 1 hour.

8. Heat oven to 375°F. (190°C.). Bake until golden and loaf sounds hollow when tapped, 25 to 30 minutes.

9. Remove from cookie sheet. Cool on wire rack.

---

*Spoon flour into dry measuring cup and level off. Do not scoop.

**If dough is too dry and stiff, too soft and sticky, or if the processor shuts off, correct problem according to directions on page 25.

BASIC BREADS

Farmer-Style Sour Cream Bread

Makes 1 loaf

2   tablespoons (30 mL) warm water (105° to 115°F. or 41° to 46°C.)
2   tablespoons (30 mL) sugar
1   package (¼ oz. or 7 g) active dry yeast
2½ to 3 cups (625 to 750 mL) all-purpose flour*
1½ teaspoons (7 mL) salt
¼   teaspoon (1 mL) baking soda
1   cup (250 mL) dairy sour cream, at room temperature
     Vegetable oil
1   tablespoon sesame or poppy seeds, optional

Sour cream adds richness and a delightful, slightly tart taste to this round, crusty loaf of bread.

1. Combine water, sugar and yeast. Stir to dissolve yeast and let stand until bubbly, about 5 minutes.

2. Fit processor with steel blade. Measure 2 cups (500 mL) of the flour, salt and soda into work bowl. Process on/off to mix.

3. Add yeast mixture to flour mixture. Process until blended, about 10 seconds.

4. Spoon sour cream evenly over flour mixture. Turn on processor and add enough of the remaining flour through feed tube so dough forms a ball that cleans the sides of the bowl. Process until ball turns around bowl about 25 times.

5. Turn dough onto lightly floured surface. Shape into a ball and place on greased cookie sheet. Flatten with hands into a circle about 8 inches (20 cm) in diameter. Brush dough with oil. Sprinkle sesame or poppy seeds over dough, if desired. Let stand in warm place (85°F. or 30°C.) until doubled, about 1 hour.

6. Heat oven to 375°F. (190°C.). Bake until golden, 25 to 30 minutes.

7. Remove from cookie sheet. Cool on wire rack.

Modern Potato Bread

Makes 1 loaf

¼   to ½ cup (60 to 125 mL) warm water (105° to 115°F. or 41° to 46°C.)
2   tablespoons (30 mL) sugar
1   package (¼ oz. or 7 g) active dry yeast
2¾ cups (680 mL) all-purpose flour*
¼   cup (60 mL) instant nonfat dry milk solids
2   tablespoons (30 mL) instant mashed potato flakes
2   tablespoons (30 mL) butter or margarine
1   teaspoon (5 mL) salt
2   eggs, beaten
     Butter or margarine

Potato breads appeared often in old farmhouse kitchens because they used up leftover mashed potatoes. Today, we can enjoy this old-fashioned bread the modern way, using instant mashed potato flakes to flavor the dough and a food processor to mix and "knead" it.

1. Combine ¼ cup (60 mL) of the water, sugar and yeast. Stir to dissolve yeast and let stand until bubbly, about 5 minutes.

2. Fit processor with steel blade. Measure flour, dry milk, potato flakes, 2 tablespoons (30 mL) of the butter and salt into work bowl. Process until mixed, about 15 seconds.

3. Add yeast mixture to flour mixture. Process until blended, about 10 seconds.

4. Turn on processor and very slowly drizzle eggs and just enough remaining water through feed tube into flour mixture so dough forms a ball that cleans the sides of the bowl. Process until ball turns around bowl about 25 times. Turn off processor and let dough stand 1 to 2 minutes.

5. Turn on processor and gradually drizzle in enough remaining water to make dough soft, smooth and satiny but not sticky.** Process until dough turns around bowl about 15 times.

6. Turn dough onto lightly greased surface. Shape into a ball and place on greased cookie sheet. Roll or pat into a circle about 8 inches (20 cm) in diameter. Cover loosely with plastic wrap and let stand in warm place (85°F. or 30°C.) until doubled, 1 to 1¼ hours.

7. Heat oven to 375°F. (190°C.). Uncover bread and bake until golden and loaf sounds hollow when tapped, about 30 minutes.

8. Remove from cookie sheet. Cool on wire rack.

---

*Spoon flour into dry measuring cup and level off. Do not scoop.

**If dough is too dry and stiff, too soft and sticky, or if the processor shuts off, correct problem according to directions on page 25.

Egg Braid

Makes 1 loaf

¼ to ½ cup (60 to 125 mL) warm water (105° to 115°F. or 41° to 46°C.)

1 package (¼ oz. or 7 g) active dry yeast

1 tablespoon (15 mL) sugar

2¾ cups (680 mL) all-purpose flour*

⅓ cup (80 mL) instant nonfat dry milk solids

¼ cup (60 mL) cold butter or margarine, cut into 4 pieces

1 teaspoon (5 mL) salt

2 eggs, beaten

1 egg
Sesame or poppy seeds, optional

This beautiful bread is very easy to make and shape. Use the richly flavored egg dough as a base for other breads, too, and add whatever ingredients sound good: raisins, currants, chopped nuts, diced dried fruits or spices.

1. Combine ¼ cup (60 mL) water, yeast and sugar. Stir to dissolve yeast and let stand until bubbly, about 5 minutes.

2. Fit processor with steel blade. Measure flour, dry milk, butter and salt into work bowl. Process until mixed, about 15 seconds.

3. Add yeast mixture to flour mixture. Process until blended, about 10 seconds.

4. Turn on processor and slowly drizzle the 2 beaten eggs through feed tube and just enough remaining water so dough forms a ball that cleans the sides of the bowl. Process until ball turns around bowl about 25 times. Turn off processor and let dough stand 1 to 2 minutes.

5. Turn on processor and gradually drizzle in enough remaining water to make dough soft, smooth and satiny but not sticky.** Process until dough turns around bowl about 15 times.

6. Turn dough onto lightly floured surface. Shape into ball and place in lightly greased bowl, turning to grease all sides. Cover with plastic wrap and let stand in warm place (85°F. or 30°C.) until doubled, about 1 hour.

7. Punch down dough. Divide into 3 equal parts. Shape each part into a strand about 18 inches (45 cm) long. Braid the strands loosely together. Tuck ends under and pinch to seal. Fit braid into greased 8½x4½x2½-inch (21.5x11.5x6.5 cm) loaf pan. Cover loosely with plastic wrap and let stand in warm place until almost doubled, about 1 hour.

8. Heat oven to 375°F. (190°C.). Beat remaining egg with fork. Brush egg over braid. Sprinkle sesame or poppy seeds over braid, if desired. Bake until evenly browned, 25 to 30 minutes.

9. Remove immediately from pan. Cool on wire rack.

Refrigerator Egg Braid Prepare dough through first rising and shape into braid as directed for Egg Braid. Place in greased loaf pan, brush with vegetable oil and cover tightly with plastic wrap. Refrigerate 4 to 24 hours. Uncover and let stand at room temperature 30 minutes. Bake as directed for Egg Braid.

Raisin Bread Prepare dough as directed for Egg Braid. Turn dough onto lightly floured surface and knead ½ cup (125 mL) dark raisins into the dough. Continue as directed for Egg Braid, eliminating sesame or poppy seeds.

Poppy Seed Pull-Apart Loaf Prepare dough as directed for Egg Braid through first rising. Punch down dough. Pinch off small pieces of dough and shape into 1 inch (2.5 cm) balls. Dip top of each ball in ¼ cup (60 mL) melted butter or margarine then in ¼ cup (60 mL) poppy seeds. Arrange balls, seed side up, in greased 2 quart (2 L) ring mold or tube pan. Cover loosely with plastic wrap and let stand in warm place (85°F. or 30°C.) until almost doubled, about 45 minutes. Heat oven to 375°F. (190°C.). Bake until loaf sounds hollow when tapped, 35 to 45 minutes. Remove immediately from pan. Cool on wire rack.

*Spoon flour into dry measuring cup and level off. Do not scoop.

**If dough is too dry and stiff, too soft and sticky, or if the processor shuts off, correct problem according to directions on page 25.

Crusty Rye Bread

Makes 1 loaf

¼ cup (60 mL) packed light brown sugar

3 strips pared orange rind (about 1x½ inches or 2.5x1.5 cm each)

1 cup (250 mL) water

1 tablespoon (15 mL) butter or margarine

1 teaspoon (5 mL) salt

1 teaspoon (5 mL) caraway seeds

2 to 2½ cups (500 to 625 mL) all-purpose flour*

½ cup (125 mL) rye flour

1 package (¼ oz. or 7 g) active dry yeast

Rye bread is a big favorite with many people. This version is especially appealing because it's baked into a round loaf so there's plenty of the chewy crust to enjoy.

1. Fit processor with steel blade. Add sugar and orange rind to work bowl. Process until rind is minced, about 1 minute.

2. Place orange mixture in a small saucepan. Add water, butter, salt and caraway seeds. Bring to boil. Remove from heat and cool to 120° to 130°F. (49° to 54°C.).

3. Refit processor with steel blade. Measure 1 cup (250 mL) of the all-purpose flour, rye flour and yeast into work bowl. Process on/off twice to mix.

4. Add cooled orange mixture to flour mixture. Process until smooth, about 20 seconds.

5. Turn on processor and add enough of the remaining flour through feed tube so dough forms a ball that cleans the sides of the bowl. Process until ball turns around bowl about 25 times.

6. Turn dough onto lightly floured surface. Shape into ball and place in lightly greased bowl, turning to grease all sides. Cover loosely with plastic wrap and let stand in warm place (85°F. or 30°C.) until doubled, about 1 hour.

7. Punch down dough. Shape into ball and place on greased cookie sheet. Roll out dough into a circle 9 inches (23 cm) in diameter. Cover loosely with plastic wrap and let stand in warm place until almost doubled, about 45 minutes.

8. Heat oven to 350°F. (180°C.). Bake until evenly brown and loaf sounds hollow when tapped, 25 to 30 minutes.

9. Remove from cookie sheet. Cool on wire rack.

Golden Honey Braid

Makes 1 loaf

½ to ¾ cup (125 to 180 mL) warm water (105° to 115°F. or 41° to 46°C.)

4 tablespoons (60 mL) honey

1 package (¼ oz. or 7 g) active dry yeast

⅛ teaspoon (0.5 mL) ground saffron, optional

2½ cups (625 mL) all-purpose flour*

¼ cup (60 mL) vegetable oil

1 teaspoon (5 mL) salt

½ cup (125 mL) golden raisins, optional

Honey

This lovely bread is made from a honey-sweetened dough that's quickly shaped into a braid. For added color and special flavor, add just a little ground saffron to the dough.

1. Combine ¼ cup (60 mL) of the water, 1 tablespoon (15 mL) of the honey, yeast and saffron, if desired. Stir to dissolve yeast and let stand until bubbly, about 5 minutes.

2. Fit processor with steel blade. Measure flour, oil, remaining 3 tablespoons (45 mL) of the honey and salt into work bowl. Process until mixed, about 15 seconds.

3. Add yeast mixture to flour mixture. Process until blended, about 10 seconds.

4. Turn on processor and very slowly drizzle just enough remaining water through feed tube into flour mixture so dough forms a ball that cleans the sides of the bowl. Process until ball turns around bowl about 25 times. Turn off processor and let dough stand 1 to 2 minutes.

5. Turn on processor and gradually drizzle in enough remaining water to make dough soft, smooth and satiny but not sticky.** Process until dough turns around bowl about 15 times. *continued*

*Spoon flour into dry measuring cup and level off. Do not scoop.

**If dough is too dry and stiff, too soft and sticky, or if the processor shuts off, correct problem according to directions on page 25.

Golden Honey Braid (continued)

6. Turn dough onto lightly floured surface. Knead raisins into dough, if desired. Shape into ball and place in lightly greased bowl, turning to grease all sides. Cover loosely with plastic wrap and let stand in warm place (85°F. or 30°C.) until doubled, about 1 hour.

7. Punch down dough. Divide dough into 3 equal parts. Shape each part into strand 20 inches (50 cm) long. Braid strands loosely together and place on greased cookie sheet or in greased 2 quart (2 L) ring mold or tube pan. Cover loosely with plastic wrap and let stand in warm place until almost doubled, about 45 minutes.

8. Heat oven to 350°F. (180°C.). Bake until golden and loaf sounds hollow when tapped, 30 to 40 minutes.

9. Remove immediately from cookie sheet or pan and place on wire rack. Brush honey over crust. Cool.

Italian Rosemary Bread

Makes 1 loaf

¼ to ½ cup (60 to 125 mL) warm water (105° to 115°F. or 41° to 46°C.)

4 tablespoons (60 mL) sugar

1 package (¼ oz. or 7 g) active dry yeast

2¾ cups (680 mL) all-purpose flour*

⅓ cup (80 mL) instant nonfat dry milk solids

1 teaspoon (5 mL) salt

1 teaspoon (5 mL) dried rosemary leaves

¼ cup (60 mL) olive oil

2 eggs

½ cup (125 mL) dark raisins
Olive oil

The distinctive flavors of rosemary, raisins and olive oil mingle in this delightful bread. It's especially good toasted as an accompaniment to egg dishes.

1. Combine ¼ cup (60 mL) of the water, 1 tablespoon (15 mL) of the sugar and yeast. Stir to dissolve yeast and let stand until bubbly, about 5 minutes.

2. Fit processor with steel blade. Measure flour, dry milk, remaining 3 tablespoons (45 mL) of the sugar, salt and rosemary into work bowl. Process on/off to mix.

3. Add yeast mixture, ¼ cup (60 mL) of the oil and eggs to flour mixture. Process until blended, about 10 seconds.

4. Turn on processor and very slowly drizzle just enough remaining water through feed tube into flour mixture so dough forms a ball that cleans the sides of the bowl. Process until ball turns around bowl about 25 times. Turn off processor and let dough stand 1 to 2 minutes.

5. Turn on processor and gradually drizzle in enough remaining water to make dough soft, smooth and satiny but not sticky.** Process until dough turns around bowl about 15 times.

6. Turn dough onto lightly floured surface. Knead raisins into dough. Shape dough into a smooth ball. Place on greased cookie sheet. Roll or pat into circle about 8 inches (20 cm) in diameter. Brush with olive oil. Cover loosely with plastic wrap and let stand in warm place (85°F. or 30°C.) until doubled, about 1 hour.

7. Heat oven to 350°F. (180°C.). Make a cross about 6 inches (15 cm) long and ¼ inch (0.5 cm) deep in top of loaf using processor's steel blade, sharp knife or razor blade. Bake until evenly brown, 30 to 35 minutes.

8. Remove from cookie sheet. Brush crust with oil. Cool on wire rack.

---

*Spoon flour into dry measuring cup and level off. Do not scoop.

**If dough is too dry and stiff, too soft and sticky, or if the processor shuts off, correct problem according to directions on page 25.

Makes 1 loaf

Cheddar Anadama Bread

¼ cup (60 mL) cornmeal
½ cup (125 mL) boiling water
½ cup (125 mL) cold water
¼ cup (60 mL) molasses
2 tablespoons (30 mL) butter
  or margarine
2½ to 3 cups (625 to 750 mL)
  all-purpose flour*
1 package (¼ oz. or 7 g)
  active dry yeast
¾ teaspoon (7 mL) salt
1 cup (250 mL) coarsely
  chopped Cheddar cheese
  Butter or margarine

Legend has it that a 19th Century fisherman became enraged with his wife, Anna, who always served him cornmeal and molasses for dinner. One day when he couldn't stand it any longer, he threw flour and yeast into it, baked it, then sat down to eat while mumbling, "Anna, damn her."

1. Stir cornmeal into boiling water. Add cold water, molasses and 2 tablespoons (30 mL) of the butter. Cool until 120° to 130°F. (49° to 54°C.). Reserve.

2. Fit processor with steel blade. Measure 1½ cups (375 mL) of the flour, yeast and salt into work bowl. Process on/off to mix.

3. Add cooled cornmeal mixture to flour mixture. Process until smooth, about 20 seconds.

4. Turn on processor and add enough of the remaining flour through feed tube so dough forms a ball that cleans the sides of the bowl. Process until ball turns around bowl about 25 times.

5. Turn dough onto lightly floured surface. Knead cheese into dough (cheese should be evenly dispersed throughout dough, not lumped together). Shape into ball and place in well greased 8- or 9-inch (20 or 23 cm) pie pan. Flatten dough to fill pan. Cover loosely with plastic wrap and let stand in warm place (85°F. or 30°C.) until doubled, about 1 hour.

6. Heat oven to 375°F. (190°C.). Bake until golden and loaf sounds hollow when tapped, 30 to 35 minutes.

7. Remove immediately from pan. Brush butter over crust. Cool on wire rack.

Makes 1 loaf

Pioneer Bread

¼ to ½ cup (60 to 125 mL)
  warm water (105° to
  115°F. or 41° to 46°C.)
3 tablespoons (45 mL) sugar
1 package (¼ oz. or 7 g)
  active dry yeast
1 egg, beaten
3 tablespoons (45 mL) butter
  or margarine, melted and
  cooled
1¾ cups (430 mL) all-purpose
  flour*
⅓ cup (80 mL) cornmeal
1 teaspoon (5 mL) salt
  Vegetable oil or melted
  butter or margarine

Flour and cornmeal were staples in the diets of many pioneers, so it was natural that they combine them frequently in bread. Today, we can enjoy this Early American favorite the easy way, by using a food processor to handle all the mixing and kneading chores.

1. Combine ¼ cup (60 mL) of the water, 1 tablespoon (15 mL) of the sugar and yeast. Stir to dissolve yeast and let stand until bubbly, about 5 minutes. Blend egg and butter into yeast mixture.

2. Fit processor with steel blade. Measure flour, cornmeal and salt into work bowl. Process on/off to mix.

3. Add yeast mixture to flour mixture. Process until blended, about 10 seconds.

4. Turn on processor and very slowly drizzle just enough remaining water through feed tube into flour mixture so dough forms a ball that cleans the sides of the bowl. Process until ball turns around bowl about 25 times. Turn off processor and let dough stand 1 to 2 minutes.

5. Turn on processor and gradually drizzle in enough remaining water to make dough soft, smooth and satiny but not sticky.** Process until dough turns around bowl about 15 times.

6. Turn dough onto lightly greased surface. Shape into ball and place in lightly greased bowl, turning to grease all sides. Cover loosely with plastic wrap and let stand in warm place (85°F. or 30°C.) until doubled, about 1 hour. *continued*

---

*Spoon flour into dry measuring cup and level off. Do not scoop.

**If dough is too dry and stiff, too soft and sticky, or if the processor shuts off, correct problem according to directions on page 25.

Pioneer Bread *(continued)*

7. Punch down dough. Shape into loaf (see Shaping in Index) and place in greased 8½x4½x2½-inch (21.5x11.5x6.5 cm) loaf pan. Brush with oil. Let stand in warm place until doubled, about 1 hour.

8. Heat oven to 400°F. (200°C.). Bake until golden and loaf sounds hollow when tapped, 25 to 30 minutes.

9. Remove immediately from pan. Brush crust with oil, if desired. Cool on wire rack.

Cottage Cheese Dill Bread

Makes 1 loaf

¼ to ½ cup (60 to 125 mL) warm water (105° to 115°F. or 41° to 46°C.)

2 tablespoons (30 mL) sugar

1 package (¼ oz. or 7 g) active dry yeast

2¾ cups (680 mL) all-purpose flour*

1 tablespoon (15 mL) instant minced onions

1 tablespoon (15 mL) butter or margarine

2 teaspoons (10 mL) dried dill weed

1 teaspoon (5 mL) salt

¼ teaspoon (1 mL) baking soda

1 cup (250 mL) creamed cottage cheese, at room temperature

1 egg, beaten
   Vegetable oil or melted butter or margarine

This round, crusty loaf of white bread has a moist, creamy crumb due to the addition of cottage cheese to the dough. Serve it warm or cool with soups, salads or meats.

1. Combine ¼ cup (60 mL) of the water, sugar and yeast. Stir to dissolve yeast and let stand until bubbly, about 5 minutes.

2. Fit processor with steel blade. Measure flour, onions, butter, dill weed, salt and soda into work bowl. Process until mixed, about 15 seconds.

3. Add yeast mixture to flour mixture. Process until blended, about 10 seconds.

4. Combine cottage cheese and beaten egg. Pour evenly over flour mixture.

5. Turn on processor and very slowly drizzle just enough remaining water through feed tube into flour mixture so dough forms a ball that cleans the sides of the bowl. Process until ball turns around bowl about 25 times. Turn off processor and let dough stand 1 to 2 minutes.

6. Turn on processor and gradually drizzle in just enough remaining water to make dough soft, smooth and satiny but not sticky.** Process until dough turns around bowl about 15 times.

7. Turn dough onto lightly greased surface. Shape into a ball and place in lightly greased bowl, turning to grease all sides. Cover loosely with plastic wrap and let stand in warm place (85°F. or 30°C.) until doubled, about 1 hour.

8. Punch down dough. Shape into smooth ball and place on greased cookie sheet. Roll or pat dough into a circle about 8 inches (20 cm) in diameter. Brush with oil and let stand in warm place until almost doubled, about 45 minutes.

9. Heat oven to 350°F. (180°C.). Bake until evenly brown, 35 to 45 minutes.

10. Remove from cookie sheet. Cool on wire rack.

---

*Spoon flour into dry measuring cup and level off. Do not scoop.

**If dough is too dry and stiff, too soft and sticky, or if the processor shuts off, correct problem according to directions on page 25.

BASIC BREADS

Whole Wheat Zucchini Yeast Bread

Makes 2 loaves

2 to 5 tablespoons (30 to 75 mL) warm water (105° to 115°F. or 41° to 46°C.)

2 tablespoons (30 mL) packed brown sugar

1 package (¼ oz. or 7 g) active dry yeast

2 cups (500 mL) all-purpose flour*

½ cup (125 mL) whole wheat flour

¼ cup (60 mL) wheat germ

3 tablespoons (45 mL) instant nonfat dry milk solids

2 tablespoons (30 mL) butter or margarine, cut into 2 pieces

2 teaspoons (10 mL) ground coriander

1 teaspoon (5 mL) salt

1 teaspoon (5 mL) grated orange rind, optional

1½ cups shredded zucchini

⅔ cup (160 mL) dark raisins or currants

This is a really good bread with a chewy crust and a moist, full flavored interior. Its hearty taste is the result of an interesting mix of ingredients: whole wheat flour, shredded zucchini, raisins, wheat germ, coriander and orange.

1. Combine 2 tablespoons (30 mL) of the water, 1 tablespoon (15 mL) of the brown sugar and yeast. Stir to dissolve yeast and let stand until bubbly, about 5 minutes.

2. Fit processor with steel blade. Measure flours, wheat germ, dry milk, butter, remaining 1 tablespoon (15 mL) of the sugar, coriander, salt and orange rind, if desired, into work bowl. Process on/off 2 or 3 times until mixed.

3. Sprinkle zucchini over flour mixture. Process until zucchini is blended in, about 5 seconds.

4. Add yeast mixture to flour mixture. Turn on processor and very slowly drizzle just enough remaining water through feed tube into flour mixture so dough forms a ball that cleans the sides of the bowl. Process until ball turns around bowl about 25 times. Turn off processor and let dough stand 1 to 2 minutes.

5. Turn on processor and gradually drizzle in enough remaining water to make dough soft, smooth and satiny but not sticky.** Process until dough turns around bowl about 15 times.

6. Turn dough onto lightly floured surface. Knead raisins into dough. Shape dough into ball, cover with plastic wrap and let stand at room temperature about 30 minutes.

7. Divide dough in half. Shape each half into smooth ball and place on greased cookie sheet. Roll or pat into circle about 5 inches (13 cm) in diameter. Cover loosely with plastic wrap and let stand in warm place (85°F. or 30°C.) until doubled, about 45 minutes.

8. Heat oven to 350°F. (180°C.). Uncover breads and bake until evenly brown and loaves sound hollow when tapped, 30 to 35 minutes.

9. Remove from cookie sheets. Cool on wire rack.

Old-Fashioned Hearth Bread

Makes 1 loaf

½ to ¾ cup (125 to 180 mL) warm water (105° to 115°F. or 41° to 46°C.)

2 tablespoons (30 mL) honey or light molasses

1 package (¼ oz. or 7 g) active dry yeast

2 cups (500 mL) all-purpose flour*

2 tablespoons (30 mL) instant nonfat dry milk solids

1 tablespoon (15 mL) wheat germ

1 tablespoon (15 mL) butter or margarine

1 teaspoon (5 mL) salt

In days gone by, breads like these were baked on flat stones in an open fire. Today, the baking methods are much improved and so are the mixing methods. A food processor mixes and kneads the bread dough literally in seconds.

1. Combine ¼ cup (60 mL) of the water, honey and yeast. Stir to dissolve yeast and let stand until bubbly, about 5 minutes.

2. Fit processor with steel blade. Measure flour, dry milk, wheat germ, butter and salt into work bowl. Process until mixed, about 15 seconds.

3. Add yeast mixture to flour mixture. Process until blended, about 10 seconds.

4. Turn on processor and very slowly drizzle just enough remaining water through feed tube into flour mixture so dough forms a ball that cleans the sides of the bowl. Process until ball turns around bowl about 25 times. Turn off processor and let dough stand 1 to 2 minutes.   *continued*

*Spoon flour into dry measuring cup and level off. Do not scoop.

**If dough is too dry and stiff, too soft and sticky, or if the processor shuts off, correct problem according to directions on page 25.

Old-Fashioned Hearth Bread *(continued)*

5. Turn on processor and gradually drizzle in enough remaining water to make dough soft, smooth and satiny but not sticky.** Process until dough turns around bowl about 15 times.

6. Turn dough onto lightly greased surface. Shape into ball and place in lightly greased bowl, turning to grease all sides. Cover loosely with plastic wrap and let stand in warm place (85°F. or 30°C.) until doubled, about 1 hour.

7. Punch down dough. Shape into smooth ball and place on greased cookie sheet. Roll or pat into circle about 6 inches (15 cm) in diameter. Cover loosely with plastic wrap and let stand in warm place until almost doubled, about 45 minutes.

8. Heat oven to 375°F. (190°C.). Bake until golden and loaf sounds hollow when tapped, about 25 to 30 minutes.

9. Remove from cookie sheet. Cool on wire rack.

Mini Herb Breads

Makes 3 small loaves

¼ to ½ cup (60 to 125 mL) warm water (105° to 115°F. or 41° to 46°C.)

2 tablespoons (30 mL) sugar

1 package (¼ oz. or 7 g) active dry yeast

2¾ cups (680 mL) all-purpose flour*

½ cup (125 mL) instant nonfat dry milk solids

2 tablespoons (30 mL) butter or margarine

1 tablespoon (15 mL) dried herbs (dill weed, savory, basil, thyme or marjoram)

1 teaspoon (5 mL) salt

2 eggs, beaten

Melted butter or margarine, optional

Flavor these little breads with your favorite dried herbs and serve them at lunch or dinner. Baked in disposable foil baking pans, they make nice gifts, too.

1. Combine ¼ cup (60 mL) of the water, sugar and yeast. Stir to dissolve yeast and let stand until bubbly, about 5 minutes.

2. Fit processor with steel blade. Measure flour, dry milk, 2 tablespoons (30 mL) of the butter, herbs and salt into the work bowl. Process until mixed, about 15 seconds.

3. Add yeast mixture to flour mixture. Process until blended, about 10 seconds.

4. Turn on processor and slowly drizzle beaten eggs through feed tube and just enough remaining water so dough forms a ball that cleans the sides of the bowl. Process until ball turns around bowl about 25 times. Turn off processor and let dough stand 1 to 2 minutes.

5. Turn on processor and gradually drizzle in enough remaining water to make dough soft, smooth and satiny but not sticky.** Process until dough turns around bowl about 15 times.

6. Turn dough onto lightly floured surface. Shape into ball and place in lightly greased bowl, turning to grease all sides. Cover with plastic wrap and let stand in warm place (85°F. or 30°C.) until doubled, about 1 hour.

7. Punch down dough. Divide into 3 equal parts. Shape each part into a small loaf and place in greased 5¾x3½x2¼-inch (15x9x5.5 cm) loaf pan. Cover pans loosely with plastic wrap and let stand in warm place until doubled, about 45 minutes.

8. Heat oven to 375°F. (190°C.). Bake until golden and loaves sound hollow when tapped, 15 to 20 minutes.

9. Remove immediately from pans. Brush crusts with melted butter, if desired. Cool on wire rack.

---

*Spoon flour into dry measuring cup and level off. Do not scoop.

**If dough is too dry and stiff, too soft and sticky, or if the processor shuts off, correct problem according to directions on page 25.

Makes 1 loaf

Three Colored Party Braid

White Dough for Party
  Braid (recipe follows)
Whole Wheat Dough for
  Party Braid (recipe
  follows)
Rye Dough for Party
  Braid (recipe follows)
Water
Sesame Seeds

Three different doughs, a white, a whole wheat and a rye, make up this pretty bread. The doughs are shaped into strands, then braided and stacked together. Slice it thinly and serve with assorted cheeses, spreads and cold cuts.

1. Prepare White Dough as directed.

2. Prepare Whole Wheat Dough as directed.

3. Prepare Rye Dough as directed.

4. Divide each dough into 3 equal parts. Shape each part into a strand about 18 inches (45 cm) long. Shape strands into three separate braids using one strand of each dough per braid.

5. Place two braids side by side on large greased cookie sheet. Tuck ends under and pinch to seal. Pinch to seal the two braids together.

6. Center remaining braid on top of the two braids. Tuck ends under and pinch to seal. Pinch to seal where braids meet. Brush water over braids. Sprinkle with sesame seeds. Let stand in warm place (85°F. or 30°C.) until doubled, about 45 minutes.

7. Heat oven to 400°F. (200°C.). Bake until loaf sounds hollow when tapped, 25 to 30 minutes.

8. Remove immediately from cookie sheet. Cool on wire rack.

White Dough For Party Braid

½ to ¾ cup (125 to 180 mL)
     warm water (105° to
     115°F. or 41° to 46°C.)
1 tablespoon (15 mL) sugar
1 package (¼ oz. or 7 g)
     active dry yeast
2 cups (500 mL) all-purpose
     flour*
1 tablespoon (15 mL) butter
     or margarine
½ teaspoon (2 mL) salt

1. Combine ¼ cup (60 mL) of the water, sugar and yeast. Stir to dissolve yeast and let stand until bubbly, about 5 minutes.

2. Fit processor with steel blade. Measure flour, butter and salt into work bowl. Process until mixed, about 15 seconds.

3. Add yeast mixture to flour mixture. Process until blended, about 10 seconds.

4. Turn on processor and very slowly drizzle just enough remaining water through feed tube into flour mixture so dough forms a ball that cleans the sides of the bowl. Process until ball turns around bowl about 25 times. Turn off processor and let dough stand 1 to 2 minutes.

5. Turn on processor and gradually drizzle in enough remaining water to make dough soft, smooth and satiny but not sticky.** Process until dough turns around bowl about 15 times.

6. Turn dough onto lightly greased surface. Shape into ball and place in lightly greased bowl, turning to grease all sides. Cover loosely with plastic wrap and let stand in warm place until doubled, about 1 hour.

7. Punch down dough. Shape as directed.

Whole Wheat Dough For Party Braid

½ to ¾ cup (125 to 180 mL)
     warm water (105° to
     115°F. or 41° to 46°C.)
1 tablespoon (15 mL) brown
     sugar
   continued

1. Combine ¼ cup (60 mL) of the water, sugar and yeast. Stir to dissolve yeast and let stand until bubbly, about 5 minutes.

2. Fit processor with steel blade. Measure flours, butter and salt into work bowl. Process until mixed, about 15 seconds.

*Spoon flour into dry measuring cup and level off. Do not scoop.

**If dough is too dry and stiff, too soft and sticky, or if the processor shuts off, correct problem according to directions on page 25.

Whole Wheat Dough For Party Braid (continued)

1 package (¼ oz. or 7 g)
  active dry yeast
1½ cups (375 mL) all-purpose
  flour*
½ cup (125 mL) whole wheat
  flour
1 tablespoon (15 mL) butter
  or margarine
½ teaspoon (2 mL) salt

3. Add yeast mixture to flour mixture. Process until blended, about 10 seconds.

4. Turn on processor and very slowly drizzle just enough remaining water through feed tube into flour mixture so dough forms a ball that cleans the sides of the bowl. Process until ball turns around bowl about 25 times. Turn off processor and let dough stand 1 to 2 minutes.

5. Turn on processor and gradually drizzle in enough remaining water to make dough soft, smooth and satiny but not sticky.** Process until dough turns around bowl about 15 times.

6. Turn dough onto lightly greased surface. Shape into ball and place in lightly greased bowl, turning to grease all sides. Cover loosely with plastic wrap and let stand in warm place until doubled, about 1 hour.

7. Punch down dough. Shape as directed.

Rye Dough For Party Braid

½ to ¾ cup (125 to 180 mL)
  warm water (105° to
  115°F. or 41° to 46°C.)
1 tablespoon (15 mL)
  molasses
1 package (¼ oz. or 7 g)
  active dry yeast
1½ cups (375 mL) all-purpose
  flour*
½ cup (125 mL) rye flour
1 tablespoon (15 mL)
  caraway seeds
1 tablespoon (15 mL) butter
  or margarine
½ teaspoon (2 mL) salt

1. Combine ¼ cup (60 mL) of the water, molasses and yeast. Stir to dissolve yeast and let stand until bubbly, about 5 minutes.

2. Fit processor with steel blade. Measure flours, caraway seeds, butter and salt into work bowl. Process until mixed, about 15 seconds.

3. Add yeast mixture to flour mixture. Process until blended, about 10 seconds.

4. Turn on processor and very slowly drizzle just enough remaining water through feed tube into flour mixture so dough forms a ball that cleans the sides of the bowl. Process until ball turns around bowl about 25 times. Turn off processor and let dough stand 1 to 2 minutes.

5. Turn on processor and gradually drizzle in enough remaining water to make dough soft, smooth and satiny but not sticky.** Process until dough turns around bowl about 15 times.

6. Turn dough onto lightly greased surface. Shape into ball and place in lightly greased bowl, turning to grease all sides. Cover loosely with plastic wrap and let stand in warm place until doubled, about 1 hour.

7. Punch down dough. Shape as directed.

*Spoon flour into dry measuring cup and level off. Do not scoop.

**If dough is too dry and stiff, too soft and sticky, or if the processor shuts off, correct problem according to directions on page 25.

BUNS AND DINNER ROLLS

Light Rye Rolls

Makes 1 dozen rolls

¾ to 1 cup (180 to 250 mL) warm water (105° to 115°F. or 41° to 46°C.)

¼ cup (60 mL) packed light brown sugar

1 package (¼ oz. or 7 g) active dry yeast

2½ cups (625 mL) all-purpose flour*

½ cup (125 mL) rye flour

⅓ cup (80 mL) wheat germ

¼ cup (60 mL) cold butter or margarine, cut into 4 pieces

¾ teaspoon (4 mL) salt

1 egg, beaten

1 egg white, slightly beaten Caraway seeds

Rye breads came to us from the Scandinavian countries where they're made in a variety of ways. This version is a light rye flavored with brown sugar and wheat germ. It can be shaped into rolls or a loaf.

1. Combine ¼ cup (60 mL) of the water, 1 tablespoon (15 mL) of the sugar and yeast. Stir to dissolve yeast and let stand until bubbly, about 5 minutes.

2. Fit processor with steel blade. Measure flours, wheat germ, butter, remaining brown sugar and salt into work bowl. Process until mixed, about 20 seconds.

3. Add yeast mixture and egg to flour mixture. Process until blended, about 10 seconds.

4. Turn on processor and very slowly drizzle just enough remaining water through feed tube into flour mixture so dough forms a ball that cleans the sides of the bowl. Process until ball turns around bowl about 25 times. Turn off processor and let dough stand 1 to 2 minutes.

5. Turn on processor and gradually drizzle in enough remaining water to make dough soft, smooth and satiny but not sticky.** Process until dough turns around bowl about 15 times.

6. Cover work bowl and let dough stand at room temperature until doubled, about 1½ hours.

7. Turn processor on/off once or twice to punch down dough.

8. Turn dough onto lightly floured surface and roll out ½-inch (1.5 cm) thick. Cut out rolls into circles 2½-inches (6.5 cm) in diameter using lightly floured round biscuit or cookie cutter. Reroll and cut leftover dough. Place rolls on greased cookie sheet about 1½ inches (4 cm) apart. Cover loosely with plastic wrap and let stand in warm place (85°F. or 30°C.) until doubled, about 1 hour.

9. Heat oven to 400°F. (200°C.). Uncover rolls and brush with beaten egg white. Sprinkle with caraway seeds. Bake until golden, 10 to 12 minutes.

10. Remove immediately from cookie sheet and cool on wire rack.

Light Rye Bread Prepare dough as directed for Light Rye Rolls through first rising. Punch down dough and shape into loaf. Place in greased 9x5x3-inch (23x13x8 cm) loaf pan. Cover loosely with plastic wrap and let stand in warm place (85°F. or 30°C.) until doubled, 45 to 60 minutes. Heat oven to 375°F. (190°C.). Brush loaf with beaten egg white and sprinkle with caraway seeds. Bake until golden and loaf sounds hollow when tapped, 25 to 30 minutes. Remove immediately from pan and cool on wire rack.

*Spoon flour into dry measuring cup and level off. Do not scoop.

**If dough is too dry and stiff, too soft and sticky, or if the processor shuts off, correct problem according to directions on page 25.

Raised Buttermilk Biscuits

Makes about 1½ dozen

¼ cup (60 mL) warm water (105° to 115°F. or 41° to 46°C.)
1 package (¼ oz. or 7 g) active dry yeast
1 tablespoon (15 mL) sugar
2¾ cups (680 mL) all-purpose flour*
¼ cup (60 mL) cold butter or margarine, cut into 4 pieces
1 teaspoon (5 mL) salt
1 teaspoon (5 mL) baking powder
½ teaspoon (2 mL) baking soda
¾ to 1 cup (180 to 250 mL) cold buttermilk
Melted butter or margarine

These tasty, crusty yeast-raised biscuits adapt to almost any meal—from breakfast to a casual soup and salad lunch to a formal dinner.

1. Combine water, yeast and sugar. Stir to dissolve yeast and let stand until bubbly, about 5 minutes.

2. Fit processor with steel blade. Measure flour, butter, salt, baking powder and soda into work bowl. Process until mixed, about 15 seconds.

3. Add yeast mixture to flour mixture. Process until blended, about 10 seconds.

4. Add the buttermilk, ¼ cup (60 mL) at a time, processing on/off 5 times after each addition. Add just enough buttermilk to make a dough that is very coarse and crumbly. It should NOT be smooth and satiny like most yeast doughs.

5. Turn dough onto lightly floured surface, sprinkle lightly with flour and cover with inverted bowl or plastic wrap. Let stand 15 to 20 minutes.

6. Roll out dough ½ inch (1.5 cm) thick. Cut into circles 2½ inches (6.5 cm) in diameter using a biscuit or cookie cutter. Place on lightly greased cookie sheet and brush with melted butter. Let stand in warm place (85°F. or 30°C.) until doubled, about 45 minutes.

7. Heat oven to 425°F. (220°C.). Bake until golden, 10 to 12 minutes.

8. Remove immediately from cookie sheet and cool on wire rack.

Saffron Raisin Buns

Makes 1 dozen buns

½ to ¾ cup (125 to 180 mL) warm water (105° to 115°F. or 41° to 46°C.)
2 tablespoons (30 mL) honey
1 package (¼ oz. or 7 g) active dry yeast
2¼ cups (560 mL) all-purpose flour*
2 tablespoons (30 mL) vegetable oil
1 teaspoon (5 mL) salt
⅛ teaspoon (0.5 mL) ground saffron
½ cup (125 mL) dark raisins
1 egg, beaten
2 to 3 tablespoons (30 to 45 mL) sugar

The combination of saffron and raisins is a classic in these sweet buns that trace their roots to Cornwall, England.

1. Combine ¼ cup (60 mL) of the water, honey and yeast. Stir to dissolve yeast and let stand until bubbly, about 5 minutes.

2. Fit processor with steel blade. Measure flour, oil and salt into work bowl. Process until mixed, about 10 seconds.

3. Add yeast mixture to flour mixture. Process until blended, about 10 seconds.

4. Stir saffron into ¼ cup (60 mL) of the remaining water. Turn on processor and slowly drizzle just enough saffron-water mixture through feed tube into flour mixture so dough forms a ball that cleans the sides of the bowl. Process until ball turns around bowl about 25 times. Turn off processor and let dough stand 1 to 2 minutes.

5. Turn on processor and gradually drizzle in enough remaining water to make dough soft, smooth and satiny but not sticky.** Process until dough turns around bowl about 15 times.

6. Let dough stand in work bowl 5 minutes. Turn dough onto lightly greased surface. Knead in the raisins. Cover dough with inverted bowl or plastic wrap and let rest about 30 minutes.

7. Uncover dough and divide into 12 equal parts. Shape each part into a ball and place on lightly greased cookie sheet. Cover loosely with plastic wrap and let stand in warm place (85°F. or 30°C.) until doubled, about 1 hour.

8. Heat oven to 375°F. (190°C.). Uncover buns and brush with beaten egg. Sprinkle with sugar. Bake until golden, 20 to 25 minutes. Remove from cookie sheet. Cool on wire rack.

---

*Spoon flour into dry measuring cup and level off. Do not scoop.

**If dough is too dry and stiff, too soft and sticky, or if the processor shuts off, correct problem according to directions on page 25.

BUNS AND DINNER ROLLS

Parkerhouse Rolls

Makes 15 to 18 rolls

½ to ¾ cup (125 to 180 mL)
   warm water (105° to
   115°F. or 41° to 46°C.)

3 tablespoons (45 mL) sugar

1 package (¼ oz. or 7 g)
   active dry yeast

2¾ cups (680 mL) all-purpose
   flour*

3 tablespoons (45 mL) instant
   nonfat dry milk solids

3 tablespoons (45 mL) cold
   butter or margarine, cut
   into 3 pieces

1 teaspoon (5 mL) salt

1 egg, beaten
   Melted butter or vegetable
   oil

Parkerhouse Rolls are a dinner roll classic in the United States. With a food processor, the dough is easy to prepare. To shape the rolls, simply cut the dough into circles and fold in half-moon shapes.

1. Combine ¼ cup (60 mL) of the water, 1 tablespoon (15 mL) of the sugar and yeast. Stir to dissolve yeast and let stand until bubbly, about 5 minutes.

2. Fit processor with steel blade. Measure flour, dry milk, remaining sugar, butter and salt into work bowl. Process until mixed, about 15 seconds.

3. Add yeast mixture and egg to flour mixture. Process until blended, about 10 seconds.

4. Turn on processor and very slowly drizzle just enough remaining water through feed tube into flour mixture so dough forms a ball that cleans sides of the bowl. Process until dough turns around bowl about 25 times. Turn off processor and let dough stand 1 to 2 minutes.

5. Turn on processor and gradually drizzle in enough remaining water to make dough soft, smooth and satiny, but not sticky.** Process until dough turns around bowl about 15 times.

6. Turn dough onto lightly floured surface. Shape into ball and place in lightly greased bowl, turning to grease all sides. Cover loosely with plastic wrap and let stand in warm place (85°F. or 30°C.) until doubled, 1 to 1½ hours.

7. Punch down dough. Roll out ¼-inch (0.5 cm) thick and brush with melted butter. Cut with 3-inch (8 cm) round cookie or biscuit cutter. Make a crease with dull edge of table knife just off center of each round. Fold larger side over other side. Pinch center of rounded edges together. Reroll and shape leftover dough.

8. Place rolls on greased cookie sheets. Brush with melted butter. Let rise in warm place until doubled, 30 to 40 minutes.

9. Heat oven to 375°F. (190°C.). Bake until golden, 12 to 15 minutes. Remove immediately from cookie sheets and cool on wire rack.

Herbed Cloverleaf Rolls

Makes 1 dozen rolls

¾ to 1 cup (180 to 250 mL)
   warm water (105° to
   115°F. or 41° to 46°C.)

1 package (¼ oz. or 7 g)
   active dry yeast

2 teaspoons (10 mL) sugar

2¾ cups (680 mL) all-purpose
   flour*

2 tablespoons (30 mL)
   vegetable oil

1 teaspoon (5 mL) salt
   Vegetable oil or melted
   butter

1 tablespoon (15 mL) mixed
   dried herbs

Cloverleaf Rolls are another old-fashioned dinner roll classic. For extra flavor, these are rolled in dried herbs, such as parsley, chives, oregano, savory, basil, thyme or tarragon. Of course, you can omit the herbs if you prefer your rolls plain.

1. Combine ¼ cup (60 mL) of the water, yeast and sugar. Stir to dissolve yeast and let stand until bubbly, about 5 minutes.

2. Fit processor with steel blade. Measure flour, 2 tablespoons (30 mL) oil, and salt into work bowl. Process until mixed, about 15 seconds.

3. Add yeast mixture to flour mixture. Process until blended, about 10 seconds.

4. Turn on processor and very slowly drizzle just enough remaining water through feed tube into flour mixture so dough forms a ball that cleans sides of the bowl. Process until ball turns around bowl about 25 times. Turn off processor and let dough stand 1 to 2 minutes. *continued*

---

*Spoon flour into dry measuring cup and level off. Do not scoop.

**If dough is too dry and stiff, too soft and sticky, or if the processor shuts off, correct problem according to directions on page 25.

Herbed Cloverleaf Rolls *(continued)*

5. Turn on processor and gradually drizzle in enough remaining water to make dough soft, smooth and satiny but not sticky.** Process until dough turns around bowl about 15 times.

6. Turn dough onto lightly floured surface. Shape into ball and place in lightly greased bowl, turning to grease all sides. Cover loosely with plastic wrap. Let stand in warm place (85°F. or 30°C.) until almost doubled, about 30 minutes.

7. Divide dough into 12 equal parts. Divide each part into 3 pieces and shape each into a smooth ball. Dip each ball in oil and roll in herbs. Place 3 balls in each greased muffin cup.

8. Let stand in warm place until doubled, 50 to 60 minutes.

9. Heat oven to 375°F. (190°C.). Bake until golden, 15 to 20 minutes.

10. Remove rolls immediately from muffin cups and cool on wire rack.

Italian Pan Rolls

Makes 16 rolls

¾ to 1 cup (180 to 250 mL) warm water (105° to 115°F. or 41° to 46°C.)

1 tablespoon (15 mL) sugar

1 package (¼ oz. or 7 g) active dry yeast

2¾ cups (680 mL) all-purpose flour*

1 tablespoon (15 mL) cold butter or margarine

1 teaspoon (5 mL) garlic salt

½ teaspoon (2 mL) Italian herb seasoning or ¼ teaspoon (1 mL) each leaf basil and oregano

2 tablespoons (30 mL) olive oil, vegetable oil or melted butter

¼ cup (60 mL) grated Parmesan cheese

These easy dinner rolls are prepared from an herb seasoned dough that's shaped into balls and rolled in grated Parmesan cheese for added flavor. They're super with barbecued or roasted meats and, of course, with any Italian style meal.

1. Combine ¼ cup (60 mL) of the water, sugar and yeast. Stir to dissolve yeast and let stand until bubbly, about 5 minutes.

2. Fit processor with steel blade. Measure flour, butter, garlic salt and herb seasoning into work bowl. Process until mixed, about 10 seconds.

3. Add yeast mixture to flour mixture. Process until blended, about 10 seconds.

4. Turn on processor and very slowly drizzle just enough remaining water through feed tube into flour mixture so dough forms a ball that cleans sides of the bowl. Process until ball turns around bowl about 25 times. Turn off processor and let dough stand 1 to 2 minutes.

5. Turn on processor and gradually drizzle in enough remaining water to make dough soft, smooth and satiny but not sticky.** Process until dough turns around bowl about 15 times.

6. Turn dough onto lightly floured surface. Shape into ball and place in lightly greased bowl, turning to grease all sides. Cover loosely with plastic wrap and let stand in warm place (85°F. or 30°C.) about 30 minutes.

7. Divide dough into quarters, then divide again into quarters, making 16 pieces. Shape each piece into a ball, dip in oil, coat with cheese and arrange in greased 8 or 9-inch (20 or 23 cm) round or square cake pan.

8. Cover loosely with plastic wrap. Let stand in warm place until doubled, 1 to 1½ hours.

9. Heat oven to 375°F. (190°C.). Uncover rolls and bake until golden, about 25 minutes.

10. Remove immediately from pan and cool on wire rack.

---

*Spoon flour into dry measuring cup and level off. Do not scoop.

**If dough is too dry and stiff, too soft and sticky, or if the processor shuts off, correct problem according to directions on page 25.

BUNS AND DINNER ROLLS

Makes 32 rolls

Easy Croissants

1 cup (250 mL) warm water (105° to 115°F. or 41° to 46°C.)

1 package (¼ oz. or 7 g) active dry yeast

1 can (5.33 oz. or 158 mL) evaporated milk

⅓ cup (80 mL) sugar

2 eggs

1½ teaspoons (7 mL) salt

5½ cups (1375 mL) all-purpose flour*

¼ cup (60 mL) butter or margarine, melted and cooled

1 cup (250 mL) cold butter or margarine, cut into ¼-inch (0.5 cm) thick slices

1 tablespoon (15 mL) cold water

Fine French pastry chefs would find it difficult to match the flavor and goodness of these marvelous rolls. And they certainly could not match the ease with which these croissants are prepared with a food processor.

1. Combine warm water and yeast in 1-quart (1 L) bowl. Stir to dissolve yeast. Add evaporated milk, sugar, 1 egg, salt and 1 cup (250 mL) of the flour. Beat mixture with whisk to make a smooth batter. Blend in the melted butter. Reserve.

2. Fit processor with steel blade. Measure 3 cups (750 mL) of the remaining flour and cold butter slices into the work bowl. Process on/off 15 to 20 times until butter is in pieces no larger than kidney beans. Transfer mixture to large mixing bowl. Stir in the remaining 1½ cups (375 mL) flour.

3. Pour yeast-milk mixture over flour mixture. Stir with wooden spoon or rubber spatula just until all flour is moistened. Cover tightly and refrigerate until thoroughly chilled, at least 4 hours or up to 3 days.

4. Turn dough onto lightly floured surface. Knead about 6 times. Divide dough into 4 equal parts. Shape 1 part at a time, keeping others in refrigerator.

5. Roll each part on well floured surface into a circle about 17 inches (43 cm) in diameter. Cut into 8 equal pie-shaped wedges. Roll up each wedge, starting at wide end and rolling towards point. Place on ungreased cookie sheets about 1½ inches (4 cm) apart. Curve ends of each roll to form crescent shapes.

6. Cover loosely with plastic wrap and let stand in warm place (85°F. or 30°C.) until doubled, 1 to 1½ hours.

7. Heat oven to 325°F. (160°C.). Beat remaining egg and cold water with a fork. Brush mixture over each roll. Bake until golden, 20 to 25 minutes.

8. Remove immediately from cookie sheets and cool on wire rack. Serve warm.

Makes 8 buns

Whole Grain Caraway Onion Buns

¾ to 1 cup (180 to 250 mL) warm water (105° to 115°F. or 41° to 46°C.)

1 tablespoon (15 mL) brown sugar

1 package (¼ oz. or 7 g) active dry yeast

1¾ cups (430 mL) all-purpose flour*

1 cup (250 mL) whole wheat flour

¼ cup (60 mL) instant minced onion

1 tablespoon (15 mL) caraway seeds

2 teaspoons (10 mL) salt
Vegetable oil

Whole grain, onion and caraway seeds give these buns a hardy flavor that makes them great for sandwiches made with hamburger patties, Polish sausage or sliced, cooked meats.

1. Combine ¼ cup (60 mL) of the water, sugar and yeast. Stir to dissolve yeast and let stand until bubbly, about 5 minutes.

2. Fit processor with steel blade. Measure the flours, onion, caraway seeds and salt into work bowl. Process until mixed, about 5 seconds.

3. Add yeast mixture to flour mixture. Process until blended, about 10 seconds.

4. Turn on processor and very slowly drizzle just enough remaining water through feed tube into flour mixture so dough forms a ball that cleans sides of bowl. Process until ball turns around bowl about 25 times. Turn off processor and let dough stand 1 to 2 minutes.

5. Turn on processor and gradually drizzle in enough remaining water to make dough soft, smooth and satiny but not sticky.** Process until dough turns around bowl about 15 times.   *continued*

---

*Spoon flour into dry measuring cup and level off. Do not scoop.

**If dough is too dry and stiff, too soft and sticky, or if the processor shuts off, correct problem according to directions on page 25.

6. Turn dough onto lightly greased surface. Shape into ball and let stand 10 minutes. Divide ball into 8 equal parts. Shape each into ball, place on lightly greased cookie sheet and flatten slightly. Brush with oil.

8. Cover loosely with plastic wrap and let stand in warm place (85°F. or 30°C.) until doubled, about 1 hour.

9. Heat oven to 375°F. (190°C.). Uncover buns and bake until done, 15 to 20 minutes.

10. Remove immediately from cookie sheet and cool on wire rack.

Hamburger Buns

Makes 1 dozen buns

¾ to 1 cup (180 to 250 mL) warm water (105° to 115°F. or 41° to 46° C.)

1 tablespoon (15 mL) sugar

1 package (¼ oz. or 7 g) active dry yeast

2¾ cups (680 mL) all-purpose flour*

2 tablespoons (30 mL) instant nonfat dry milk solids

1½ tablespoons (22 mL) butter or margarine

1 teaspoon (5 mL) salt

1 egg, beaten

Hamburgers and hot dogs are great when paired with homemade buns fresh from the oven, or try the Onion Rolls with bratwurst or Polish sausage. With a food processor, all are a snap to prepare, too.

1. Combine ¼ cup (60 mL) of the water, sugar and yeast. Stir to dissolve yeast and let stand until bubbly, about 5 minutes.

2. Fit processor with steel blade. Measure flour, dry milk, butter and salt into work bowl. Process until mixed about 15 seconds.

3. Add yeast mixture to flour mixture. Process until blended, about 10 seconds.

4. Turn on processor and very slowly drizzle just enough remaining water through feed tube into flour mixture so dough forms a ball that cleans sides of bowl. Process until ball turns around bowl about 25 times. Turn off processor and let dough stand 1 to 2 minutes.

5. Turn on processor and gradually drizzle in enough remaining water to make dough soft, smooth and satiny but not sticky.** Process until dough turns around bowl about 15 times.

6. Turn dough onto lightly greased surface. Cover with inverted bowl or plastic wrap. Let stand 30 minutes.

7. Knead dough 3 or 4 times. Divide dough into 12 equal pieces. Shape each into a smooth ball and place on greased cookie sheet. Flatten balls using palm of hand. Let stand in warm place (85°F. or 30°C.) until doubled, about 45 minutes.

8. Heat oven to 375°F. (190°C.). Brush buns with beaten egg. Bake until golden, 20 to 25 minutes.

9. Remove immediately from cookie sheet and cool on wire rack.

Hot Dog Buns
Prepare dough as directed for Hamburger Buns and divide into 12 equal pieces. Shape each piece into bun 6 inches (15 cm) long. Let rise and bake as for Hamburger Buns.

Onion Rolls
Prepare dough as directed for Hamburger Buns adding 1 tablespoon (15 mL) instant minced onions and 1 teaspoon (5 mL) caraway seeds to work bowl with flour, dry milk, butter and salt. Divide dough into 12 equal parts. Shape each part into bun 6 inches (15 cm) long. Let rise and bake as directed for Hamburger Buns.

---

*Spoon flour into dry measuring cup and level off. Do not scoop.

**If dough is too dry and stiff, too soft and sticky, or if the processor shuts off, correct problem according to directions on page 25.

BUNS AND DINNER ROLLS

Rye Pull-Apart Rolls

Makes 20 rolls

¾ to 1 cup (180 to 250 mL)
    warm water (105° to
    115°F. or 41° to 46°C.)

2 tablespoons (30 mL)
    molasses

1 package (¼ oz. or 7 g)
    active dry yeast

2¼ cups (560 mL) all-purpose
    flour*

½ cup (125 mL) rye flour

⅓ cup (80 mL) instant nonfat
    dry milk solids

1 tablespoon (15 mL) butter
    or margarine

1½ teaspoons (7 mL) salt

1½ teaspoons (7 mL) caraway
    seeds
    Vegetable oil

These delicious rye-caraway flavored rolls are made from a "log" of dough that's sliced before baking. After baking, the rolls simply pull apart.

1. Combine ¼ cup (60 mL) of the water, molasses and yeast. Stir to dissolve yeast and let stand until bubbly, about 5 minutes.

2. Fit processor with steel blade. Measure flours, dry milk, butter, salt and caraway seeds into work bowl.

3. Add yeast mixture to flour mixture. Process until blended, about 10 seconds.

4. Turn on processor and very slowly drizzle just enough remaining water through feed tube into flour mixture so dough forms a ball that cleans sides of bowl. Process until ball turns around bowl about 25 times. Turn off processor and let dough stand 1 to 2 minutes.

5. Turn on processor and gradually drizzle in enough remaining water to make dough soft, smooth and satiny but not sticky.** Process until dough turns around bowl about 15 times.

6. Turn dough onto lightly greased surface. Cover with inverted bowl or plastic wrap and let stand 20 minutes.

7. Shape dough into a roll about 10 inches (25 cm) long. Place on large greased cookie sheet and flatten so roll is about 3-inches (8 cm) wide. Cut with sharp knife straight across dough to make slices ½ to ¾-inch (1.5 to 2 cm) wide and 3 inches (8 cm) long. Do not separate slices. Brush with oil and cover loosely with plastic wrap. Let stand in warm place (85°F. or 30°C.) until doubled, about 1 hour.

8. Heat oven to 375°F. (190°C.). Uncover rolls and bake until golden, about 15 minutes.

9. Remove from cookie sheet and cool on wire rack.

Wheat Germ Pan Rolls

Makes 16 rolls

1 to 1¼ cups (250 to 310 mL)
    warm water (105° to
    115°F. or 41° to 46°C.)

1 tablespoon (15 mL)
    molasses

1 package (¼ oz. or 7 g)
    active dry yeast

2¼ cups (560 mL) all-purpose
    flour*

½ cup (125 mL) whole wheat
    flour

¼ cup (60 mL) wheat germ

1 tablespoon (15 mL)
    vegetable oil

1 teaspoon (5 mL) salt
    Vegetable oil or melted
    butter or margarine
    Wheat germ

Whole wheat flour, wheat germ and molasses add natural goodness to these easy rolls. They're baked in a cake pan and pulled apart for eating.

1. Combine ¼ cup (60 mL) of the water, molasses and yeast. Stir to dissolve yeast and let stand until bubbly, about 5 minutes.

2. Fit processor with steel blade. Measure the flours, ¼ cup (60 mL) wheat germ, 1 tablespoon (15 mL) oil and salt into work bowl. Process until mixed, about 5 seconds.

3. Add yeast mixture to flour mixture. Process until blended, about 10 seconds.

4. Turn on processor and very slowly drizzle just enough remaining water through feed tube into flour mixture so dough forms a ball that cleans sides of bowl. Process until ball turns around bowl about 25 times. Turn off processor and let dough stand 1 to 2 minutes.

5. Turn on processor and gradually drizzle in enough remaining water to make dough soft, smooth and satiny but not sticky.** Process until dough turns around bowl about 15 times. *continued*

*Spoon flour into dry measuring cup and level off. Do not scoop.

**If dough is too dry and stiff, too soft and sticky, or if the processor shuts off, correct problem according to directions on page 25.

6. Turn dough onto lightly floured surface. Shape into ball and let stand 10 minutes. Divide ball into 16 equal parts and shape each into smooth ball.

7. Arrange balls in greased 8- or 9-inch (20 or 23 cm) round or square cake pan. Brush with oil.

8. Cover loosely with plastic wrap and let stand in warm place (85°F. or 30°C.) until doubled, about 1 hour.

9. Heat oven to 350°F. (180°C.). Uncover rolls and bake until golden, 25 to 30 minutes.

10. Remove from pan and cool on wire rack.

Cottage Cheese Pan Rolls

Makes 16 rolls

2   to 5 tablespoons (30 to 75 mL) warm water (105° to 115°F. or 41° to 46°C.)

1   tablespoon (15 mL) sugar

1   package (¼ oz. or 7 g) active dry yeast

2¾ cups (680 mL) all-purpose flour*

2   tablespoons (30 mL) cold butter or margarine

2   teaspoons (10 mL) baking powder

1   teaspoon (5 mL) salt

¼   teaspoon (1 mL) baking soda

1   cup (250 mL) large curd creamed cottage cheese, at room temperature

1   egg, beaten
    Vegetable oil

Cottage cheese is the special ingredient that makes these rolls so moist and light. They're great for breakfast or brunch when served with cream cheese and fruit preserves. They're nice dinner rolls, too, and can be flavored with 2 teaspoons (10 mL) dill weed or leaf oregano, if desired.

1. Combine 2 tablespoons (30 mL) of the water, sugar and yeast. Stir to dissolve yeast and let stand until bubbly, about 5 minutes.

2. Fit processor with steel blade. Measure flour, butter, baking powder, salt and soda into work bowl. Process until mixed, about 10 seconds.

3. Add yeast mixture to flour mixture. Process until blended, about 10 seconds.

4. Combine cottage cheese and egg. Pour half of mixture evenly over flour mixture. Process until blended, about 15 seconds. Pour other half of cheese mixture over flour mixture. Process 15 to 20 seconds. Turn off processor and let dough stand 1 to 2 minutes.

5. Turn on processor and gradually drizzle in enough remaining water to make dough soft, smooth and satiny but not sticky.** Process until dough turns around bowl, about 15 times.

6. Turn dough onto lightly floured surface. Shape into ball and cover with an inverted bowl or plastic wrap. Let stand 20 minutes.

7. Divide dough into 16 equal pieces. Shape each into a ball and arrange in greased 8 inch (20 cm) round cake pan. Brush with oil and let stand in warm place (85°F. or 30°C.) until doubled, 60 to 70 minutes.

8. Heat oven to 350°F. (180°C.). Bake until golden, 25 to 30 minutes.

9. Remove immediately from pan and cool on wire rack.

---

*Spoon flour into dry measuring cup and level off. Do not scoop.

**If dough is too dry and stiff, too soft and sticky, or if the processor shuts off, correct problem according to directions on page 25.

BUNS AND DINNER ROLLS

Crusty Water Rolls

Makes 9 rolls

¼ to ½ cup (60 to 125 mL)
    warm water (105° to
    115°F. or 41° to 46°C.)
1 package (¼ oz. or 7 g)
    active dry yeast
1 teaspoon (5 mL) sugar
¾ teaspoon (4 mL) salt
2 egg whites
2¼ cups (560 mL) all-purpose
    flour*
2 tablespoons (30 mL)
    vegetable oil
    Cornmeal
    Cold water

These rolls also can be called hard rolls, because that's basically what they are—rolls that are crusty-hard on the outside, moist and light on the inside.

1. Combine ¼ cup (60 mL) of the water, yeast, sugar and salt. Stir to dissolve yeast and let stand until bubbly, about 5 minutes. Blend in egg whites.

2. Fit processor with steel blade. Measure flour and oil into work bowl. Process until mixed, about 10 seconds.

3. Turn processor on and very slowly drizzle the yeast mixture through feed tube into flour mixture. Process until blended, about 10 seconds.

4. Turn on processor and very slowly drizzle just enough remaining water into flour mixture so dough forms a ball that cleans sides of bowl. Process until ball turns around bowl about 25 times. Turn off processor and let dough stand 1 to 2 minutes.

5. Turn on processor and gradually drizzle in enough remaining water to make dough soft, smooth and satiny but not sticky.** Process until dough turns around bowl about 15 times.

6. Turn dough onto lightly floured surface. Shape into ball and place in lightly greased bowl, turning to grease all sides. Cover with plastic wrap and let stand in warm place (85°F. or 30°C.) until doubled, about 1 hour.

7. Punch down dough, cover and let rest 10 minutes. Divide dough into 9 equal pieces. Shape each into a ball. Dip bottom side in cornmeal and place on greased cookie sheet about 1½ inches (4 cm) apart. Cover loosely with plastic wrap and let stand in warm place until doubled, about 1 hour.

8. Place a shallow pan of water on bottom rack of oven. Heat oven to 400°F. (200°C.). Brush rolls with cold water. Bake until golden, 15 to 18 minutes. Brush or spray rolls with cold water once or twice during baking, if desired, for crisper crusts.

9. Remove rolls immediately from cookie sheet and cool on wire rack.

Bolillos

Makes 8 rolls

¾ to 1 cup (180 to 250 mL)
    warm water (105° to
    115°F. or 41° to 46°C.)
1 package (¼ oz. or 7 g)
    active dry yeast
1½ teaspoons (7 mL) sugar
1 tablespoon (15 mL) butter
    or margarine
2¾ cups (680 mL) all-purpose
    flour*
¾ teaspoon (4 mL) salt
½ cup (125 mL) cold water
1 teaspoon (5 mL) cornstarch

These spindle-shaped rolls are the Mexican version of hard rolls. For extra crispy crusts, they're brushed before baking with a cornstarch-water mixture.

1. Combine ¼ cup (60 mL) of the warm water, yeast and sugar. Stir to dissolve yeast and let stand until bubbly, about 5 minutes.

2. Stir butter into remaining warm water until butter melts. Reserve.

3. Fit processor with steel blade. Measure flour and salt into work bowl. Add yeast mixture and process until blended, about 10 seconds.

4. Turn on processor and very slowly drizzle enough remaining water-butter mixture through feed tube into flour mixture so dough forms a ball that cleans sides of bowl. Process until ball turns around bowl about 25 times. Turn off processor and let dough stand 1 to 2 minutes. *continued*

---

*Spoon flour into dry measuring cup and level off. Do not scoop.

**If dough is too dry and stiff, too soft and sticky, or if the processor shuts off, correct problem according to directions on page 25.

Bolillos (continued)

5. Turn on processor and gradually drizzle in enough remaining water-butter mixture to make dough soft, smooth and satiny but not sticky.** Process until dough turns around bowl about 15 times.

6. Turn dough onto lightly greased surface and cover with an inverted bowl or plastic wrap. Let stand 30 minutes at room temperature.

7. Knead dough 3 or 4 times. Divide dough into 8 equal pieces. Shape each piece into an oval roll with a slight taper and point at each end. Place rolls on greased cookie sheet 2 or 3 inches (5 or 8 cm) apart. Cover loosely with plastic wrap and let stand in warm place (85°F. or 30°C.) until doubled, about 45 minutes.

8. Heat oven to 375°F. (190°C.). Uncover rolls. Combine cold water and cornstarch in small saucepan. Bring mixture to a boil and brush over rolls. Cut a 2-inch (5 cm) long slash in the top of each roll using a sharp knife or razor blade.

9. Bake until rolls are golden, 25 to 30 minutes.

10. Remove immediately from cookie sheet and cool on wire rack.

Buttery Pan Rolls

Makes 16 rolls

¼ cup (60 mL) warm water (105° to 115°F. or 41° to 46°C.)
2 tablespoons (30 mL) sugar
1 package (¼ oz. or 7 g) active dry yeast
2 cups (500 mL) all-purpose flour*
8 tablespoons (125 mL) butter or margarine, melted and cooled
½ teaspoon (2 mL) salt
1 egg, beaten
¼ to ½ cup (60 to 125 mL) cold milk

Light and fluffy, these simple rolls are wonderful! They're baked in butter and are best served out of the baking pan right from the oven.

1. Combine water, sugar and yeast. Stir to dissolve yeast and let stand until bubbly, about 5 minutes.

2. Fit processor with steel blade. Measure flour, 3 tablespoons (45 mL) of the melted butter and salt into work bowl. Process until mixed, about 15 seconds.

3. Add yeast mixture and egg to flour mixture. Process until blended, about 15 seconds.

4. Turn on processor and very slowly drizzle just enough milk through feed tube into flour mixture to make a smooth batter. Process 10 to 15 seconds. Cover processor and let batter stand at room temperature until light and bubbly, about 45 minutes.

5. Pour half of the remaining melted butter into 8-inch (20 cm) square baking pan. Tilt pan to completely coat bottom with butter.

6. Turn processor on/off twice to beat down batter. Drop batter by rounded tablespoonsful into pan, making 16 rolls. Drizzle remaining butter over rolls. Cover loosely with plastic wrap and let stand in warm place (85°F. or 30°C.) until almost doubled, 30 to 40 minutes.

7. Heat oven to 400°F. (200°C.). Uncover rolls and bake until golden, 12 to 15 minutes. Cool slightly in pan on wire rack.

---

*Spoon flour into dry measuring cup and level off. Do not scoop.

**If dough is too dry and stiff, too soft and sticky, or if the processor shuts off, correct problem according to directions on page 25.

Makes 8 large or 12 small buns

Whole Wheat Sesame Burger Buns

¾ to 1 cup (180 to 250 mL) warm water (105° to 115°F. or 41° to 46°C.)

1 tablespoon (15 mL) brown sugar

1 package (¼ oz. or 7 g) active dry yeast

2¼ cups (560 mL) all-purpose flour*

½ cup (125 mL) whole wheat flour

2 tablespoons (30 mL) wheat germ

2 tablespoons (30 mL) melted butter, margarine or lard

1 teaspoon (5 mL) salt

1 egg white, lightly beaten
Sesame seeds

Homemade hamburger buns are a special treat, especially when they're as good as these are. With a food processor, they're not at all difficult to prepare, either.

1. Combine ¼ cup (60 mL) of the water, sugar and yeast. Stir to dissolve yeast and let stand until bubbly, about 5 minutes.

2. Fit processor with steel blade. Measure flours, wheat germ, butter and salt into work bowl. Process until mixed, about 10 seconds.

3. Add yeast mixture to flour mixture. Process until blended, about 10 seconds.

4. Turn on processor and very slowly drizzle just enough remaining water through feed tube into flour mixture so dough forms a ball that cleans sides of bowl. Process until ball turns around bowl about 25 times. Turn off processor and let dough stand 1 to 2 minutes.

5. Turn on processor and gradually drizzle in enough remaining water to make dough soft, smooth and satiny but not sticky.** Process until dough turns around bowl about 15 times.

6. Turn dough onto lightly floured surface. Shape into ball and let stand 10 minutes.

7. Divide ball into 8 equal parts to make large buns or 12 equal parts to make small buns. Shape each part into smooth ball and place on greased cookie sheet. Let stand in warm place (85°F. or 30°C.) 30 minutes. Flatten buns with palms of hand. Let stand in warm place until almost doubled, about 30 minutes.

8. Brush bun tops with egg white and sprinkle with sesame seeds. Heat oven to 350°F. (180°C.). Bake until golden, 25 to 30 minutes.

9. Remove immediately from cookie sheet and cool on wire rack.

---

*Spoon flour into dry measuring cup and level off. Do not scoop.

**If dough is too dry and stiff, too soft and sticky, or if the processor shuts off, correct problem according to directions on page 25.

Clockwise: Old-Fashioned
Hearth Bread, Old-
Fashioned Cinnamon
Braid, Old-Fashioned
Oatmeal Bread

Whole Wheat Bread (top),
Whole Wheat Zucchini
Yeast Bread (center),
Crusty Rye Bread (bottom)

Clockwise: Crusty Water Rolls, Easy Croissants, Cloverleaf Rolls

Whole Wheat Sesame
Burger Buns and Hot Dog
Buns

SWEET YEAST BREADS

Makes 1 loaf, coffee cake, or 18 rolls ## Basic Sweet Dough

½	to ¾ cup (125 to 180 mL) warm water (105° to 115°F. or 41° to 46°C.)
3	tablespoons (45 mL) sugar
1	package (¼ oz. or 7 g) active dry yeast
2¾	cups (680 mL) all-purpose flour*
2	tablespoons (30 mL) instant nonfat dry milk solids
2	tablespoons (30 mL) butter or margarine, cut into 2 pieces
1	teaspoon (5 mL) salt
1	egg, beaten Vegetable oil or melted butter

This handy recipe really is a basic for many breads, coffee cakes and rolls. You can add nuts, candied or dried fruits and spices to the dough. Shape it any way you like—in rolls or buns, regular or round loaves, braids, twists, pretzels, rings, wreaths—whatever suits your fancy or the occasion.

1. Combine ¼ cup (60 mL) of the water, 1 tablespoon (15 mL) of the sugar and yeast. Stir to dissolve yeast and let stand until bubbly, about 5 minutes.

2. Fit processor with steel blade. Measure flour, dry milk, butter, remaining 2 tablespoons (30 mL) of the sugar and salt into work bowl. Process until mixed, about 15 seconds.

3. Add yeast mixture and egg to flour mixture. Process until blended, about 10 seconds.

4. Turn on processor and very slowly drizzle just enough remaining water through feed tube into flour mixture so dough forms a ball that cleans the sides of the bowl. Process until ball turns around bowl about 25 times. Turn off processor and let dough stand 1 to 2 minutes.

5. Turn on processor and gradually drizzle in enough remaining water to make dough soft, smooth and satiny but not sticky.** Process until dough turns around bowl about 15 times.

6. Turn dough onto lightly floured surface. Shape into ball and place in lightly greased bowl, turning to grease all sides. Cover loosely with plastic wrap and let stand in warm place (85°F. or 30°C.) until doubled, 1 to 1½ hours.

7. Punch down dough. Shape into rolls, loaf or coffee cake, as desired. Place in greased pan or on greased cookie sheet. Brush with oil. Let stand in warm place until doubled, 45 to 60 minutes.

8. Heat oven to 375°F. (190°C.). Bake until done, 15 to 20 minutes for rolls, 20 to 30 minutes for loaf or coffee cake.

9. Remove immediately from pan or cookie sheet. Brush crust with oil, if desired. Cool on wire rack. Frost or decorate as desired.

Refrigerator Sweet Dough Prepare dough as directed for Basic Sweet Dough through first rising period. Shape as desired and place in greased pan. Cover tightly and refrigerate 4 to 24 hours. Uncover and let stand at room temperature 20 minutes before baking. Bake as directed for Basic Sweet Dough.

---

*Spoon flour into dry measuring cup and level off. Do not scoop.

**If dough is too dry and stiff, too soft and sticky, or if the processor shuts off, correct problem according to directions on page 25.

SWEET YEAST BREADS

Danish Coffee Pretzel

Makes 1 coffee cake

Basic Sweet Dough (see Index for page number)

2 tablespoons (30 mL) butter or margarine, at room temperature

3 tablespoons (45 mL) sugar

½ teaspoon (2 mL) ground cinnamon

Vegetable oil

Honey Glaze (recipe follows)

¼ cup (60 mL) slivered blanched almonds

This handsome bread, sweetly spiced with cinnamon and topped with a honey glaze, is super for many occasions. The Danes, who originated the recipe, even decorate it with candles and serve it as a birthday cake!

1. Prepare Basic Sweet Dough as directed through first rising. Punch down dough. Roll out dough into an 8x18-inch (20x45 cm) rectangle. Spread butter over dough.

2. Mix sugar and cinnamon. Sprinkle over butter on dough. Roll up dough jelly-roll fashion, starting on 18-inch (45 cm) side. Pinch seam to seal well. Twist roll by pushing ends in opposite directions, making the roll about 36-inches (90 cm) long. Place dough on large greased cookie sheet and shape into pretzel. Tuck ends under and pinch to seal well. Brush with oil. Let stand in warm place (85°F or 30°C.) until doubled, about 1 hour.

3. Heat oven to 350°F. (180°C.). Bake until evenly brown, 25 to 30 minutes.

4. Prepare Honey Glaze while pretzel is baking. Remove pretzel from cookie sheet and place on wire rack. Brush with warm Honey Glaze and sprinkle with almonds.

Honey Glaze

¼ cup (60 mL) honey

2 tablespoons (30 mL) sugar

1 tablespoon (15 mL) butter or margarine

1. Combine ingredients in small saucepan. Cook over medium heat, stirring constantly, until mixture boils. Boil and stir 1 minute. Keep glaze warm.

Orange Sugar Twists

Makes 1½ dozen rolls

Basic Sweet Dough (see Index for page number)

¼ cup (60 mL) sugar

Rind of 1 orange, pared

Vegetable oil

Orange Glaze (recipe follows)

Fresh orange flavor and a pretty twist shape distinguish these simple sweet rolls prepared from the Basic Sweet Dough.

1. Prepare Basic Sweet Dough as directed through first rising. Punch down dough.

2. Fit processor with steel blade. Add sugar and orange rind to work bowl. Process until rind is finely chopped, 15 to 20 seconds.

3. Roll out dough into a 12x14-inch (30x35 cm) rectangle. Sprinkle sugar mixture over dough. Fold over dough to make a 6x14-inch (15x35 cm) rectangle. Cut into ¾-inch (2 cm) wide strips. Twist each strip twice and place on greased cookie sheet. Brush with oil. Let stand in warm place (85°F. or 30°C.) until doubled, 50 to 60 minutes.

4. Heat oven to 375°F. (190°C.). Prepare Orange Glaze.

5. Bake rolls until golden, 25 to 30 minutes. Remove rolls from pan and place on wire rack. Drizzle with Orange Glaze. Serve warm or at room temperature.

Orange Glaze

½ cup (125 mL) powdered sugar

3 to 4 teaspoons (15 to 20 mL) orange juice

1. Mix sugar and enough juice to make a smooth mixture thin enough to pour.

Makes 1 loaf

Cinnamon Breakfast Braid

½ to ¾ cup (125 to 180 mL) warm water (105° to 115°F. or 41° to 46°C.)

4 tablespoons (60 mL) sugar

1 package (¼ oz. or 7 g) active dry yeast

2¾ cups (680 mL) all-purpose flour*

¼ cup (60 mL) cold butter or margarine, cut into 4 pieces

1 teaspoon (5 mL) salt

1 egg, beaten
   Cinnamon Sugar (recipe follows)

1 egg white, slightly beaten

¼ cup (60 mL) sliced almonds

A sweet mixture of cinnamon and sugar is tucked inside each of the strands of dough that makes this pretty braided bread.

1. Combine ¼ cup (60 mL) of the water, 1 tablespoon (15 mL) of the sugar and yeast. Stir to dissolve yeast and let stand until bubbly, about 5 minutes.

2. Fit processor with steel blade. Measure flour, butter, remaining sugar and salt into work bowl. Process until mixed, about 15 seconds.

3. Add yeast mixture and egg to the flour mixture. Process until blended, about 10 seconds.

4. Turn on processor and very slowly drizzle just enough remaining water through feed tube into flour mixture so dough forms a ball that cleans the sides of the bowl. Process until ball turns around bowl about 25 times. Turn off processor and let dough stand 1 to 2 minutes.

5. Turn on processor and gradually drizzle in enough remaining water to make dough soft, smooth and satiny, but not sticky.** Process until dough turns around bowl about 15 times.

6. Turn dough onto lightly greased surface. Cover with inverted bowl and let stand 20 minutes.

7. Prepare Cinnamon Sugar while dough is standing. Roll out dough into a 9x15-inch (23x38 cm) rectangle. Cut into three 3x15-inch (8x38 cm) strips. Spoon ⅓ of Cinnamon Sugar lengthwise down center of each strip. Pull one edge of each strip over Cinnamon Sugar to meet other edge of same strip. Pinch seam to seal.

8. Braid the strips together to form a loaf. Tuck ends under and pinch to seal. Place braid on greased cookie sheet. Brush with beaten egg white and sprinkle with almonds. Let stand in warm place (85°F. or 30°C.) until doubled, about 1 hour.

9. Heat oven to 375°F. (190°C.). Bake until evenly brown and loaf sounds hollow when tapped, 30 to 35 minutes.

10. Remove from cookie sheet and cool on wire rack.

Cinnamon Sugar

¼ cup (60 mL) sugar

2 teaspoons (10 mL) ground cinnamon

1 tablespoon (15 mL) butter or margarine, at room temperature

1. Mix ingredients.

---

*Spoon flour into dry measuring cup and level off. Do not scoop.

**If dough is too dry and stiff, too soft and sticky, or if the processor shuts off, correct problem according to directions on page 25.

Poppy Seed Coffee Bread

Makes 1 loaf

This delicious coffee cake encases a sweet poppy seed-almond filling. The interesting lattice top, that looks a little like a braid, is made simply by overlapping diagonal strips of dough.

Poppy Seed Filling (recipe follows)

¼ cup (60 mL) warm water (105° to 115°F. or 41° to 46°C.)

4 tablespoons (60 mL) sugar

1 package (¼ oz. or 7 g) active dry yeast

1 egg, beaten

2¼ cups (560 mL) all-purpose flour*

¼ cup (60 mL) cold butter or margarine, cut into 4 pieces

½ teaspoon (2 mL) salt

¼ to ⅓ cup (60 to 80 mL) evaporated milk, at room temperature

1 egg white

1 teaspoon (5 mL) cold water

2 tablespoons (30 mL) sliced almonds

Powdered sugar

1. Prepare Poppy Seed Filling. Reserve.

2. Combine water, 1 tablespoon (15 mL) of the sugar and yeast. Stir to dissolve yeast and let stand until bubbly, about 5 minutes. Stir egg into yeast mixture.

3. Fit processor with steel blade. Measure flour, butter, remaining 3 tablespoons (45 mL) of the sugar and salt into work bowl. Process until mixed, about 10 seconds.

4. Turn on processor and slowly add yeast mixture through feed tube to flour mixture. Drizzle very slowly just enough evaporated milk into flour mixture so dough forms a ball that cleans the sides of the bowl. Process until ball turns around bowl about 25 times. Turn off processor and let dough stand 1 to 2 minutes.

5. Turn on processor and gradually drizzle in enough remaining evaporated milk to make dough soft, smooth and satiny but not sticky.** Process until dough turns around bowl about 15 times.

6. Cover processor and let dough stand in work bowl at room temperature 30 minutes. Process on/off twice to punch down dough.

7. Roll out dough on a large greased cookie sheet into a 10x15-inch (25x38 cm) rectangle. Spread Poppy Seed Filling lengthwise down center ⅓ of dough. Cut 10 diagonal strips with a sharp knife 1 inch (2.5 cm) apart in each of the other 2 sections of dough, cutting from outer edge to within 1 inch (2.5 cm) of the filling. Fold the strips over the filling, alternating from the left and right sides.

8. Beat egg white and cold water with fork and brush loaf with mixture. Sprinkle with almonds.

9. Let loaf stand in warm place (85°F. or 30°C.) until almost doubled, about 30 minutes.

10. Heat oven to 350°F. (180°C.). Bake until evenly brown, about 30 minutes.

11. Remove from cookie sheet and cool on wire rack. Sprinkle with powdered sugar.

Poppy Seed Filling

¾ cup (180 mL) poppy seeds

¾ cup (180 mL) whole almonds

3 pieces pared lemon rind (each about 1½x¼-inches or 4x0.5 cm)

½ cup (125 mL) sugar

⅓ cup (80 mL) milk

3 tablespoons (45 mL) butter or margarine

1 tablespoon (15 mL) lemon juice

1. Fit processor with steel blade. Measure poppy seeds, almonds and lemon rind into work bowl. Process until mixture is the consistency of cornmeal, about 2 minutes.

2. Place poppy seed mixture in saucepan. Add sugar, milk, butter and lemon juice. Cook over low heat, stirring frequently, until thickened, about 10 minutes. Cool.

*Spoon flour into dry measuring cup and level off. Do not scoop.

**If dough is too dry and stiff, too soft and sticky, or if the processor shuts off, correct problem according to directions on page 25.

Cinnamon Doughnut Twists

Makes 1½ dozen doughnuts

¼ cup (60 mL) warm water (105° to 115°F. or 41° to 46°C.)

12 tablespoons (180 mL) sugar

1 package (¼ oz. or 7 g) active dry yeast

⅓ to ½ cup milk (80 to 125 mL)

2 tablespoons (30 mL) butter or margarine

3 teaspoons (15 mL) ground cinnamon

½ teaspoon (2 mL) salt

1 egg

2¾ cups (680 mL) all-purpose flour*

Vegetable oil

These easy-to-prepare doughnuts are certain to be a hit with everyone. To make them light and airy, be sure that they rise until doubled and that the oil has a chance to reach proper temperature between fryings.

1. Combine water, 1 tablespoon (15 mL) of the sugar and yeast. Stir to dissolve yeast and let stand until bubbly, about 5 minutes.

2. Measure milk, 3 tablespoons (45 mL) of the remaining sugar, butter, ½ teaspoon (2 mL) of the cinnamon and salt into small saucepan. Heat over low heat, stirring constantly, just until butter is melted (mixture should be about 110°F. or 43°C.). Remove from heat and blend in egg.

3. Fit processor with steel blade. Measure flour into work bowl. Turn on processor and slowly add yeast mixture through feed tube to flour mixture. Drizzle just enough milk mixture slowly into flour mixture so dough forms a ball that cleans the sides of the bowl. Process until ball turns around bowl about 25 times. Turn off processor and let dough stand 1 to 2 minutes.

4. Turn on processor and gradually drizzle in enough remaining milk mixture to make dough soft, smooth and satiny but not sticky.** Process until dough turns around bowl about 15 times.

5. Turn dough onto lightly floured surface. Roll dough into an 8x18-inch (20x45 cm) rectangle. Cut into strips 1 inch (2.5 cm) wide and 8 inches (20 cm) long. Twist strips and place on greased cookie sheet. Brush with oil and let stand in warm place (85°F. or 30°C.) until doubled, about 30 to 40 minutes.

6. Pour about 2 inches (5 cm) oil into large saucepan. Heat oil to 350°F. (180°C.). Fry twists in oil 1½ minutes on each side. Drain on paper toweling.

7. Mix remaining ½ cup (125 mL) sugar and 2½ teaspoons (12 mL) cinnamon. Roll twists in mixture.

Fried Cinnamon Puffs

Makes about 3 dozen

2¾ cups (680 mL) all-purpose flour*

¾ cup (180 mL) sugar

1 package (¼ oz. or 7 g) active dry yeast

3 teaspoons (15 mL) ground cinnamon

1 teaspoon (5 mL) salt

½ cup (125 mL) milk

¼ cup (60 mL) water

¼ cup (60 mL) butter or margarine

2 eggs, beaten

Vegetable oil for deep frying

A sweet cinnamon sugar coating makes these light, puffy, spiced doughnut balls even more tempting.

1. Fit processor with steel blade. Measure flour, ¼ cup (60 mL) of the sugar, yeast, 1 teaspoon (5 mL) of the cinnamon and salt into work bowl. Process until mixed, about 10 seconds.

2. Combine milk, water and butter in saucepan. Heat over low heat until warm (120° to 130°F. or 49° to 54°C.). Mix in eggs with fork.

3. Turn processor on and pour milk mixture through feed tube into flour mixture. Process until batter is smooth, about 30 seconds.

4. Let batter stand in work bowl, covered, until bubbly, about 30 minutes. Process on/off once to stir batter down.

5. Pour about 2 inches (5 cm) of oil into large saucepan. Heat oil to 400°F. (200°C.). Mix remaining ½ cup (125 mL) of the sugar and 2 teaspoons (10 mL) of the cinnamon. Drop batter by level tablespoonsful into oil. Fry until brown, about 1½ minutes on each side. Drain on paper toweling. Roll in cinnamon sugar mixture.

---

*Spoon flour into dry measuring cup and level off. Do not scoop.

**If dough is too dry and stiff, too soft and sticky, or if the processor shuts off, correct problem according to directions on page 25.

SWEET YEAST BREADS

Makes 1 dozen

Caramel Sticky Buns

¼ to ½ cup (60 to 125 mL) warm water (105° to 115°F. or 41° to 46°C.)

3 tablespoons (45 mL) sugar

1 package (¼ oz. or 7 g) active dry yeast

1 egg, beaten

2¼ cups (560 mL) all-purpose flour*

2 tablespoons (30 mL) instant nonfat dry milk solids

1 teaspoon (5 mL) salt

Caramel Topping (recipe follows)

3 tablespoons (45 mL) butter or margarine, melted

These classic buns are coffeetime favorites. They bake on top of a rich caramel nut mixture. One minute after coming out of the oven, they should be inverted onto a serving plate so the hot caramel can drizzle down over the buns.

1. Combine ¼ cup (60 mL) of the water, 1 tablespoon (15 mL) of the sugar and yeast. Stir to dissolve yeast and let stand until bubbly, about 5 minutes. Stir in egg.

2. Fit processor with steel blade. Measure flour, dry milk, remaining 2 tablespoons (30 mL) of the sugar and salt into work bowl. Process until mixed, about 5 seconds.

3. Turn on processor and slowly pour yeast mixture through feed tube into flour mixture. Slowly drizzle just enough remaining water into flour mixture so dough forms a ball that cleans sides of the bowl. Process until ball turns around bowl about 25 times. Turn off processor and let dough stand 1 to 2 minutes.

4. Turn on processor and gradually drizzle in enough remaining water to make dough soft, smooth and satiny but not sticky.** Process until dough turns around bowl about 15 times.

5. Cover processor and let dough stand at room temperature until it begins to rise, about 30 minutes.

6. Prepare Caramel Topping while dough is rising. Pour topping into greased 9-inch (23 cm) round cake or pie pan.

7. Process on/off. Turn dough onto lightly greased surface. Divide into 12 equal parts. Shape each into ball, dip in melted butter and arrange over Caramel Topping in pan. Let stand in warm place (85°F or 30°C.) until doubled, about 1 hour.

8. Heat oven to 400°F. (200°C.). Bake buns until brown, 10 to 12 minutes. Cool about one minute, then invert buns onto serving plate. Serve warm or at room temperature.

Caramel Topping

3 tablespoons (45 mL) packed brown sugar

3 tablespoons (45 mL) butter or margarine

2 tablespoons (30 mL) dark corn syrup

¼ cup (60 mL) chopped walnuts or pecans

1. Combine brown sugar, butter, and corn syrup in small saucepan. Cook over medium heat, stirring constantly, until bubbly and brown sugar dissolves.

2. Remove from heat. Stir in nuts.

---

*Spoon flour into dry measuring cup and level off. Do not scoop.

**If dough is too dry and stiff, too soft and sticky, or if the processor shuts off, correct problem according to directions on page 25.

Cardamom Buns

¼ cup (60 mL) warm water (105° to 115°F. or 41° to 46°C.)

1 package (¼ oz. or 7 g) active dry yeast

1 teaspoon (5 mL) sugar

2¾ cups (680 mL) all-purpose flour*

¼ cup (60 mL) butter or margarine, at room temperature

1 teaspoon (5 mL) salt

1 teaspoon (5 mL) ground cardamom

1 egg, beaten

⅓ to ½ cup (80 to 125 mL) evaporated or fresh milk

1 egg white, slightly beaten

1 tablespoon (15 mL) sugar

1 tablespoon (15 mL) ground almonds

These sweet, delicately spiced buns are best when served fresh from the oven for breakfast or brunch.

1. Combine water, yeast and sugar. Stir to dissolve yeast and let stand until bubbly, about 5 minutes.

2. Fit processor with steel blade. Measure flour, butter, salt and cardamom into work bowl. Process until mixed, about 10 seconds.

3. Add yeast mixture and 1 beaten egg to flour mixture. Process until blended, about 10 seconds.

4. Turn on processor and very slowly drizzle just enough milk through feed tube so dough forms a ball that cleans the sides of the bowl. Process until ball turns around bowl about 25 times. Turn off processor and let dough stand 1 to 2 minutes.

5. Turn on processor and gradually drizzle in enough remaining milk to make dough soft, smooth and satiny but not sticky.** Process until dough turns around bowl about 15 times.

6. Turn dough onto lightly greased surface. Shape into a ball. Cover with plastic wrap or inverted bowl and let stand at room temperature until almost doubled, 30 to 45 minutes.

7. Uncover dough and divide into 12 equal parts. Shape each into smooth ball and place on greased cookie sheet. Let rise in warm place (85°F. or 30°C.) until doubled, about 1 hour.

8. Heat oven to 375°F. (190°C.). Brush rolls with egg white. Mix sugar and ground almonds and sprinkle over rolls. Bake until golden, 25 to 30 minutes. Remove from cookie sheet and cool on wire rack.

Kolaches

Basic Sweet Dough (see Index for page number)

1 cup (250 mL) dried, pitted apricots, peaches or prunes

1 cup (250 mL) water

⅓ cup (80 mL) honey

2 teaspoons (10 mL) lemon juice

1 egg, beaten

2 tablespoons (30 mL) milk

These little rounds of sweet dough are baked with a filling in the center. The apricot, peach or prune fillings here are delicious. If you prefer, you could use canned poppy seed or date cake and pastry filling instead.

1. Prepare Basic Sweet Dough as directed until dough is soft, smooth and satiny but not sticky. Let stand, covered, in work bowl at room temperature until doubled, 1 to 1½ hours.

2. While dough is rising, combine dried fruit and water in small saucepan. Cook over medium heat until fruit is soft and water is absorbed, 20 to 25 minutes. Stir honey and lemon juice into fruit. Cool mixture.

3. Process on/off twice to punch down dough. Turn dough onto lightly greased surface and divide into 12 equal parts. Shape each part into smooth ball and place on greased cookie sheet. Flatten each ball until ½-inch (1.5 cm) thick. Let stand in warm place (85°F. or 30°C.) until almost doubled, about 30 minutes.

4. Make indentation in center of each round of dough using thumb or back of a spoon. Spoon fruit mixture into each indentation. Let stand in warm place until doubled, 20 to 30 minutes longer.

5. Heat oven to 350°F. (180°C.). Mix egg and milk. Brush mixture over dough. Bake until golden, 15 to 20 minutes.

6. Remove from cookie sheet. Cool on wire rack.

---

*Spoon flour into dry measuring cup and level off. Do not scoop.

**If dough is too dry and stiff, too soft and sticky, or if the processor shuts off, correct problem according to directions on page 25.

SWEET YEAST BREADS

Makes 1 loaf

Pulla

½ to ¾ cup (125 to 180 mL) warm water (105° to 115°F. or 41° to 46°C.)

4 tablespoons (60 mL) sugar

1 package (¼ oz. or 7 g) active dry yeast

2 eggs

2¾ cups (680 mL) all-purpose flour*

¼ cup (60 mL) cold butter or margarine, cut into 4 pieces

1 teaspoon (5 mL) salt

½ teaspoon (2 mL) ground cardamom

Crushed sugar cubes, pearl sugar and/or sliced almonds

Cardamom is the spice that flavors this interesting Finnish braided sweet bread. It's good with coffee or tea, especially when sliced and toasted.

1. Combine ¼ cup (60 mL) of the water, 1 tablespoon (15 mL) of the sugar and yeast. Stir to dissolve yeast and let stand until bubbly, about 5 minutes. Add 1 egg and stir until blended.

2. Fit processor with steel blade. Measure flour, butter, remaining 3 tablespoons (45 mL) of the sugar, salt and cardamom into work bowl. Process until mixed, about 15 seconds.

3. Add yeast mixture to flour mixture. Process until blended, about 10 seconds.

4. Turn on processor and very slowly drizzle just enough remaining water through feed tube into flour mixture so dough forms a ball that cleans the sides of the bowl. Process until ball turns around bowl about 25 times. Turn off processor and let dough stand 1 to 2 minutes.

5. Turn on processor and gradually drizzle in enough remaining water to make dough soft, smooth and satiny but not sticky.** Process until dough turns around bowl about 15 times.

6. Turn dough onto lightly floured surface. Shape into ball and place in lightly greased bowl, turning to grease all sides. Cover with plastic wrap and let stand in warm place (85°F. or 30°C.) until doubled, about 1 hour.

7. Punch down dough. Divide dough into 3 equal parts. Shape each part into 18-inch (45 cm) strand. Braid strands together and place on greased cookie sheet. Tuck ends under and pinch to seal. Cover loosely with plastic wrap. Let stand in warm place until doubled, about 1 hour.

8. Heat oven to 375°F. (190°C.). Beat remaining egg with fork. Brush egg over braid. Sprinkle with sugar and/or almonds.

9. Bake until loaf is evenly brown, 20 to 25 minutes. Remove from cookie sheet and cool on wire rack.

Makes 1 ring

Date Tea Ring

Basic Sweet Dough (see Index for page number)

1 package (8 oz. or 250 mL) chopped, pitted dates

⅓ cup (80 mL) water

½ cup (125 mL) chopped nuts

¼ cup (60 mL) butter or margarine, at room temperature

Vegetable oil

Sugar Icing (recipe follows)

This richly flavored bread is great for breakfast, brunch or morning coffee parties. For holidays, a sprinkling of chopped nuts and candied fruits give it a festive appearance.

1. Prepare Basic Sweet Dough as directed through first rising.

2. While dough is rising, combine dates and water in a small saucepan. Cook over medium heat, stirring frequently, until most of the water is absorbed, about 2 minutes. Remove from heat. Stir in nuts. Cool.

3. Punch down dough. Roll out dough into a 9x15-inch (23x38 cm) rectangle. Spread butter over dough. Spread date mixture over butter. Roll up dough jelly-roll fashion, beginning at 15-inch (38 cm) side. Pinch seam to seal. Arrange in circle on large greased cookie sheet. Pinch ends of dough together to seal. With scissors, cut ⅔ of the way through ring at 1-inch (2.5 cm) intervals, leaving center of the ring intact. Gently lay each section on its side, cut side up to show date filling.

4. Brush with oil. Cover loosely with plastic wrap and let stand in warm place (85°F. or 30°C.) until doubled, about 1 hour. *continued*

---

*Spoon flour into dry measuring cup and level off. Do not scoop.

**If dough is too dry and stiff, too soft and sticky, or if the processor shuts off, correct problem according to directions on page 25.

Date Tea Ring (continued)

5. Heat oven to 350°F. (180°C.). Prepare Sugar Icing.

6. Uncover dough and bake until evenly brown, 45 to 50 minutes. Remove from cookie sheet to wire rack. Spread with Sugar Icing. Cool.

Sugar Icing

1   cup (250 mL) powdered sugar

1   teaspoon (5 mL) butter, at room temperature

2   to 3 tablespoons (30 to 45 mL) milk

1. Mix sugar, butter and enough milk to make a smooth mixture thick enough to spread.

Lemon Raisin Bread

Makes 1 loaf

¼   to ½ cup (60 to 125 mL) warm water (105° to 115°F. or 41° to 46°C.)

4   tablespoons (60 mL) granulated sugar

1   package (¼ oz. or 7 g) active dry yeast

1   egg, beaten

¼   cup (60 mL) blanched whole almonds

¼   cup (60 mL) mixed candied fruit

¼   cup (60 mL) dark raisins or currants

2   pieces pared lemon rind (About 1½x¼-inches or 4x0.5 cm)

2¼   cups (560 mL) all-purpose flour*

2   tablespoons (30 mL) butter or margarine, at room temperature

½   teaspoon (2 mL) salt

1   cup (250 mL) powdered sugar

¼   teaspoon (1 mL) vanilla

2   to 3 tablespoons (30 to 45 mL) milk

Lemon, almonds and fruit richly flavor this appealing round bread that can be cut in wedges or slices to serve. If desired, the amount of raisins may be doubled and the candied fruit omitted.

1. Combine ¼ cup (60 mL) of the water, 1 tablespoon (15 mL) of the granulated sugar and yeast. Stir to dissolve yeast and let stand until bubbly, about 5 minutes. Stir in egg.

2. Fit processor with steel blade. Measure almonds, candied fruit and raisins into work bowl. Process on/off 3 or 4 times until mixture is coarsely chopped. Remove from work bowl and reserve.

3. Place remaining granulated sugar and lemon rind in work bowl. Process until rind is minced, 1 to 2 minutes.

4. Add flour, butter and salt to sugar mixture. Process until mixed, about 5 minutes.

5. Turn on processor and gradually drizzle yeast mixture through feed tube into flour mixture. Drizzle just enough of the remaining water into flour mixture so dough forms a ball that cleans the sides of the bowl. Process until dough turns around the bowl about 25 times. Turn off processor and let dough stand 1 to 2 minutes.

6. Turn on processor and very slowly drizzle in enough remaining water to make dough soft, smooth and satiny but not sticky.** Process until dough turns around bowl about 15 times.

7. Sprinkle nut-fruit mixture evenly over dough. Process on/off just until mixed.

8. Turn dough onto large greased cookie sheet. Shape into a ball. Cover with inverted bowl or plastic wrap and let stand 20 to 30 minutes. Roll out to an 8-inch (20 cm) circle. Cover loosely with plastic wrap and let stand in warm place (85°F. or 30°C.) until doubled, about 45 minutes.

9. Heat oven to 375°F. (190°C.). Uncover loaf and bake until evenly brown, 25 to 30 minutes.

10. Remove bread from cookie sheet and place on wire rack. Blend powdered sugar, vanilla and enough milk to make a smooth mixture thick enough to spread. Spread over bread.

---

*Spoon flour into dry measuring cup and level off. Do not scoop.

**If dough is too dry and stiff, too soft and sticky, or if the processor shuts off, correct problem according to directions on page 25.

SWEET YEAST BREADS

Makes 2½ dozen rolls

Cream Dream Rolls

¼ cup (60 mL) warm water (105° to 115°F. or 41° to 46°C.)

7 tablespoons (105 mL) sugar

1 package (¼ oz. or 7 g) active dry yeast

1 cup (250 mL) whipping cream

3 egg yolks, beaten

3½ cups (875 mL) all-purpose flour*

½ cup (125 mL) cold butter or margarine, cut into 8 pieces

1 teaspoon (5 mL) salt
Almond Icing (recipe follows)

1 teaspoon (5 mL) ground cinnamon

¼ cup (60 mL) chopped walnuts or pecans
All-purpose flour

These elegant sweet rolls are made from a rich, creamy dough that's rolled around in spicy cinnamon sugar. Prepare them the day ahead, refrigerate overnight, then bake them the next morning for breakfast.

1. Combine water, 1 tablespoon (15 mL) of the sugar and yeast. Stir to dissolve yeast and let stand until bubbly, about 5 minutes. Blend in cream and egg yolks.

2. Fit processor with steel blade. Measure 2 cups (500 mL) of the flour, butter, 4 tablespoons (60 mL) of the sugar and salt into work bowl. Process on/off 5 or 6 times until butter is size of kidney beans.

3. Transfer flour-butter mixture to a large mixing bowl. Stir in remaining 1½ cups (375 mL) flour.

4. Add cream mixture to flour mixture. Stir just enough to moisten flour. (Dough should be crumbly like a biscuit dough, not smooth and satiny like most yeast doughs.) Cover with plastic wrap and refrigerate 12 to 24 hours.

5. Turn dough onto well floured surface. Cut dough into 4 equal parts. Roll each part into a rectangle 6x12 inches (15x30 cm). Cut each rectangle into 12 strips 1 inch (2.5 cm) wide and 6 inches (15 cm) long. Shape into knots, circles, figure 8's, spirals, braids or ovals as desired. Place on greased cookie sheets. Let rise in warm place (85°F. or 30°C.) until doubled, about 45 minutes.

6. Heat oven to 350°F. (180°C.). Prepare Almond Icing. Mix remaining 2 tablespoons (30 mL) sugar with cinnamon. Bake rolls until evenly brown, about 15 minutes. Remove from cookie sheet, dip in Almond Icing, then in cinnamon mixture or nuts. Cool on wire rack.

Almond Icing

1⅓ cups (330 mL) sifted powdered sugar

2 tablespoons (30 mL) milk

1 tablespoon (15 mL) hot water

½ teaspoon (2 mL) almond extract

1. Blend ingredients until smooth.

Makes 3 dozen rolls

Sunday Breakfast Rolls

¼ cup (60 mL) warm water (105° to 115°F. or 41° to 46°C.)

1 package (¼ oz. or 7 g) active dry yeast

½ cup (125 mL) milk, heated (105° to 115°F or 41° to 46°C.)

2 eggs, at room temperature
continued

Leisurely Sunday breakfasts are a treat, especially when you serve these delicious cinnamon rolls fresh from the oven. Don't worry about having to get up early to make them. All preparation except baking can be done on Saturday.

1. Combine water and yeast. Stir to dissolve yeast. Blend in milk and eggs.

2. Fit processor with steel blade. Add ¼ cup (60 mL) of the sugar and lemon rind to work bowl. Process until rind is minced, about 1 minute.

*Spoon flour into dry measuring cup and level off. Do not scoop.

Sunday Breakfast Rolls *(continued)*

1¼ cups (310 mL) sugar

4 pieces pared lemon rind (each about 1x¼-inch or 2.5x0.5 cm)

3½ cups (875 mL) all-purpose flour*

1 cup (250 mL) cold butter or margarine, cut into 12 pieces

1 teaspoon (5 mL) salt

1 tablespoon (15 mL) ground cinnamon

3. Add 2 cups (500 mL) of the flour, butter and salt to sugar-lemon mixture. Process on/off about 10 times until butter is about the size of peas. Transfer flour mixture to a large mixing bowl. Stir in remaining flour.

4. Pour yeast mixture over the flour mixture. Stir just enough to moisten flour. (Dough will be lumpy, not smooth and satiny like most yeast doughs.) Cover with plastic wrap and refrigerate overnight.

5. Turn dough onto lightly floured surface. Divide in half. Roll out each half into a 12x18-inch (30x45 cm) rectangle.

6. Mix remaining 1 cup (250 mL) of the sugar and cinnamon. Sprinkle half of cinnamon mixture over each rectangle. Roll up jelly-roll fashion, beginning at 18-inch (45 cm) side. Pinch seam to seal. Cut into 1-inch (2.5 cm) slices and place cut side up on greased cookie sheets. Flatten with palm of hand to about ½-inch (1.5 cm) thick. Let stand in warm place (85°F. or 30°C.) until almost doubled, 30 to 45 minutes.

7. Heat oven to 400°F. (200°C.). Bake until golden, 10 to 12 minutes.

8. Remove from cookie sheets and cool on wire rack.

Makes 20 rolls

Brown Sugar Sticky Rolls

1 cup (250 mL) packed brown sugar

1 cup (250 mL) whipping cream

8 tablespoons (120 mL) granulated sugar

3 tablespoons (45 mL) cold butter, cut in 3 pieces

2 teaspoons (10 mL) ground cinnamon

2¾ to 3¼ cups (680 to 810 mL) all-purpose flour*

1 package (¼ oz. or 7 g) active dry yeast

1 teaspoon (5 mL) salt

¾ cup (180 mL) hot water (120° to 130°F. or 49° to 54°C.)

1 egg, beaten

These cinnamon spiced rolls are simply delicious with their easy brown sugar topping. They're speedy to prepare, too, since the dough requires just one rising period.

1. Sprinkle brown sugar evenly over bottom of greased 13x9x2-inch (33x23x5 cm) baking pan. Pour cream evenly over brown sugar. Reserve.

2. Fit processor with steel blade. Measure 6 tablespoons (90 mL) of the sugar, 1 tablespoon (15 mL) of the butter and cinnamon into work bowl. Process on/off 2 or 3 times until mixed. Remove from work bowl and reserve.

3. Measure 1 cup (250 mL) of the flour, remaining 2 tablespoons (30 mL) sugar and butter, yeast and salt into work bowl. Process on/off 3 or 4 times to blend.

4. Turn processor on and pour water through feed tube into flour mixture. Process until mixture is smooth, about 30 seconds. Add egg and process until blended, 5 seconds.

5. Add 1¾ cups (430 mL) of the remaining flour to batter in work bowl. Process until flour is blended in, about 15 seconds. Gradually add just enough of the remaining flour to make a soft and pliable dough that cleans the sides of the bowl. Turn off processor and let dough stand in work bowl 10 minutes.

6. Turn dough onto lightly greased surface and roll into 15x7-inch (38x18 cm) rectangle. Sprinkle cinnamon mixture over dough. Roll up dough jelly-roll fashion. Pinch seam with fingers to seal. Cut into 20 slices. Place slices cut side down on the cream mixture.

7. Cover pan and let stand in a warm place (85°F. or 30°C.) until doubled, about 1 hour.

8. Heat oven to 400°F. (200°C.). Bake rolls until golden, 20 to 25 minutes. Cool 5 minutes in pan. Invert onto serving platter. Serve warm or at room temperature.

---

*Spoon flour into dry measuring cup and level off. Do not scoop.

SWEET YEAST BREADS

Cinnamon Rolls

Basic Sweet Dough (see Index for page number)
¼ cup (60 mL) butter or margarine, at room temperature
½ cup (125 mL) sugar
1 tablespoon (15 mL) ground cinnamon
Vegetable oil
Sugar Glaze (recipe follows)

What better way to start the day than with these classic rolls? For fresh rolls at breakfast, prepare, shape and refrigerate the dough the night before, then let it stand at room temperature in the morning while the oven is preheating.

1. Prepare Basic Sweet Dough as directed through first rising. Punch down dough. Roll out dough into a 15-inch (38 cm) square.

2. Spread butter over dough. Combine sugar and cinnamon and sprinkle over butter. Roll up dough jelly-roll fashion. Pinch seam to seal. Cut into 1-inch (2.5 cm) wide slices and place cut side down in greased 13x9x2-inch (33x23x5 cm) baking pan. Brush with oil. Let stand in warm place (85°F. or 30°C.) until doubled, 50 to 60 minutes.

3. Heat oven to 375°F. (190°C.). Prepare Sugar Glaze.

4. Bake rolls until golden, 15 to 20 minutes. Remove rolls from pan and place on wire rack. Drizzle with Sugar Glaze. Serve warm or at room temperature.

Sugar Glaze

1 cup (250 mL) powdered sugar
1 to 2 tablespoons (15 to 30 mL) milk or strong coffee

1. Mix sugar and enough milk to make a smooth mixture thin enough to pour.

Kuchen

Basic Sweet Dough (see Index for page number)
1 cup (250 mL) whipping cream
½ cup (125 mL) sugar
2 eggs
Cinnamon Topping (recipe follows)

In German kuchen means "cake." In America this classic is what almost everyone thinks of simply as coffee cake. It's easy to prepare from the Basic Sweet Dough. Top it with a simple sweet custard and add any of many fruits for variety.

1. Prepare Basic Sweet Dough as directed through first rising. Punch down dough. Divide into 2 equal parts. Shape each part into ball and roll out to a circle 7½ inches (19.5 cm) in diameter. Fit each circle into greased 8- or 9-inch (20 or 23 cm) round cake or pie pan. Press dough to sides of pan to cover pan bottom completely.

2. Heat oven to 350°F. (180°C.). Sprinkle ¼ cup (60 mL) of the sugar over dough in each pan. Beat cream and eggs with whisk until blended. Pour half of cream mixture over sugar in each pan.

3. Prepare Cinnamon Topping. Sprinkle topping evenly over cream mixture in each pan. Bake until knife inserted in center of cream mixture comes out clean, 25 to 30 minutes. Cool Kuchen in pans on wire rack.

Fruit Kuchen Follow directions for Kuchen through fitting dough in pie pan and sprinkling with ¼ cup (60 mL) of the sugar. Arrange 1 cup (250 mL) fruit or berries (blueberries, raspberries, blackberries, sliced strawberries, peaches, apples or pears) over sugared dough in pans. Pour cream mixture over fruit. Sprinkle with Cinnamon Topping and bake as directed for Kuchen.

Cinnamon Topping

2 tablespoons (30 mL) sugar
1 teaspoon (5 mL) ground cinnamon

1. Mix sugar and cinnamon.

Makes 2 dozen

Elephant Ears

These big rounds of pastry-like yeast dough are rolled thinly, covered with a tempting cinnamon-nut topping and baked until golden and crispy.

¼ to ½ cup (60 to 125 mL) warm water (105° to 115°F. or 41° to 46°C.)
8 tablespoons (120 mL) granulated sugar
1 package (¼ oz. or 7 g) active dry yeast
1 egg, beaten
2¼ cups (560 mL) all-purpose flour*
¼ cup (60 mL) cold butter or margarine, cut into 4 pieces
1 teaspoon (5 mL) salt
⅓ cup (80 mL) packed brown sugar
3 tablespoons (45 mL) butter or margarine, at room temperature
½ teaspoon (2.5 mL) ground cinnamon
  Cinnamon-Nut Topping (recipe follows)

1. Combine ¼ cup (60 mL) of the water, 1 tablespoon (15 mL) of the granulated sugar and yeast. Stir to dissolve yeast and let stand until bubbly, about 5 minutes. Stir in egg.

2. Fit processor with steel blade. Measure flour, cold butter, 3 tablespoons (45 mL) of the remaining granulated sugar and salt into work bowl. Process until mixed, about 15 seconds.

3. Turn on processor and slowly drizzle yeast mixture through feed tube into flour mixture. Drizzle just enough of the remaining water into flour mixture so dough forms a ball that cleans the sides of the bowl. Process until dough turns around the bowl about 25 times. Turn off processor and let dough stand 1 to 2 minutes.

4. Turn on processor and very slowly drizzle in enough remaining water to make dough soft, smooth and satiny but not sticky.** Process until dough turns around bowl about 15 times.

5. Turn dough onto lightly floured surface. Shape into ball and place in lightly greased bowl, turning to grease all sides. Cover with plastic wrap and let stand in warm place (85°F. or 30°C.) until doubled, about 1 hour.

6. Punch down dough. Divide dough in half. Roll out each half into a 12-inch (30 cm) square. Mix remaining 4 tablespoons (60 mL) of the granulated sugar, brown sugar, 3 tablespoons (45 mL) of the room temperature butter and cinnamon. Spread half of the mixture over each square of dough. Roll up dough jelly-roll fashion. Pinch seam to seal. Cut each roll into 1-inch (2.5 cm) slices. Place slices 3 inches (8 cm) apart on greased cookie sheets. Cover with waxed paper and let stand at room temperature about 30 minutes.

7. Prepare Cinnamon-Nut Topping while dough is standing.

8. Roll out each slice to 5-inch (13 cm) circle. Remove waxed paper. Brush with melted butter. Sprinkle Cinnamon-Nut Topping over each circle. Cover with waxed paper and roll topping into each circle. Remove paper.

9. Heat oven to 400°F. (200°C.). Bake rolls until brown, 10 to 12 minutes.

10. Remove from cookie sheets and cool on wire rack.

Cinnamon-Nut Topping

1 cup (250 mL) granulated sugar
½ cup (125 mL) chopped walnuts or pecans
1 teaspoon (5 mL) ground cinnamon

1. Mix ingredients.

---

*Spoon flour into dry measuring cup and level off. Do not scoop.

**If dough is too dry and stiff, too soft and sticky, or if the processor shuts off, correct problem according to directions on page 25.

Makes 1 loaf

Sweet Egg Braid

¼ to ½ cup (60 to 125 mL)
warm water (105° to
115°F. or 41° to 46°C.)

4 tablespoons (60 mL) sugar

1 package (¼ oz. or 7 g)
active dry yeast

2¾ cups (680 mL) all-purpose
flour*

½ cup (125 mL) instant nonfat
dry milk solids

¼ cup (60 mL) cold butter or
margarine, cut into 4
pieces

1 teaspoon (5 mL) salt

2 eggs, beaten

1 egg

1 teaspoon cold water

Sliced almonds, sesame
seeds or candied fruit, if
desired

A sprinkling of sliced almonds or sesame seeds will distinguish this handsome braided loaf made from an egg-rich sweet dough. For the holidays, a simple powdered sugar icing and a generous sprinkle of candied fruit turn it into a festive favorite.

1. Combine ¼ cup (60 mL) of water, 1 tablespoon (15 mL) of the sugar and yeast. Stir to dissolve yeast and let stand until bubbly, about 5 minutes.

2. Fit processor with steel blade. Measure flour, dry milk, butter, remaining 3 tablespoons sugar and salt into work bowl. Process until mixed, about 15 seconds.

3. Add yeast mixture to flour mixture. Process until blended, about 10 seconds.

4. Turn on processor and slowly drizzle beaten eggs through feed tube, and just enough remaining water so dough forms a ball that cleans the sides of the bowl. Process until ball turns around bowl about 25 times. Turn off processor and let dough stand 1 to 2 minutes.

5. Turn on processor and gradually drizzle in enough remaining water to make dough soft, smooth and satiny but not sticky.** Process until dough turns around bowl about 15 times.

6. Turn dough onto lightly floured surface. Shape into ball and place in lightly greased bowl, turning to grease all sides. Cover with plastic wrap and let stand in warm place (85°F. or 30°C.) until doubled, about 1 hour.

7. Punch down dough. Divide into 3 equal parts. Shape each part into a strand about 18-inches (45 cm) long. Braid the strands together. Tuck ends under and pinch to seal. Place on greased cookie sheet. Cover with plastic wrap and let stand in warm place until doubled, about 1 hour.

8. Heat oven to 375°F. (190°C.). Beat egg and cold water with fork. Brush egg mixture over loaf. Sprinkle with almonds, sesame seeds or candied fruit, if desired.

9. Bake until evenly browned, 25 to 30 minutes. Remove from cookie sheet and cool on wire rack.

*Spoon flour into dry measuring cup and level off. Do not scoop.

**If dough is too dry and stiff, too soft and sticky, or if the processor shuts off, correct problem according to directions on page 25.

HOLIDAY BREADS

Dresden Stollen

Makes 1 loaf

Richly laden with brandy or rum-soaked fruits and nuts, Dresden Stollen is a Christmas classic from Germany. Shaped like a large Parkerhouse roll, this sweet bread will keep at least a week in the refrigerator. Slice it thin and serve with whipped butter and coffee or wine.

¼ cup (60 mL) golden raisins

¼ cup (60 mL) chopped candied cherries

¼ cup (60 mL) slivered almonds

¼ cup (60 mL) candied orange peel

2 tablespoons (30 mL) brandy or dark rum

¼ cup (60 mL) warm water (105° to 115°F. or 41° to 46°C.)

4 tablespoons (60 mL) sugar

2 packages (¼ oz. or 7 g each) active dry yeast

4 pieces pared lemon rind (each about 2x½-inch or 5x1.5 cm)

2¾ cups (680 mL) all-purpose flour*

⅓ cup (80 mL) cold butter or margarine, cut into 5 pieces

½ teaspoon (2 mL) salt

1 egg

½ teaspoon (2 mL) almond extract

2 to 5 tablespoons (30 to 75 mL) milk

   All-purpose flour

2 tablespoons (30 mL) butter or margarine, melted

1 egg white

3 tablespoons (45 mL) powdered sugar

1. Mix raisins, cherries, almonds, orange peel and brandy. Reserve.

2. Combine water, 1 tablespoon (15 mL) of the sugar and yeast. Stir to dissolve yeast and let stand until bubbly, about 5 minutes.

3. Fit processor with steel blade. Add remaining 3 tablespoons (45 mL) of the sugar and lemon rind to work bowl. Process until rind is minced.

4. Add 2¾ cups (680 mL) of the flour, butter and salt to sugar mixture in work bowl. Process until mixed, about 15 seconds.

5. Add yeast mixture, egg and almond flavoring to flour mixture. Process until blended, about 10 seconds.

6. Turn on processor and very slowly drizzle just enough milk through feed tube into flour mixture so dough forms a ball that cleans the sides of the bowl. Process until ball turns around bowl about 25 times. Turn off processor and let dough stand 1 to 2 minutes.

7. Turn on processor and gradually drizzle in enough remaining milk to make dough soft, smooth and satiny but not sticky.** Process until dough turns around bowl about 15 times.

8. Turn dough onto lightly floured surface. Shape into ball, cover with inverted bowl or plastic wrap and let stand 20 minutes.

9. Uncover dough and knead fruit mixture into dough on well floured surface. Sprinkle with additional flour, if necessary, to keep dough from becoming sticky. Shape dough into ball and place in lightly greased bowl, turning to grease all sides. Cover loosely with plastic wrap and let stand in warm place (85°F. or 30°C.) until doubled, about 1 hour.

10. Punch down dough. Roll or pat dough on a large greased cookie sheet into a 7x9-inch (18x23 cm) oval. Brush with melted butter. Make a crease lengthwise with handle of wooden spoon just off the center. Fold lengthwise, bringing smaller section over the larger one. Brush top with egg white. Cover loosely with plastic wrap and let stand in warm place until almost doubled, about 45 minutes.

11. Heat oven to 350°F. (180°C.). Uncover bread and bake until evenly browned, 25 to 30 minutes.

12. Remove immediately from cookie sheet and place on wire rack. Brush melted butter over bread. Sift powdered sugar over bread. Cool.

---

*Spoon flour into dry measuring cup and level off. Do not scoop.

**If dough is too dry and stiff, too soft and sticky, or if the processor shuts off, correct problem according to directions on page 25.

Dutch Easter Bread

Makes 1 loaf

½   cup (125 mL) milk
¼   cup (60 mL) water
2   tablespoons (30 mL) butter
      or margarine
1   egg, beaten
2½ to 2¾ cups (625 to 680
      mL) all-purpose flour*
2   tablespoons (30 mL) sugar
1   package (¼ oz. or 7 g)
      active dry yeast
1   teaspoon (5 mL) salt
½   cup (125 mL) dark raisins
½   cup (125 mL) currants
¼   cup (60 mL) chopped citron
      or mixed candied fruits
      Vegetable oil
      Sugar Icing (see Index for
      page number)

Holland gives us this white bread that's richly studded with raisins, currants and candied fruits. It's especially good when sliced, toasted and served with fresh butter.

1. Combine milk, water and butter in small saucepan. Heat over low heat until 120° to 130°F. (49° to 54°C.). Blend egg into milk mixture.

2. Measure 1 cup (250 mL) of the flour, sugar, yeast and salt into work bowl. Process until mixed, about 5 seconds.

3. Turn on processor and add milk mixture through feed tube to flour mixture. Process until smooth, about 30 seconds.

4. Turn on processor and add enough of the remaining flour ¼ cup (60 mL) at a time through feed tube so dough forms a ball that cleans the sides of the bowl. Process until ball turns around bowl about 25 times.

5. Cover processor and let dough stand in work bowl at room temperature until almost doubled, 1 to 1¼ hours.

6. Uncover processor. Sprinkle raisins, currants and citron over dough. Process on/off 3 or 4 times to mix fruit into dough.

7. Shape dough into loaf and place in greased 9x5x3-inch (23x13x8 cm) loaf pan. Brush with oil and let stand in warm place (85°F. or 30°C.) until almost doubled, 45 to 50 minutes.

8. Heat oven to 375°F. (190°C.). Bake until golden and loaf sounds hollow when tapped, 25 to 30 minutes.

9. Prepare Sugar Icing while bread is baking.

10. Remove loaf immediately from pan. Spread Sugar Icing over top crust. Cool on wire rack.

Hot Cross Buns

Makes 1½ dozen buns

½   cup (125 mL) milk
¼   cup (60 mL) butter or
      margarine
¼   cup (60 mL) sugar
½   teaspoon (2 mL) salt
1   egg, beaten
2½ to 2¾ cups (625 to 680
      mL) all-purpose flour*
1   package (¼ oz. or 7 g)
      active dry yeast
¼   teaspoon (1 mL) ground
      cinnamon or nutmeg
½   cup (125 mL) currants or
      dark raisins
2   tablespoons (30 mL)
      chopped candied orange
      peel
1   egg
1   tablespoon (15 mL) water
      Almond Icing (see Index
      for page number)

These simple sweet buns have a long history, but it's the English who popularized them. They used to be served only on Good Friday. Now they're popular not only during the Lenten season but all year around.

1. Combine milk, butter, sugar and salt in small saucepan. Heat over low heat until 120° to 130°F (49° to 54°C.). (Butter may not melt completely.) Blend beaten egg into milk mixture.

2. Fit processor with steel blade. Measure 1½ cups (375 mL) of the flour, yeast and cinnamon into work bowl. Process on/off 2 or 3 times to mix.

3. Turn on processor and add milk mixture through feed tube to flour mixture. Process until smooth, about 20 seconds.

4. Turn on processor and add enough of the remaining flour through feed tube so dough forms a ball that cleans the sides of the bowl. Process until ball turns around bowl about 25 times.

5. Turn dough onto lightly greased surface. Knead raisins and orange peel into dough. Shape into ball and place in lightly greased bowl, turning to grease all sides. Cover loosely with plastic wrap and let stand in warm place (85°F. or 30°C.) until doubled, about 1 hour.

6. Punch down dough. Divide dough into 18 equal parts. Shape each part into a smooth ball. Place balls 2 inches (5 cm) apart on greased cookie sheets.   *continued*

*Spoon flour into dry measuring cup and level off. Do not scoop.

7. Beat egg and water with a fork. Brush egg mixture over each bun. Let stand in warm place until almost doubled, 30 to 40 minutes.

8. Heat oven to 400°F. (200°C.). Bake buns until golden, about 10 minutes.

9. Prepare Almond Icing while buns are baking.

10. Remove buns immediately from cookie sheets and place on wire rack. Cool 5 minutes. Drizzle Almond Icing over each bun to form a cross.

Nut Filled Christmas Wreath

Makes 1 loaf

3	tablespoons (45 mL) sugar
2	tablespoons (30 mL) warm water (105° to 115°F. or 41° to 46°C.)
1	package (¼ oz. or 7 g) active dry yeast
2¾	cups (680 mL) all-purpose flour*
¾	teaspoon (4 mL) salt
½	teaspoon (2 mL) ground cardamom
¼	cup (60 mL) butter or margarine, melted and cooled
2	eggs
2	to 5 tablespoons (30 to 75 mL) milk
	Cherry Nut Filling (recipe follows)
	Almond Icing (see Index for page number)

This cheery, colorful bread is ideal for the Christmas season, but it's so good you may want to serve it all year around, too. It's a ring of dough that's wrapped around a delicious candied cherry-nut filling and topped with a simple icing.

1. Combine 1 tablespoon (15 mL) of the sugar, water and yeast. Stir to dissolve yeast and let stand until bubbly, about 5 minutes.

2. Fit processor with steel blade. Measure flour, remaining 2 tablespoons (30 mL) of the sugar, salt and cardamom into work bowl. Process until mixed, about 5 seconds.

3. Add yeast mixture, melted butter and eggs to flour mixture. Process until blended, about 10 seconds.

4. Turn on processor and very slowly drizzle just enough milk through feed tube into flour mixture so dough forms a ball that cleans the sides of the bowl. Process until ball turns around bowl about 25 times. Turn off processor and let dough stand 1 to 2 minutes.

5. Turn on processor and gradually drizzle in enough remaining milk to make dough soft, smooth and satiny but not sticky.** Process until dough turns around bowl about 15 times.

6. Turn dough onto lightly floured surface. Shape into ball and place in lightly greased bowl, turning to grease all sides. Let stand in warm place (85°F. or 30°C.) until doubled, about 1 hour.

7. Prepare Cherry Nut Filling while dough is rising.

8. Punch down dough. Roll out dough into a 9x24-inch (23x60 cm) rectangle. Sprinkle Filling over dough to within 1 inch (2.5 cm) from edges. Roll up dough jelly-roll fashion beginning on 24-inch (60 cm) side. Pinch seam to seal.

9. Cut roll in half lengthwise using a sharp knife. Turn each half cut side up. Carefully twist halves together, keeping cut sides up to expose the filling. Place dough on greased cookie sheet and shape into a ring. Pinch ends together to seal. Let stand in warm place until almost doubled, about 45 minutes.

10. Heat oven to 375°F. (190°C.). Bake until evenly browned, about 20 minutes.

11. Prepare Almond Icing while bread is baking.

12. Remove bread immediately from cookie sheet and place on wire rack. Drizzle Almond Icing over bread. Cool.

---

*Spoon flour into dry measuring cup and level off. Do not scoop.

**If dough is too dry and stiff, too soft and sticky, or if the processor shuts off, correct problem according to directions on page 25.

Cherry Nut Filling

¾ cup (180 mL) chopped filberts, almonds, walnuts or pecans

¼ cup (60 mL) all-purpose flour*

¼ cup (60 mL) chopped candied red cherries

¼ cup (60 mL) chopped candied green cherries

¼ cup (60 mL) butter or margarine, at room temperature

2 tablespoons (30 mL) brown sugar

½ teaspoon (2 mL) almond extract

1. Fit processor with steel blade. Measure all ingredients into work bowl. Process on/off 6 to 8 times until mixed.

Makes 1 loaf

Babovka

¼ cup (60 mL) warm water (105° to 115°F. or 41° to 46°C.)

4 tablespoons (60 mL) packed light brown sugar

2 packages (¼ oz. or 7 g each) active dry yeast

¼ cup (60 mL) cold butter or margarine, cut into 4 pieces

2 eggs

½ teaspoon (2 mL) salt

2¼ to 2½ cups (560 to 625 mL) all-purpose flour*

¼ cup (60 mL) dark raisins

½ cup (125 mL) granulated sugar

2 tablespoons (30 mL) ground cinnamon

1 cup (250 mL) powdered sugar

This European bread is traditional for Christmas. Baked in a tube pan, it's made from a sweet dough rolled jelly-roll fashion around cinnamon sugar. After baking, it should be inverted immediately onto a serving plate so the melted sugar can drizzle down over the bread like caramel.

1. Combine water, 1 tablespoon (15 mL) of the brown sugar and yeast. Stir to dissolve yeast and let stand until bubbly, about 5 minutes.

2. Fit processor with steel blade. Add butter and remaining 3 tablespoons (45 mL) brown sugar to work bowl. Process until mixed, 10 to 15 seconds. Stop processor once or twice, if necessary, to scrape sides of bowl.

3. Add eggs and salt to butter mixture. Process until blended, about 10 seconds. Stop processor and scrape sides of bowl, if necessary.

4. Add 1¼ cups (310 mL) of the flour and yeast mixture to butter mixture. Process on/off 8 to 10 times until blended.

5. Turn on processor and add enough of the remaining flour through feed tube so dough forms a ball that cleans the sides of the bowl. Process until ball turns around bowl about 25 times.

6. Turn dough onto lightly greased surface. Knead raisins into dough. Shape dough into ball and place in lightly greased bowl, turning to grease all sides. Cover loosely with plastic wrap and let stand in warm place (85°F. or 30°C.) until almost doubled, about 1 hour.

7. Punch down dough. Let stand 10 minutes. Roll out dough into a 16-inch (40 cm) square. Combine granulated sugar and 1 tablespoon (15 mL) of the cinnamon and sprinkle over dough. Roll up dough jelly-roll fashion. Pinch seam to seal. Cut into 8 equal slices. Place slices cut side down in greased tube or Bundt pan. Let stand in warm place until almost doubled, about 1 hour.

8. Heat oven to 350°F. (180°C.). Bake until done, 30 to 35 minutes.

9. Remove bread immediately from pan and invert onto wire rack. Combine powdered sugar and remaining 1 tablespoon (15 mL) cinnamon. Sprinkle mixture over bread. Cool.

---

*Spoon flour into dry measuring cup and level off. Do not scoop.

Makes 1 loaf

Vanochka

3 tablespoons (45 mL) warm water (105° to 115°F. or 41° to 46°C.)

1 package (¼ oz. or 7 g) active dry yeast

5 tablespoons (75 mL) packed light brown sugar

1 egg, beaten

2¼ cups (560 mL) all-purpose flour*

¼ cup (60 mL) cold butter or margarine, cut into 4 pieces

½ teaspoon (2 mL) salt

½ teaspoon (2 mL) grated lemon rind

¼ teaspoon (1 mL) crushed anise seeds

¼ teaspoon (1 mL) ground mace

¼ to ½ cup (60 to 125 mL) half and half, evaporated or fresh milk

¼ cup (60 mL) dark raisins

¼ cup (60 mL) toasted slivered almonds

1 egg yolk

1 tablespoon (15 mL) cold milk

2 tablespoons (30 mL) sliced almonds

Powdered sugar

This Czechoslovakian bread is a Christmas tradition. An authentic Vanochka is shaped with a four-strand braid on the bottom, topped with a three strand braid. This version, developed to fit the food processor's work bowl, consists of a three strand braid topped with a two strand twist. It's evry bit as pretty and delicious as the original.

1. Combine water, yeast and 1 tablespoon (15 mL) of the brown sugar. Stir to dissolve yeast and let stand until bubbly, about 5 minutes. Stir beaten egg into yeast mixture.

2. Fit processor with steel blade. Measure flour, butter, remaining 4 tablespoons (60 mL) of the brown sugar, salt, lemon rind, anise and mace into work bowl. Process until mixed, about 10 seconds.

3. Add yeast mixture to flour mixture. Process until blended, about 10 seconds.

4. Turn on processor and very slowly drizzle just enough half and half through feed tube into flour mixture so dough forms a ball that cleans the sides of the bowl. Process until ball turns around bowl about 25 times. Turn off processor and let dough stand 1 to 2 minutes.

5. Turn on processor and gradually drizzle in enough remaining half and half to make dough soft, smooth and satiny but not sticky.** Process until dough turns around bowl about 15 times.

6. Cover processor and let dough stand in work bowl at room temperature until doubled, about 1 hour. Process on/off twice to punch down dough.

7. Turn dough onto lightly greased surface. Knead raisins and almonds into dough.

8. Cut off about ½ cup (125 mL) of the dough and reserve. Divide remaining dough into 3 equal parts. Shape each part into strand 25 inches (63 cm) long. Braid the strands together and place on greased cookie sheet.

9. Divide reserved dough into 2 equal parts. Shape each part into strand 25 inches (63 cm) long. Twist the 2 strands together.

10. Beat egg yolk and cold milk with a fork. Brush egg mixture over braided strands. Place twisted strands on top of braided strands. Brush egg mixture over twisted strands. Sprinkle sliced almonds over loaf. Let stand in warm place (85°F. or 30°C.) until almost doubled, about 45 minutes.

11. Heat oven to 375°F. (190°C.). Bake until golden, 20 to 25 minutes.

12. Remove bread from cookie sheet and place on wire rack. Dust heavily with powdered sugar. Cool.

---

*Spoon flour into dry measuring cup and level off. Do not scoop.

**If dough is too dry and stiff, too soft and sticky, or if the processor shuts off, correct problem according to directions on page 25.

HOLIDAY BREADS

Julekage

¼ cup (60 mL) warm water (105° to 115°F. or 41° to 46°C.)

4 tablespoons (60 mL) sugar

1 package (¼ oz. or 7 g) active dry yeast

¼ cup (60 mL) butter or margarine, melted and cooled

1 egg, beaten

2½ cups (625 mL) all-purpose flour*

1 teaspoon (5 mL) ground cardamom or nutmeg

½ teaspoon (2 mL) salt

2 to 5 tablespoons (30 to 75 mL) evaporated or fresh milk

1 cup (250 mL) dark raisins

¼ cup (60 mL) finely chopped candied citron

Vegetable oil

1 egg yolk

2 tablespoons (30 mL) cold water

This is the traditional Christmas bread of Norway. It is shaped into a round loaf that's made shiny with an egg glaze. For a festive look, it may be decorated with a simple powdered sugar icing and additional candied fruits.

1. Combine water, 1 tablespoon (15 mL) of the sugar and yeast. Stir to dissolve yeast and let stand until bubbly, about 5 minutes. Blend melted butter and egg into yeast mixture.

2. Fit processor with steel blade. Measure flour, remaining 3 tablespoons (45 mL) sugar, cardamom and salt into work bowl. Process until mixed, about 10 seconds.

3. Add yeast mixture to flour mixture. Process until blended, about 20 seconds.

4. Turn on processor and very slowly drizzle just enough milk through feed tube into flour mixture so dough forms a ball that cleans the sides of the bowl. Process until ball turns around bowl about 25 times. Turn off processor and let dough stand 1 to 2 minutes.

5. Turn on processor and gradually drizzle in enough remaining milk to make dough soft, smooth and satiny but not sticky.** Process until dough turns around bowl about 15 times.

6. Turn dough onto lightly greased surface. Knead in raisins and citron. Shape into ball and place in lightly greased bowl, turning to grease all sides. Cover loosely with plastic wrap and let stand in warm place (85°F. or 30°C.) until doubled, about 1 hour.

7. Punch down dough. Roll or pat into circle 8 inches (20 cm) in diameter. Place in greased 9-inch (23 cm) round cake or pie pan. Brush with oil. Let stand in warm place until doubled, about 45 minutes.

8. Heat oven to 350°F. (180°C.). Beat egg yolk and cold water with fork. Brush over bread. Bake until evenly browned, 35 to 40 minutes.

9. Remove from pan immediately. Cool on wire rack.

Makes 1 loaf

Cresca

¼ to ½ cup (60 to 125 mL) warm water (105° to 115°F. or 41° to 46°C.)

1 package (¼ oz. or 7 g) active dry yeast

1 teaspoon (5 mL) sugar

2¼ cups (560 mL) all-purpose flour*

⅓ cup (80 mL) grated Parmesan or Romano cheese

1 tablespoon (15 mL) olive or vegetable oil

¼ teaspoon (1 mL) salt

¼ teaspoon (1 mL) pepper

2 eggs

Olive or vegetable oil

This bread comes from northern Italy where it's a traditional Easter bread. It's a non-sweet bread flavored with Parmesan or Romano cheese, and it's good with any meal, Easter or otherwise.

1. Combine ¼ cup (60 mL) of the water, yeast and sugar. Stir to dissolve yeast and let stand until bubbly, about 5 minutes.

2. Fit processor with steel blade. Measure flour, cheese, 1 tablespoon (15 mL) of the oil, salt and pepper into work bowl. Process until mixed, about 15 seconds.

3. Add yeast mixture and eggs to flour mixture. Process until blended, about 10 seconds.

4. Turn on processor and very slowly drizzle just enough remaining water through feed tube into flour mixture so dough forms a ball that cleans the sides of the bowl. Process until ball turns around bowl about 25 times. Turn off processor and let dough stand 1 to 2 minutes. *continued*

---

*Spoon flour into dry measuring cup and level off. Do not scoop.

**If dough is too dry and stiff, too soft and sticky, or if the processor shuts off, correct problem according to directions on page 25.

Cresca *(continued)*

5. Turn on processor and gradually drizzle in enough remaining water to make dough soft, smooth and satiny but not sticky.** Process until dough turns around bowl about 15 times.

6. Cover processor and let dough stand in work bowl at room temperature until doubled, 1 to 1¼ hours. Or, turn dough onto lightly floured surface and shape into ball. Place in lightly greased bowl, turning to grease all sides. Cover loosely with plastic wrap and let stand in warm place (85°F. or 30°C.) until doubled, about 45 minutes.

7. Punch down dough. Roll or pat dough into a circle 8 inches (20 cm) in diameter. Place in greased 9-inch (23 cm) round pie or cake pan. Brush with oil. Let stand in warm place until doubled, 50 to 60 minutes.

8. Heat oven to 350°F. (180°C.). Bake until done and loaf sounds hollow when tapped, 30 to 35 minutes.

9. Remove immediately from pan. Brush crust with oil, if desired. Cool on wire rack.

Makes 1 loaf

Panettone

¼ to ½ cup (60 to 125 mL) warm water (105° to 115°F. or 41° to 46°C.)

4 tablespoons (60 mL) sugar

1 package (¼ oz. or 7 g) active dry yeast

3 cups (750 mL) all-purpose flour*

¼ cup (60 mL) butter or margarine, at room temperature

1½ teaspoons (7 mL) anise seeds

½ teaspoon (2 mL) salt

3 eggs

¼ cup (60 mL) golden raisins

¼ cup (60 mL) chopped citron

2 tablespoons (30 mL) pine nuts or slivered almonds
Vegetable oil

1 tablespoon (15 mL) cold water

This sweet bread originated in Milan and now is a favorite throughout Italy. It's made from a dough rich in egg and butter. Anise gives it a special flavor. Italians serve it at Christmas, Easter, weddings and other special occasions.

1. Combine ¼ cup (60 mL) of the water, 1 tablespoon (15 mL) of the sugar and yeast. Stir to dissolve yeast and let stand until bubbly, about 5 minutes.

2. Fit processor with steel blade. Measure flour, butter, remaining 3 tablespoons (45 mL) of the sugar, anise and salt into work bowl. Process until mixed, about 15 seconds.

3. Add yeast mixture and 2 of the eggs to flour mixture. Process until blended, about 10 seconds.

4. Turn on processor and very slowly drizzle just enough remaining water through feed tube into flour mixture so dough forms a ball that cleans the sides of the bowl. Process until ball turns around bowl about 25 times. Turn off processor and let dough stand 1 to 2 minutes.

5. Turn on processor and gradually drizzle in enough remaining water to make dough soft, smooth and satiny but not sticky.** Process until dough turns around bowl about 15 times.

6. Turn dough onto lightly greased surface. Knead in raisins, citron and nuts. Shape into ball and place in lightly greased bowl, turning to grease all sides. Cover loosely with plastic wrap and let stand in warm place (85°F. or 30°C.) until doubled, about 1 hour.

7. Punch down dough. Shape into smooth ball and place on greased cookie sheet. Roll or pat into circle about 6 inches (15 cm) in diameter. Cut a cross ½-inch (1.5 cm) deep in the top of dough using a sharp knife or razor blade. Brush with oil. Let stand in warm place until doubled, 50 to 60 minutes.

8. Heat oven to 350°F. (180°C.). Beat remaining egg and cold water with fork. Brush over bread. Bake until done, 35 to 40 minutes.

9. Remove immediately from cookie sheet. Cool on wire rack.

---

*Spoon flour into dry measuring cup and level off. Do not scoop.

**If dough is too dry and stiff, too soft and sticky, or if the processor shuts off, correct problem according to directions on page 25.

Saint Lucia Crown

Makes 1 loaf

¼ cup (60 mL) warm water (105° to 115°F. or 41° to 46°C.)

4 tablespoons (60 mL) sugar

1 package (¼ oz. or 7 g) active dry yeast

2¾ cups (680 mL) all-purpose flour*

¼ cup (60 mL) butter or margarine, at room temperature

1 teaspoon (5 mL) salt

3 eggs

2 to 5 tablespoons (30 to 75 mL) evaporated or fresh milk

⅛ teaspoon (0.5 mL) powdered saffron

½ cup (125 mL) golden raisins

¼ cup (60 mL) chopped blanched almonds

1 tablespoon (15 mL) cold water

Vegetable oil

Sugar Icing (see Index for page number)

In Sweden this beautiful bread is traditionally served on St. Lucia's Day, December 13th. It's made from three strands of sweet, saffron spiced dough that are braided together to form a ring which looks like a crown.

1. Combine warm water, 1 tablespoon (15 mL) of the sugar and yeast. Stir to dissolve yeast and let stand until bubbly, about 5 minutes.

2. Fit processor with steel blade. Measure flour, butter, remaining 3 tablespoons (45 mL) of the sugar and salt into work bowl. Process until mixed, about 15 seconds.

3. Add yeast mixture and 2 of the eggs to flour mixture. Process until blended, about 10 seconds.

4. Stir saffron into 2 tablespoons (30 mL) of the milk. Turn on processor and very slowly drizzle just enough milk through feed tube into flour mixture so dough forms a ball that cleans the sides of the bowl. Process until ball turns around bowl about 25 times. Turn off processor and let dough stand 1 to 2 minutes.

5. Turn on processor and gradually drizzle in enough remaining milk to make dough soft, smooth and satiny but not sticky.** Process until dough turns around bowl about 15 times. Cover work bowl and let dough stand in bowl at room temperature until doubled, 1 to 1½ hours.

6. Punch down dough. Cut off about ⅓ cup (80 mL) of the dough and reserve. Divide remaining dough into 3 equal parts. Shape each part into a strand 25 inches (63 cm) long. Braid strands together and place on greased cookie sheet. Shape into a ring about 8 inches (20 cm) in diameter. Pinch ends together to seal.

7. Shape reserved ⅓ cup (80 mL) of dough into a strand 12 inches (30 cm) long. Shape into a bow and place over seam of braided ring. Cover loosely with plastic wrap and let stand in warm place (85°F. or 30°C.) until doubled, about 45 minutes.

8. Heat oven to 350°F. (180°C.). Beat the remaining egg with cold water. Brush over ring. Bake until evenly browned, 25 to 30 minutes.

9. Prepare Sugar Icing while bread is baking.

10. Remove bread from cookie sheet and place on wire rack. Drizzle Sugar Icing over bread. Cool. If desired, make 4 to 6 small holes in bread and insert candles into holes.

Golden Eggnog Holiday Braid

Makes 1 loaf

2 tablespoons (30 mL) warm water (105° to 115°F. or 41° to 46°C.)

2 tablespoons (30 mL) sugar

1 package (¼ oz. or 7 g) active dry yeast

2½ cups (625 mL) all-purpose flour*

2 tablespoons (30 mL) butter or margarine

continued

This lovely braided bread will soon become a perennial favorite. It's delicious with its sweet dough that's richly flavored with dairy eggnog and nutmeg. Serve it all through the holidays with coffee, sweet wine or eggnog, of course.

1. Combine water, sugar and yeast. Stir to dissolve yeast and let stand until bubbly, about 5 minutes.

2. Fit processor with steel blade. Measure flour, butter, salt and nutmeg into work bowl. Process until mixed, about 15 seconds.

3. Add yeast mixture to flour mixture. Process until blended, about 10 seconds.

*Spoon flour into dry measuring cup and level off. Do not scoop.

**If dough is too dry and stiff, too soft and sticky, or if the processor shuts off, correct problem according to directions on page 25.

Golden Eggnog Holiday Braid *(continued)*

1 teaspoon (5 mL) salt

¼ teaspoon (1 mL) ground nutmeg

½ to ¾ cup (125 to 180 mL) dairy eggnog, at room temperature
Dairy eggnog
Crushed sugar cubes or sliced almonds

4. Turn on processor and very slowly drizzle just enough eggnog through feed tube into flour mixture so dough forms a ball that cleans the sides of the bowl. Process until ball turns round bowl about 25 times. Turn off processor and let dough stand 1 to 2 minutes.

5. Turn on processor and gradually drizzle in enough remaining eggnog to make dough soft, smooth and satiny but not sticky.** Process until dough turns around bowl about 15 times.

6. Let dough stand in work bowl 10 minutes. Turn dough onto lightly floured surface and shape into ball. Place in lightly greased bowl, turning to grease all sides. Cover loosely with plastic wrap and let stand in warm place (85°F. or 30°C.) until doubled, about 1 hour.

7. Punch down dough. Let stand 10 minutes. Divide into 3 equal parts. Shape each part into strand 20 inches (50 cm) long. Braid the 3 strands together. Place on greased cookie sheet. Brush with oil and let stand in warm place until doubled, about 45 minutes.

8. Heat oven to 375°F. (190°C.). Brush braid with eggnog and sprinkle with sugar or almonds. Bake until done, 25 to 30 minutes.

9. Remove braid from cookie sheet. Cool on wire rack.

Apricot Holiday Bread

Makes 1 loaf

½ cup (125 mL) pecan or walnut pieces

½ cup (125 mL) dried apricots or peaches

2½ to 3 cups (625 to 750 mL) all-purpose flour*

2 tablespoons (30 mL) sugar

2 tablespoons (30 mL) butter or margarine

1 package (¼ oz. or 7 g) active dry yeast

1 teaspoon (5 mL) salt

¼ teaspoon (1 mL) ground ginger

¼ teaspoon (1 mL) ground nutmeg

⅔ cup (160 mL) milk

1 egg
Vegetable oil
Sugar Icing (see Index for page number), optional

Dried apricots, chopped nuts and spices flavor this appealing bread for either the Christmas or Easter holidays. It's easily shaped into a round loaf that can be decorated after baking with a simple icing.

1. Fit processor with steel blade. Place nuts into work bowl. Process on/off 3 or 4 times to chop nuts. Transfer nuts to small bowl. Place apricots in work bowl. Process on/off 10 to 12 times to coarsely chop apricots. Add apricots to the nuts in bowl. Reserve.

2. Refit processor with steel blade. Measure 1½ cups (375 mL) of the flour, sugar, butter, yeast, salt, ginger and nutmeg into work bowl. Process until mixed, about 5 seconds.

3. Heat milk over low heat until 120° to 130°F. (49° to 54°C.). Turn on processor and add milk through feed tube to flour mixture. Process until smooth, about 30 seconds.

4. Add egg to batter. Process until blended, about 10 seconds.

5. Turn on processor and add enough of the remaining flour ¼ cup (60 mL) at a time through feed tube so dough forms a ball that cleans the sides of the bowl. Process until ball turns around bowl about 25 times.

6. Turn dough onto lightly floured surface. Shape into ball. Place in lightly greased bowl, turning to grease all sides. Cover loosely with plastic wrap and let stand in warm place (85°F. or 30°C.) until doubled, about 1 hour.

7. Punch down dough. Roll or pat dough with hands into a circle 8 inches in diameter. Place in greased 9-inch (23 cm) round cake or pie pan. Brush with oil. Let stand in warm place until doubled, 45 to 55 minutes.

8. Heat oven to 375°F. (190°C.). Bake until done, 25 to 30 minutes.

9. Remove immediately from pan. Cool on wire rack. Spread Sugar Icing over loaf, if desired.

---

*Spoon flour into dry measuring cup and level off. Do not scoop.

**If dough is too dry and stiff, too soft and sticky, or if the processor shuts off, correct problem according to directions on page 25.

HOLIDAY BREADS

Mexican Three Kings Bread

Makes 1 loaf

¼ cup (60 mL) warm water (105° to 115° or 41° to 46°C.)

4 tablespoons (60 mL) sugar

1 package (¼ oz. or 7 g) active dry yeast

½ cup (125 mL) cold butter or margarine, cut into 8 pieces

2 eggs

½ teaspoon (2 mL) salt

2½ to 3 cups (625 to 750 mL) all-purpose flour*

2 tablespoons (30 mL) instant nonfat dry milk solids

¼ cup (60 mL) dark raisins

¼ cup (60 mL) chopped walnuts

¼ cup (60 mL) chopped candied cherries

Sugar Icing (see Index for page number)

In Mexico this bread is traditionally served at festivities honoring Twelfth Night, the twelfth day after Christmas. It's customary to place a small china doll, a ring or a coin in the dough. Whoever finds it is assured good luck throughout the year.

1. Combine water, 1 tablespoon (15 mL) of the sugar and yeast. Stir to dissolve yeast and let stand until bubbly, about 5 minutes.

2. Fit processor with steel blade. Add butter and remaining 3 tablespoons (45 mL) of the sugar to work bowl. Process until mixed, 10 to 15 seconds. Stop processor once or twice, if necessary, to scrape sides of bowl.

3. Add eggs and salt to butter mixture. Process until blended, about 10 seconds. Stop processor and scrape sides of bowl, if necessary.

4. Add 1½ cups (375 mL) of the flour, dry milk and yeast mixture to butter mixture. Process on/off 8 to 10 times until blended.

5. Turn on processor and add enough of the remaining flour through feed tube so dough forms a ball that cleans the sides of the bowl. Process until ball turns around bowl about 25 times.

6. Turn dough onto lightly greased surface. Knead raisins, walnuts and cherries into dough. Shape into ball and place in lightly greased bowl, turning to grease all sides. Cover loosely with plastic wrap and let stand in warm place (85°F. or 30°C.) until almost doubled, about 1 hour.

7. Punch down dough. Shape into strand about 15 inches (38 cm) long. Place strand on greased cookie sheet and shape into a ring. Pinch ends together to seal. Cover loosely with plastic wrap and let stand in warm place until almost doubled, about 45 minutes.

8. Heat oven to 375°F. (190°C.). Bake until evenly browned, 30 to 35 minutes.

9. Prepare Sugar Icing while bread is baking.

10. Remove bread immediately from cookie sheet and place on wire rack. Spread Sugar Icing over bread. Cool.

Italian Easter Bread

Makes 1 loaf

⅓ cup (80 mL) sugar

Rind of half a lemon, pared into 1-inch (2.5 cm) pieces

2¼ to 2½ cups (560 to 625 mL) all-purpose flour*

1 package (¼ oz. or 7 g) active dry yeast

½ teaspoon (2 mL) salt

¼ cup (60 mL) milk

¼ cup (60 mL) butter or margarine, cut into 4 pieces

1 egg, beaten

1 egg yolk

continued

This is a delightful bread made from a lemony, sweet dough that's filled with almond paste and shaped into a ring.

1. Fit processor with steel blade. Add ⅓ cup (80 mL) of the sugar and lemon rind to work bowl. Process until rind is minced.

2. Add 1¼ cups (310 mL) of the flour, yeast and salt to sugar mixture in the work bowl. Process until mixed, about 5 seconds.

3. Combine milk and butter in small saucepan. Heat over low heat just until 120° to 130°F. (49° to 54°C.). (Butter may not melt completely.) Blend beaten egg, egg yolk and vanilla into milk mixture.

4. Turn on processor and add milk mixture through feed tube to flour mixture. Process until smooth, about 30 seconds.

5. Turn on processor and add enough of the remaining flour ¼ cup (60 mL) at a time through feed tube so dough forms a ball that cleans the sides of the bowl. Process until ball turns around bowl about 25 times.

6. Turn dough onto lightly floured surface. Shape into ball and place in lightly greased bowl, turning to grease all sides. Cover loosely with plastic

*Spoon flour into dry measuring cup and level off. Do not scoop.

Italian Easter Bread (continued)

1 teaspoon (5 mL) vanilla
¼ cup (60 mL) almond paste
1 egg white
1 teaspoon (5 mL) sugar
18 to 20 whole blanched almonds

wrap and let stand in warm place (85°F. or 30°C.) until doubled, about 1 hour.

7. Punch down dough. Shape dough into strand 18 to 20 inches (45 to 50 cm) long. Flatten strand so it is 4 inches (10 cm) wide. Place almond paste in a long strand down center of dough. Fold dough lengthwise, bringing one side of dough over almond paste to meet other side. Pinch seam to seal.

8. Place dough on greased cookie sheet and shape into a ring. Pinch ends together to seal. Cover loosely with plastic wrap and let stand in warm place until almost doubled, about 1 hour.

9. Heat oven to 325°F. (160°C.). Cut slashes about ¼ inch (0.5 cm) across dough in 8 places using sharp knife or razor blade. Beat egg white with fork or whisk and brush over dough. Place whole almonds in the slashes. Bake until done and evenly browned, 45 to 50 minutes.

10. Remove immediately from cookie sheet. Cool on wire rack.

Makes 1 loaf

Kulich

¼ cup (60 mL) warm water (105° to 115°F. or 41° to 46°C.)
4 tablespoons (60 mL) sugar
1 package (¼ oz. or 7 g) active dry yeast
1 egg, beaten
2¾ cups (680 mL) all-purpose flour*
2 tablespoons (30 mL) butter or margarine, at room temperature
1 teaspoon (5 mL) salt
½ teaspoon (2 mL) ground cardamom
¼ to ⅓ cup (60 to 80 mL) evaporated or fresh milk
½ cup (125 mL) chopped blanched almonds
¼ cup (60 mL) golden raisins
¼ cup (60 mL) candied orange peel
Sugar Icing (see Index for page number
Candied cherries and whole almonds, optional

This is the traditional Easter bread of Russia. It's a handsome bread—tall, round and decorated with a simple icing. Cut it into crosswise slices and serve for breakfast, brunch or snacks.

1. Combine water, 1 tablespoon (15 mL) of the sugar and yeast. Stir to dissolve yeast and let stand until bubbly, about 5 minutes. Blend egg into yeast mixture.

2. Fit processor with steel blade. Measure flour, remaining 3 tablespoons (45 mL) of the sugar, butter, salt and cardamom into work bowl. Process until mixed, about 5 seconds.

3. Add yeast mixture to flour mixture. Process until blended, about 10 seconds.

4. Turn on processor and very slowly drizzle just enough milk through feed tube into flour mixture so dough forms a ball that cleans the sides of the bowl. Process until ball turns around bowl about 25 times. Turn off processor and let dough stand 1 to 2 minutes.

5. Turn on processor and gradually drizzle in enough remaining milk to make dough soft, smooth and satiny but not sticky.** Process until dough turns around bowl about 15 times.

6. Turn dough onto lightly greased surface. Knead almonds, raisins and orange peel into dough. Shape dough into ball and place in lightly greased bowl, turning to grease all sides. Let stand in warm place (85°F. or 30°C.) until doubled, about 1 hour.

7. Punch down dough. Shape dough into smooth ball and place in well greased 2-pound (900 g) coffee can or two 1-pound (450 g) coffee cans . Cover can with plastic lid. Let stand in warm place until doubled (lid should pop off), about 1 hour.

8. Heat oven to 350°F. (180°C.). Bake bread on lowest rack of oven until wooden pick or cake tester inserted in center comes out clean, 45 to 50 minutes.

9. Let bread cool in can 10 minutes, then remove from can and place upright on wire rack. Spread Sugar Icing over top of loaf. Decorate with candied cherries and almonds, if desired. Cool.

*Spoon flour into dry measuring cup and level off. Do not scoop.

**If dough is too dry and stiff, too soft and sticky, or if the processor shuts off, correct problem according to directions on page 25.

HOLIDAY BREADS

Pääsiäisleipä

¼ cup (60 mL) warm water (105° to 115°F. or 41° to 46°C.)

4 tablespoons (60 mL) sugar

1 package (¼ oz. or 7 g) active dry yeast

2¾ cups (680 mL) all-purpose flour*

¼ cup (60 mL) instant nonfat dry milk solids

¼ cup (60 mL) butter or margarine, at room temperature

1 teaspoon (5 mL) ground cardamom

½ teaspoon (2 mL) salt

2 eggs

2 to 5 tablespoons (30 to 75 mL) evaporated or fresh milk

½ cup (125 mL) golden raisins or chopped candied fruit

¼ cup (60 mL) chopped almonds

Almond Icing (see Index for page number)

Don't worry if you can't pronounce this bread—you can still enjoy it! It's rich, almost cake-like in texture and it's delicious. From Finland, it's an Easter bread that's traditionally baked in a pail. However, a coffee can works fine.

1. Combine water, 1 tablespoon (15 mL) of the sugar and yeast. Stir to dissolve yeast and let stand until bubbly, about 5 minutes.

2. Fit processor with steel blade. Measure flour, dry milk, butter, remaining 3 tablespoons (45 mL) of the sugar, cardamom and salt into work bowl. Process until mixed, about 20 seconds.

3. Add yeast mixture and eggs to flour mixture. Process until blended, about 10 seconds.

4. Turn on processor and very slowly drizzle just enough milk through feed tube into flour mixture so dough forms a ball that cleans the sides of the bowl. Process until ball turns around bowl about 25 times. Turn off processor and let dough stand 1 to 2 minutes.

5. Turn on processor and gradually drizzle in enough remaining milk to make dough soft, smooth and satiny but not sticky.** Process until dough turns around bowl about 15 times.

6. Turn dough onto lightly floured surface. Shape into ball and place in lightly greased bowl, turning to grease all sides. Cover loosely with plastic wrap and let stand in warm place (85°F. or 30°C.) until doubled, about 1 hour.

7. Punch down dough. Shape into smooth ball. Place in a well greased 2-pound (900 g) coffee can or 1½ quart (1.5 L) souffle dish. Flatten dough slightly with palm of hand. Brush with oil and let stand in warm place until doubled, about 1 hour.

8. Heat oven to 350°F. (180°C.). Bake until wooden pick or cake tester inserted in center comes out clean, 45 to 55 minutes. (If loaf browns too quickly, cover top loosely with aluminum foil.)

9. Prepare Almond Icing while bread is baking.

10. Remove bread immediately from pan or dish. Drizzle Almond Icing over top of loaf. Cool on wire rack.

---

*Spoon flour into dry measuring cup and level off. Do not scoop.

**If dough is too dry and stiff, too soft and sticky, or if the processor shuts off, correct problem according to directions on page 25.

FOREIGN BREADS

French Bread

¾ to 1 cup (180 to 250 mL) warm water (105° to 115°F. or 41° to 46°C.)

1 package (¼ oz. or 7 g) active dry yeast

2 teaspoons (10 mL) sugar

2¾ cups (680 mL) all-purpose flour*

1 tablespoon (15 mL) butter or margarine

1 teaspoon (5 mL) salt

½ cup (125 mL) water

1 teaspoon (5 mL) cornstarch

This is the classic bread with the moist, chewy interior and the crisp, crusty exterior. A cornstarch glaze before baking helps make the crust crispy. For a really crisp crust, place a pan of boiling water on the bottom shelf of the oven during baking.

1. Combine ¼ cup (60 mL) of the warm water, yeast and sugar. Stir to dissolve yeast and let stand until bubbly, about 5 minutes.

2. Fit processor with steel blade. Measure flour, butter and salt into work bowl. Process until mixed, about 10 seconds.

3. Add yeast mixture to flour mixture. Process until blended, about 10 seconds.

4. Turn on processor and very slowly drizzle just enough remaining warm water through feed tube into flour mixture so dough forms a ball that cleans the sides of the bowl. Process until ball turns around bowl about 25 times. Turn off processor and let dough stand 1 to 2 minutes.

5. Turn on processor and gradually drizzle in enough remaining warm water to make dough soft, smooth and satiny but not sticky.** Process until dough turns around bowl about 15 times.

6. Turn dough onto lightly greased surface. Shape into ball and place in lightly greased bowl, turning to grease all sides. Cover loosely with plastic wrap and let stand in warm place (85°F. or 30°C.) until doubled, about 1 hour.

7. Punch down dough. Shape into a strand 12 to 14 inches (30 to 35 cm) long. Place diagonally on large greased cookie sheet. Cut 3 slashes, each about 3 inches (8 cm) long, in top of dough using the processor's steel blade, sharp knife or razor blade. Cover loosely with plastic wrap and let stand in warm place until almost doubled, about 45 minutes.

8. Heat oven to 375°F. (190°C.). Combine ½ cup (125 mL) water and cornstarch in small saucepan. Bring to a boil. Brush hot mixture over loaf. Bake until golden and loaf sounds hollow when tapped, 35 to 40 minutes.

9. Remove from cookie sheet and cool on wire rack.

Note: For a crisper crust, place a shallow pan of boiling water on bottom shelf of oven to create steam during baking.

Crusty Cuban Bread Prepare dough as directed for French Bread through first rising. Punch down dough and turn onto lightly greased surface. Shape into a ball. Roll or pat into a circle about 8 inches (20 cm) in diameter. Grease a cookie sheet and sprinkle lightly with cornmeal. Place dough on cookie sheet. Cut a cross about 4 inches (10 cm) long and ¼ inch (0.5 cm) deep in top of loaf using the processor's steel blade, sharp knife or razor blade. Cover loosely with plastic wrap and let stand in warm place until almost doubled, about 1 hour. Bake as directed for French Bread.

*Spoon flour into dry measuring cup and level off. Do not scoop.

**If dough is too dry and stiff, too soft and sticky, or if the processor shuts off, correct problem according to directions on page 25.

Italian Bread

Makes 1 loaf

¾ to 1 cup (180 to 250 mL) warm water (105° to 115°F. or 41° to 46°C.)
1 package (¼ oz. or 7 g) active dry yeast
1 teaspoon (5 mL) sugar
2½ cups (625 mL) all-purpose flour*
¾ teaspoon (4 mL) salt
¼ cup (60 mL) cold water
1 egg, beaten
Cornmeal

This classic is an every day staple on Italian tables. The crusty bread is made from a simple dough that can be shaped into either a round or an oblong loaf.

1. Combine ¼ cup (60 mL) of the warm water, yeast and sugar. Stir to dissolve yeast and let stand until bubbly, about 5 minutes.

2. Fit processor with steel blade. Add flour and salt to work bowl. Process on/off to mix.

3. Add yeast mixture to flour mixture. Process until blended, about 10 seconds.

4. Turn on processor and very slowly drizzle just enough remaining warm water through feed tube into flour mixture so dough forms a ball that cleans sides of the bowl. Turn off processor and let dough stand 1 to 2 minutes.

5. Turn on processor and gradually drizzle in enough remaining warm water to make dough soft, smooth and satiny but not sticky.** Process until dough turns around bowl about 15 times.

6. Turn dough onto lightly floured surface. Shape into ball and place in lightly greased bowl, turning to grease all sides. Cover loosely with plastic wrap and let stand in warm place (85°F. or 30°C.) until doubled, about 1 hour.

7. Punch down dough. Shape dough into a round loaf about 7 inches (18 cm) in diameter or a long loaf about 12 inches (30 cm) long.

8. Grease a cookie sheet and sprinkle lightly with cornmeal. Place loaf on cookie sheet. Cover loosely with plastic wrap. Let stand in warm place until almost doubled, 30 to 40 minutes.

9. Heat oven to 350°F. (180°C.). Cut slashes about 3 inches (8 cm) long in top of loaf using processor's steel blade, sharp knife or razor blade.

10. Combine cold water and egg. Brush mixture over loaf. Bake until loaf sounds hollow when tapped, 30 to 35 minutes.

11. Remove immediately from cookie sheet. Cool on wire rack.

Chapatis

Makes 16 chapatis

2 cups (500 mL) whole wheat flour (or a combination of whole wheat and all-purpose flour)
1 tablespoon (15 mL) vegetable oil
1 teaspoon (5 mL) salt
¾ to 1 cup (180 to 250 mL) warm water

Made from whole wheat flour, Chapatis are thin rounds of unleavened bread from India that are cooked in an ungreased pan on top of the stove. Their mild flavor makes them an ideal accompaniment to the highly seasoned food so typical of Indian cookery. Fry the rounds of dough in oil and they become Puris.

1. Fit processor with steel blade. Measure flour, oil and salt into work bowl.

2. Turn on processor and slowly drizzle water through feed tube into flour mixture so dough forms a ball that cleans the sides of the bowl. Let dough stand 1 to 2 minutes.

3. Turn on processor and slowly add more water until dough is soft but not sticky. If dough is hard or dry, uncover processor, cut it into quarters, sprinkle water over the quarters, and cover processor. Process until dough forms soft ball, gradually adding more water if dough will absorb it. Let dough stand in work bowl 5 minutes. *continued*

*Spoon flour into dry measuring cup and level off. Do not scoop.

**If dough is too dry and stiff, too soft and sticky, or if the processor shuts off, correct problem according to directions on page 25.

Chapatis *(continued)*

4. Turn dough onto lightly greased surface and shape into a ball. Cover with inverted bowl or plastic wrap and let dough stand at room temperature about 1 hour.

5. Uncover dough. Divide dough into 16 equal parts. Roll out each part on lightly floured surface to a thin circle 6 to 8 inches (15 to 20 cm) in diameter. Heat an ungreased griddle to 375°F. (190°C.), or heat a large, ungreased fry pan over medium heat until hot enough to sizzle a drop of water. Cook each Chapati until golden, about 1 minute on each side. (Press Chapati with wide pancake turner or folded cloth to cook evenly.) Serve hot.

Puris Prepare dough and roll out into circles as directed for Chapatis. Pour about 1 inch (2.5 cm) vegetable oil into fry pan or large saucepan. Heat to 375°F. (190°C.). Fry Puris one at a time in oil until puffy, about 1 minute on each side. Drain on paper toweling. Serve hot.

Pain d'Anis

Makes 1 loaf

¼ cup (60 mL) warm water (105° to 115°F. or 41° to 46°C.)

1 tablespoon (15 mL) granulated sugar

1 package (¼ oz. or 7 g) active dry yeast

2 teaspoons (10 mL) anise seeds

1 egg, beaten

2¼ cups (560 mL) all-purpose flour*

¼ cup (60 mL) cold butter or margarine, cut into 4 pieces

¼ teaspoon (1 mL) salt

2 to 5 tablespoons (30 to 75 mL) milk

⅓ cup (80 mL) packed light brown sugar

¼ teaspoon (1 mL) ground cinnamon

Sugar Glaze (see Index for page number) or powdered sugar

This anise spiced bread is from France. It's made from a sweet yeast dough that's wrapped jelly-roll fashion around a brown sugar-cinnamon mixture and baked in a tube or Bundt pan.

1. Combine water, granulated sugar, yeast and anise seeds. Stir to dissolve yeast and let stand until bubbly, about 5 minutes. Blend egg into yeast mixture.

2. Fit processor with steel blade. Measure flour, butter and salt into work bowl. Process until mixed, about 10 seconds.

3. Turn on processor and slowly add yeast mixture through feed tube to flour mixture. Drizzle very slowly just enough milk into flour mixture so dough forms a ball that cleans the sides of the bowl. Process until ball turns around bowl about 25 times. Turn off processor and let dough stand 1 to 2 minutes.

4. Turn on processor and gradually drizzle in enough remaining milk to make dough soft, smooth and satiny but not sticky.** Process until dough turns around bowl about 15 times.

5. Turn dough onto lightly floured surface. Shape into ball and place in lightly greased bowl, turning to grease all sides. Cover loosely with plastic wrap and let stand in warm place (85°F. or 30°C.) until doubled, about 1½ hours.

6. Punch down dough. Roll out dough into a 12x22-inch (30x55 cm) rectangle. Mix brown sugar with cinnamon and sprinkle evenly over dough. Roll up dough jelly-roll fashion, beginning at 22-inch (55 cm) side. Pinch seam to seal. Fit dough into greased 5 or 6 cup (1250 mL or 1.5 L) ring mold or Bundt cake pan. Pinch ends together to seal. Cover loosely with plastic wrap and let stand in warm place until doubled, about 1 hour.

7. Heat oven to 350°F. (180°C.). Bake until wooden pick or cake tester inserted in bread comes out clean, 30 to 35 minutes.

8. Prepare Sugar Glaze, if desired, while bread is baking.

9. Remove bread immediately from pan and place on wire rack. Drizzle glaze over bread or sprinkle powdered sugar over bread. Cool.

---

*Spoon flour into dry measuring cup and level off. Do not scoop.

**If dough is too dry and stiff, too soft and sticky, or if the processor shuts off, correct problem according to directions on page 25.

FOREIGN BREADS

Makes 1 bread

Focaccia

Italian Bread Dough (see Index for page number)

½ cup (125 mL) pizza sauce

1 teaspoon (5 mL) garlic salt

¼ cup (60 mL) grated Romano or Parmesan cheese

3 tablespoons (45 mL) olive or vegetable oil

This delicious bread is very similar to pizza. It's made from Italian bread dough that's rolled thin to fit a jelly roll pan. Then it's topped with pizza sauce, grated cheese and a drizzle of olive oil.

1. Prepare Italian Bread Dough as directed through first rising. Punch down dough. Roll out dough into a rectangle about 15x11 inches (38x28 cm). Fit dough into a greased 15½x10½x1-inch (39x27x2.5 cm) jelly roll baking pan. Press dough to sides of pan. With fingers make indentations in dough at 1 inch (2.5 cm) intervals.

2. Blend pizza sauce and garlic salt. Spread evenly over dough. Sprinkle cheese evenly over sauce. Drizzle oil over cheese and sauce. Let stand in warm place (85°F. or 30°C.) until almost doubled, 20 to 30 minutes.

3. Heat oven to 450°F. (230°C.). Bake until well browned at edges, 12 to 15 minutes. Cut in half lengthwise, then cut each half into 6 or 7 pieces. Serve hot.

Makes 1 loaf

Gannat (French Cheese Bread)

4 ounces (115 g) Emmenthaler Swiss, Gruyere, sharp Cheddar or Swiss cheese

3 to 6 tablespoons (45 to 90 mL) warm water (105° to 115°F. or 41° to 46°C.)

1 package (¼ oz. or 7 g) active dry yeast

1 teaspoon (5 mL) sugar

2½ cups (625 mL) all-purpose flour*

¼ cup (60 mL) butter or margarine, at room temperature

1 teaspoon (5 mL) salt

2 eggs
Vegetable oil

This bread is an excellent accompaniment to any meal from breakfast through dinner. It's also nice for sandwich making, toasting or snacking. Emmenthaler Swiss is the classic cheese to use, but substitute Cheddar or domestic Swiss if you prefer.

1. Fit processor with shredding disc. Fit cheese into feed tube, cutting it if necessary. Process until all cheese is shredded. Remove cheese from work bowl and reserve.

2. Combine 3 tablespoons (45 mL) of the water, yeast and sugar. Stir to dissolve yeast and let stand until bubbly, about 5 minutes.

3. Fit processor with steel blade. Measure flour, butter and salt into work bowl. Process until mixed, about 15 seconds.

4. Add yeast mixture and eggs to flour mixture. Process until blended, about 15 seconds.

5. Turn on processor and very slowly drizzle just enough remaining water through feed tube into flour mixture so dough forms a ball that cleans the sides of the bowl. Process until ball turns around bowl about 25 times. Turn off processor and let dough stand 1 to 2 minutes.

6. Turn on processor and gradually drizzle in enough remaining water to make dough soft, smooth and satiny but not sticky.** Process until dough turns around bowl about 15 times.

7. Turn dough onto lightly floured surface. Shape into ball and place in lightly greased bowl, turning to grease all sides. Cover loosely with plastic wrap and let stand in warm place (85°F. or 30°C.) until doubled, about 1 hour.

8. Punch down dough. Place dough on lightly greased surface and knead cheese into dough. Roll or pat into circle 8 inches (20 cm) in diameter. Place in well greased 9-inch (23 cm) round cake or pie pan. Brush with oil. Let stand in warm place until doubled, about 45 minutes.

9. Heat oven to 375°F. (190°C.). Bake until evenly browned and bread sounds hollow when tapped, 30 to 35 minutes.

10. Remove immediately from pan. Cool on wire rack.

---

*Spoon flour into dry measuring cup and level off. Do not scoop.

**If dough is too dry and stiff, too soft and sticky, or if the processor shuts off, correct problem according to directions on page 25.

Brioche

Makes 1 loaf

2	to 5 tablespoons (30 to 75 mL) warm water (105° to 115°F. or 41° to 46°C.)
1	package (¼ oz. or 7 g) active dry yeast
1	tablespoon (15 mL) sugar
2¼	cups (560 mL) all-purpose flour*
⅓	cup (80 mL) cold butter or margarine, cut into 5 pieces
1	teaspoon (5 mL) salt
2	eggs, at room temperature, beaten
2	tablespoons (30 mL) milk
1	egg

A golden, egg-rich bread with a beautiful sheen to its crust, the classic French Brioche has a top knot and is baked in a flared, fluted pan. It can be shaped into a single large loaf or several petites brioches.

1. Combine 2 tablespoons (30 mL) of the water, yeast and sugar. Stir to dissolve yeast and let stand until bubbly, about 5 minutes.

2. Fit processor with steel blade. Measure flour, butter and salt into work bowl. Process until mixed, about 20 seconds.

3. Add yeast mixture to flour mixture. Process until blended, about 10 seconds.

4. Turn on processor and gradually drizzle the 2 beaten eggs through feed tube into flour mixture. Continue processing while very slowly drizzling just enough remaining water through feed tube so dough forms a ball that cleans the sides of the bowl. Process until ball turns around bowl about 25 times. Turn off processor and let dough stand, covered, in work bowl at room temperature 30 minutes.

5. Turn on processor and gradually drizzle in enough remaining water to make dough soft, smooth and satiny but not sticky.** Process until dough turns around bowl about 25 times. Turn off processor and let dough stand, covered, in work bowl at room temperature 30 minutes.

6. Process again until dough turns around bowl about 25 times. Turn dough onto lightly greased surface. Pinch off about ½ cup (125 mL) of the dough, shape into a smooth ball and reserve.

7. Shape remaining dough into a smooth ball and place in well greased brioche pan about 6½ inches (16.5 cm) in diameter. Make indentation about 1½ inches (4 cm) wide in center of dough and insert smaller ball of dough. Cover loosely with plastic wrap and let stand in warm place (85°F. or 30°C.) until doubled, about 1 hour.

8. Heat oven to 350°F. (180°C.). Beat milk and remaining egg with fork. Brush mixture over brioche. Bake until evenly browned and loaf begins to pull away from sides of the pan, 45 to 55 minutes.

9. Cool bread 5 minutes in pan. Carefully remove from pan and cool on wire rack.

Petites Brioches Prepare dough as directed for Brioche up to shaping. Divide dough into 10 equal parts. Pinch off about ⅙ of each part and shape into a small smooth ball. Shape remaining ⅚ of each part into a smooth ball and place in greased muffin pan. Make an indentation in center top of each larger part and insert smaller ball. Let rise as directed for Brioche. Heat oven to 425°F. (220°C.). Brush each brioche with egg-milk mixture as directed for Brioche. Bake until golden, 15 to 20 minutes. Remove immediately from muffin pan and cool on wire rack. Makes 10 small brioches.

---

*Spoon flour into dry measuring cup and level off. Do not scoop.

**If dough is too dry and stiff, too soft and sticky, or if the processor shuts off, correct problem according to directions on page 25.

FOREIGN BREADS

Bath Buns

Makes 1 dozen buns

2¾ to 3¼ cups (680 to 810 mL) all-purpose flour*

¼ cup (60 mL) sugar

¼ cup (60 mL) cold butter or margarine, cut into 4 pieces

1 package (¼ oz. or 7 g) active dry yeast

½ teaspoon (2 mL) salt

½ cup (125 mL) milk

1 egg, beaten

½ teaspoon (2 mL) almond extract

½ cup (125 mL) finely chopped mixed candied fruit

1 egg white

1 tablespoon (15 mL) cold milk

Sugar

A classic from Bath, England, these delicate sugar glazed buns are traditionally served hot for breakfast with fresh butter and a pot of steaming tea.

1. Fit processor with steel blade. Measure 1 cup (250 mL) of the flour, ¼ cup (60 mL) of the sugar, butter, yeast and salt into work bowl. Process until mixed, about 15 seconds.

2. Heat milk in small saucepan over low heat until 120° to 130°F. (49° to 54°C.). Blend egg and almond extract into milk.

3. Turn on processor and add milk mixture through feed tube to flour mixture. Process until smooth, about 30 seconds.

4. Turn on processor and add enough of the remaining flour, ¼ cup (60 mL) at a time, through feed tube so dough forms a ball that cleans the sides of the bowl. Process until ball turns around bowl about 25 times.

5. Turn dough onto lightly greased surface. Knead candied fruit into dough. Shape into ball and place in lightly greased bowl, turning to grease all sides. Cover tightly with plastic wrap. Refrigerate 4 to 24 hours.

6. Uncover dough and let stand at room temperature 20 minutes. Divide dough into 12 equal parts. Shape each part into a smooth ball and place on greased cookie sheet. Flatten dough with palm of hand.

7. Beat egg white and cold milk with fork. Brush mixture over buns. Sprinkle with sugar. Let stand at room temperature 10 minutes.

8. Heat oven to 350°F. (180°C.). Bake until golden, 15 to 20 minutes.

9. Remove from cookie sheet and cool on wire rack.

Finnish Rye Bread

Makes 1 loaf

¾ to 1 cup (180 to 250 mL) warm water (105° to 115°F. or 41° to 46°C.)

1 tablespoon (15 mL) brown sugar

1 package (¼ oz. or 7 g) active dry yeast

2¼ cups (560 mL) all-purpose flour*

½ cup (125 mL) rye flour

1 tablespoon (15 mL) butter or margarine

1 teaspoon (5 mL) salt

Butter or margarine

Unlike many other rye breads, this light rye contains no seeds or other flavorings. It needs just one rising, so it's fast to prepare.

1. Combine ¼ cup (60 mL) of the water, brown sugar and yeast. Stir to dissolve yeast and let stand until bubbly, about 5 minutes.

2. Fit processor with steel blade. Measure flours, 1 tablespoon (15 mL) of the butter and salt into work bowl. Process until mixed, about 5 seconds.

3. Add yeast mixture to flour mixture. Process until blended, about 10 seconds.

4. Turn on processor and very slowly drizzle just enough remaining water through feed tube into flour mixture so dough forms a ball that cleans the sides of the bowl. Process until ball turns around bowl about 25 times. Turn off processor and let dough stand 1 to 2 minutes.

5. Turn on processor and gradually drizzle in enough remaining water to make dough soft, smooth and satiny but not sticky.** Process until dough turns around bowl about 15 times.

6. Turn dough onto lightly greased surface. Shape into a smooth ball and place on greased cookie sheet. Flatten slightly with palm of hand. Cover loosely with plastic wrap and let stand in warm place (85°F. or 30°C.) until doubled, about 1 hour.

7. Heat oven to 375°F. (190°C.). Bake until loaf sounds hollow when tapped, 25 to 30 minutes.

8. Remove from cookie sheet. Brush crust with butter, if desired. Cool on wire rack.

---

*Spoon flour into dry measuring cup and level off. Do not scoop.

**If dough is too dry and stiff, too soft and sticky, or if the processor shuts off, correct problem according to directions on page 25.

Clockwise: Fruit Kuchen, Caramel
Sticky Buns, Sweet Egg Braid

Danish Coffee Pretzel (top), Fried
Cinnamon Puffs (center), Cinnamon
Rolls (bottom)

Kulich (top), Dutch Easter Bread
(center), Hot Cross Buns (bottom)

Clockwise: Julekage, Dresden Stollen,
Golden Eggnog Holiday Braid

Pan Dulce

Makes 8 buns

These round buns are the Mexican version of sweet rolls. They're prepared from a rich tasting dough and topped with a spicy cinnamon crumb topping. They almost always are served for breakfast and are good, too, for snacking.

Cinnamon-Spiced Crumb Topping (recipe follows)

¼ cup (60 mL) warm water (105° to 115°F. or 41° to 46°C.)

3 tablespoons (45 mL) sugar

1 package (¼ oz. or 7 g) active dry yeast

2¾ cups (680 mL) all-purpose flour*

2 tablespoons (30 mL) butter or margarine

½ teaspoon (2 mL) salt

2 eggs, beaten

2 to 5 tablespoons (30 to 75 mL) evaporated or fresh milk

1 egg white

1. Prepare Cinnamon-Spiced Crumb Topping. Reserve.

2. Combine water, 1 tablespoon (15 mL) of the sugar and yeast. Stir to dissolve yeast and let stand until bubbly, about 5 minutes.

3. Fit processor with steel blade. Measure flour, butter, remaining 2 tablespoons (30 mL) of the sugar and salt into work bowl. Process until mixed, about 15 seconds.

4. Add yeast mixture and the 2 beaten eggs to flour mixture. Process until blended, about 10 seconds.

5. Turn on processor and very slowly drizzle just enough milk through feed tube into flour mixture so dough forms a ball that cleans the sides of the bowl. Process until ball turns around bowl about 25 times. Turn off processor and let dough stand 1 to 2 minutes.

6. Turn on processor and gradually drizzle in enough remaining milk to make dough soft, smooth and satiny but not sticky.** Process until dough turns around bowl about 15 times.

7. Turn dough onto lightly floured surface. Shape into ball and place in lightly greased bowl, turning to grease all sides. Cover loosely with plastic wrap and let stand in warm place (85°F. or 30°C.) until doubled, about 45 minutes.

8. Punch down dough. Divide dough into 8 equal parts. Shape each part into a smooth ball and place about 2½ inches (6.5 cm) apart on greased cookie sheet. Flatten balls slightly with palm of hand.

9. Beat egg white until frothy with fork. Brush egg white over buns. Sprinkle Cinnamon-Spiced Crumb Topping over buns. Let stand in warm place until almost doubled, about 30 minutes.

10. Heat oven to 375°F. (190°C.). Bake until evenly browned, about 20 minutes.

11. Remove immediately from cookie sheet and cool on wire rack.

Cinnamon-Spiced Crumb Topping

⅓ cup (80 mL) all-purpose flour*

¼ cup (60 mL) sugar

2 tablespoons (30 mL) cold butter or margarine

½ teaspoon (2 mL) ground cinnamon

1 egg yolk

1. Fit processor with steel blade. Measure all ingredients into work bowl. Process until mixture resembles cornmeal, about 15 seconds.

---

*Spoon flour into dry measuring cup and level off. Do not scoop.

**If dough is too dry and stiff, too soft and sticky, or if the processor shuts off, correct problem according to directions on page 25.

FOREIGN BREADS

Austrian Streizel

Makes 1 loaf

¼ cup (60 mL) warm water (105° to 115°F. or 41° to 46°C.)

4 tablespoons (60 mL) sugar

1 package (¼ oz. or 7 g) active dry yeast

¼ cup (60 mL) butter or margarine, melted and cooled

1 egg, beaten

2½ cups (625 mL) all-purpose flour*

1 teaspoon (5 mL) grated lemon rind

½ teaspoon (2 mL) salt

2 to 6 tablespoons (30 to 90 mL) milk

1 cup (250 mL) golden raisins
Vegetable oil

Beautiful, braided loaves of bread are common throughout Europe. This Austrian version is made from a basic sweet dough that's speckled with golden raisins and flavored with a hint of lemon.

1. Combine water, 1 tablespoon (15 mL) of the sugar and yeast. Stir to dissolve yeast and let stand until bubbly, about 5 minutes. Blend melted butter and egg into yeast mixture.

2. Fit processor with steel blade. Measure flour, lemon rind and salt into work bowl. Process on/off to mix.

3. Add yeast mixture to flour mixture. Process until blended, about 15 seconds.

4. Turn on processor and slowly drizzle just enough milk through feed tube into flour mixture so dough forms a ball that cleans the sides of the bowl. Process until ball turns around bowl about 25 times. Turn off processor and let dough stand 1 to 2 minutes.

5. Turn on processor and very slowly drizzle in enough remaining milk to make dough soft, smooth and satiny but not sticky.** Process until dough turns around bowl about 15 times.

6. Cover processor and let stand in work bowl at room temperature about 30 minutes. Process on/off to punch down dough.

7. Turn dough onto lightly greased surface. Knead raisins into dough. Let dough stand 10 minutes.

8. Divide dough into 5 equal parts. Shape each part into strand 20 inches (50 cm) long. Braid 3 of the strands together and place on a greased cookie sheet. Tuck ends of braid under and pinch to seal. Twist 2 remaining strands together and place on top of braid. Tuck ends under and pinch to seal.

9. Brush loaf with oil and let stand in warm place (85°F. or 30°C.) until doubled, about 45 minutes.

10. Heat oven to 350°F. (180°C.). Bake until done, 40 to 50 minutes.

11. Remove immediately from cookie sheet. Brush with oil, if desired. Cool on wire rack.

Brazilian Beer Buns

Makes 1 dozen buns

2 tablespoons (30 mL) warm water (105° to 115°F. or 41° to 46°C.)

1 package (¼ oz. or 7 g) active dry yeast

1 tablespoon (15 mL) sugar

2½ cups (625 mL) all-purpose flour*

¼ cup (60 mL) butter or margarine, at room temperature

1 teaspoon (5 mL) salt

1 egg
continued

Beer goes into the dough and is brushed on top of these buns before baking. Just enough of its zesty flavor lingers after baking to provide an intriguing taste.

1. Combine water, yeast and sugar. Stir to dissolve yeast and let stand until bubbly, about 5 minutes.

2. Fit processor with steel blade. Measure flour, butter and salt into work bowl. Process until mixed, about 15 seconds.

3. Add yeast mixture and egg to flour mixture. Process until blended, about 10 seconds.

4. Turn on processor and very slowly drizzle just enough beer through feed tube into flour mixture so dough forms a ball that cleans sides of the bowl. Process until ball turns around bowl about 25 times. Turn off processor and let dough stand 1 to 2 minutes.

*Spoon flour into dry measuring cup and level off. Do not scoop.

**If dough is too dry and stiff, too soft and sticky, or if the processor shuts off, correct problem according to directions on page 25.

¼ to ½ cup (60 to 125 mL)
   beer, at room
   temperature
Beer
Coarse salt, optional

5. Turn on processor and gradually drizzle in enough remaining beer to make dough soft, smooth and satiny but not sticky.** Process until dough turns around bowl about 15 times.

6. Turn dough onto lightly greased surface. Shape into ball. Cover with inverted bowl or plastic wrap and let stand 20 minutes. Divide dough into 12 equal parts. Shape each part into smooth ball and place in greased muffin pan. Cover loosely with plastic wrap and let stand in warm place (85°F. or 30°C.) until doubled, about 1 hour.

7. Heat oven to 400°F. (200°C.). Slash top of each bun using processor's steel blade, sharp knife or razor blade. Brush with beer and sprinkle with coarse salt, if desired. Bake until golden, 10 to 12 minutes.

8. Remove immediately from pan. Cool on wire rack.

Makes 1 loaf

Ragbrod (Scandinavian Rye Bread)

Rind of 2 oranges, pared
   into 1-inch (2.5 cm)
   pieces
2 tablespoons (30 mL) sugar
1 tablespoon (15 mL) fennel
   seeds
1 tablespoon (15 mL)
   caraway seeds
½ to ¾ cup (125 to 180 mL)
   hot water (120° to
   130°F. or 49° to 54°C.)
1 tablespoon (15 mL) butter
   or margarine
1 teaspoon (5 mL) salt
1 tablespoon (15 mL) soy
   sauce
1¾ cups (430 mL) all-purpose
   flour*
1 cup (250 mL) rye flour
2 packages (¼ oz. or 7 g
   each) active dry yeast
Molasses

This round loaf of dark rye bread has a heavy texture, similar to pumpernickel. It's well flavored with orange zest, fennel and caraway seeds and should be sliced thin for serving.

1. Fit processor with steel blade. Add orange rind and sugar to work bowl. Process until rind is minced, about 2 minutes.

2. Place orange mixture, fennel and caraway seeds in a small saucepan. Add ¼ cup (60 mL) of the water, butter and salt. Bring to boil. Remove from heat and stir in soy sauce. Cool until 120° to 130°F. (49° to 54°C.).

3. Refit processor with steel blade. Place flours and yeast in work bowl. Process on/off twice to mix.

4. Add cooled orange mixture to flour mixture. Process until blended, about 10 seconds.

5. Turn on processor and very slowly drizzle just enough remaining water through feed tube into flour mixture so dough forms a ball that cleans the sides of the bowl. Process until ball turns around bowl about 25 times. Turn off processor and let dough stand 1 to 2 minutes.

6. Turn on processor and gradually drizzle in enough remaining water to make dough soft, smooth and satiny but not sticky.** Process until dough turns around bowl about 15 times.

7. Turn dough onto lightly greased surface. Shape into ball and place in lightly greased bowl, turning to grease all sides. Cover loosely with plastic wrap and let stand in warm place (85°F. or 30°C.) until doubled, about 1½ hours.

8. Punch down dough. Shape into a ball and place on greased cookie sheet. Roll or pat into a circle about 8 inches (20 cm) in diameter. Cut a large cross about ¼-inch (0.5 cm) deep in top of loaf using the processor's steel blade, sharp knife or razor blade. Cover loaf loosely with plastic wrap and let stand in warm place until almost doubled, about 1 hour.

9. Heat oven to 375°F. (190°C.). Bake until bread sounds hollow when tapped, 35 to 40 minutes.

10. Remove immediately from cookie sheet and place on wire rack. Brush molasses over bread. Cool.

---

*Spoon flour into dry measuring cup and level off. Do not scoop.

**If dough is too dry and stiff, too soft and sticky, or if the processor shuts off, correct problem according to directions on page 25.

FOREIGN BREADS

Challah

Makes 1 loaf

½ to ¾ cup (125 to 180 mL) warm water (105° to 115°F. or 41° to 46°C.)

1 package (¼ oz. or 7 g) active dry yeast

1 tablespoon (15 mL) sugar

2¾ cups (680 mL) all-purpose flour*

1 tablespoon (15 mL) butter or margarine

1 teaspoon (5 mL) salt

1 egg
Vegetable oil

1 egg yolk

2 tablespoons (30 mL) cold water

Poppy or sesame seeds, optional

Challah is one of the traditional foods associated with the Jewish Sabbath. It's a pretty braided bread that can be sprinkled with poppy or sesame seeds.

1. Combine ¼ cup (60 mL) of the warm water, yeast and sugar. Stir to dissolve yeast and let stand until bubbly, about 5 minutes.

2. Fit processor with steel blade. Measure flour, butter and salt into work bowl. Process until mixed, about 10 seconds.

3. Add yeast mixture and 1 egg to flour mixture. Process until blended, about 10 seconds.

4. Turn on processor and very slowly drizzle just enough remaining warm water through feed tube into flour mixture so dough forms a ball that cleans the sides of the bowl. Process until ball turns around bowl about 25 times. Turn off processor and let dough stand 1 to 2 minutes.

5. Turn on processor and gradually drizzle in enough remaining warm water to make dough soft, smooth and satiny but not sticky.** Process until dough turns around bowl about 15 times.

6. Turn dough onto lightly greased surface. Shape into ball and place in lightly greased bowl, turning to grease all sides. Cover loosely with plastic wrap and let stand in warm place (85°F. or 30°C.) until doubled, about 1 hour.

7. Punch down dough. Divide dough into 3 equal parts. Shape each part into a strand about 24 inches (60 cm) long. Braid the strands loosely together. Tuck ends under and pinch to seal. Place on greased cookie sheet. Brush braid with oil and let stand in warm place until almost doubled, about 40 minutes.

8. Heat oven to 375°F. (190°C.). Beat egg yolk and cold water together with a fork. Brush mixture over braid. Sprinkle with poppy or sesame seeds, if desired. Bake until evenly browned, 25 to 30 minutes.

9. Remove immediately from cookie sheet. Cool on wire rack.

Spinach Torta Rustica

Makes 1 bread

Italian Bread Dough (see Index for page number)

2 ounces (60 g) Parmesan cheese in a piece or ⅔ cup (160 mL) grated Parmesan

1 package (10 oz. or 285 g) frozen chopped spinach, cooked and well drained

1 cup (250 mL) ricotta cheese

1 egg yolk

½ teaspoon (2 mL) garlic salt

⅛ teaspoon (0.5 mL) pepper

1 egg, beaten

2 tablespoons (30 mL) milk

This attractive torta is made from Italian bread dough that forms a crust around a savory filling of spinach, ricotta and Parmesan cheeses. Serve this as an accompaniment to a salad or soup, or as an hors d'oeurve.

1. Prepare Italian Bread Dough as directed through first rising. Punch down dough and divide in half. Roll out one half of dough on lightly floured surface into a circle 12 inches (30 cm) in diameter. Fit into a greased 10-inch (25 cm) tart pan with removable bottom or a 10-inch (25 cm) pie pan bringing dough up pan sides to cover.

2. Fit processor with steel blade. Cut Parmesan cheese into 1-inch (2.5 cm) pieces. Turn on processor and drop cheese through feed tube. Process until cheese is coarsely grated.

3. Add drained spinach, ricotta cheese, egg yolk, salt and pepper to cheese in work bowl. Process until blended, about 10 seconds. Spread spinach-cheese mixture evenly over dough in tart pan. *continued*

---

*Spoon flour into dry measuring cup and level off. Do not scoop.

**If dough is too dry and stiff, too soft and sticky, or if the processor shuts off, correct problem according to directions on page 25.

Spinach Torta Rustica *(continued)*

4. Divide remaining dough into 10 equal parts. Shape each part into a strand about 10-inches (25 cm) long. Weave the strands together lattice-fashion over the spinach-cheese filling. Pinch ends of strands to bottom layer of dough to seal.

5. Combine beaten egg and milk. Brush mixture over dough. Let stand in warm place (85°F. or 30°C.) until almost doubled, about 45 minutes.

6. Heat oven to 350°F. (180°C.). Brush dough with remaining egg-milk mixture. Bake until evenly golden, about 45 minutes. Cool 5 minutes in pan. Remove from pan and place on wire rack. Serve hot, warm or cold. Cut in wedges to serve.

Barmbrack

Makes 1 loaf

4 tablespoons (60 mL) sugar
3 tablespoons (45 mL) warm water (105° to 115°F. or 41° to 46°C.)
1 package (¼ oz. or 7 g) active dry yeast
1 egg, beaten
2 cups (500 mL) all-purpose flour*
2 tablespoons (30 mL) butter or margarine
½ teaspoon (2 mL) salt
¼ to ½ cup (60 to 125 mL) milk
1 cup (250 mL) golden raisins
1 cup (250 mL) currants
½ cup (125 mL) chopped candied orange or lemon peel
   Vegetable oil
1 tablespoon (15 mL) cold water

In Ireland this rich, cake-like bread is traditionally served on Halloween. It also can be called "freckled" bread for the freckles of raisins, currants and candied fruit peel generously dotting the round loaf.

1. Combine 1 tablespoon (15 mL) of the sugar, warm water and yeast. Stir to dissolve yeast and let stand until bubbly, about 5 minutes. Blend egg into yeast mixture.

2. Fit processor with steel blade. Measure flour, butter, 2 tablespoons (30 mL) of the remaining sugar and salt into work bowl. Process until mixed, about 15 seconds.

3. Turn on processor and slowly add yeast mixture through feed tube to flour mixture. Process until blended, about 10 seconds.

4. Turn on processor and very slowly drizzle just enough milk into flour mixture so dough forms a ball that cleans the sides of the bowl. Process until ball turns around bowl about 25 times. Turn off processor and let dough stand 1 to 2 minutes.

5. Turn on processor and gradually drizzle in enough remaining milk to make dough soft, smooth and satiny but not sticky.** Process until dough turns around bowl about 15 times.

6. Turn dough onto lightly greased surface. Knead raisins, currants and candied fruit peel into dough. Shape into smooth ball and place on greased cookie sheet. Flatten ball into a circle about 6 inches (15 cm) in diameter. Brush with oil and let stand in warm place (85°F. or 30°C.) until doubled, about 1 hour.

7. Heat oven to 350°F. (180°C.). Bake until bread sounds hollow when tapped, 40 to 50 minutes.

8. Mix cold water with remaining 1 tablespoon (15 mL) of the sugar.

9. Remove bread immediately from cookie sheet and place on wire rack. Brush with sugar-water mixture. Cool.

---

*Spoon flour into dry measuring cup and level off. Do not scoop.

**If dough is too dry and stiff, too soft and sticky, or if the processor shuts off, correct problem according to directions on page 25.

FOREIGN BREADS

Swedish Limpa

Makes 1 loaf

½ to ¾ cup (125 to 180 mL) warm water (105° to 115°F. or 41° to 46°C.)

2 tablespoons (30 mL) molasses

1 package (¼ oz. or 7 g) active dry yeast

1 teaspoon (5 mL) instant coffee

2¼ cups (560 mL) all-purpose flour*

½ cup (125 mL) rye flour

2 tablespoons (30 mL) butter or margarine

1½ teaspoons (7 mL) grated orange rind

1 teaspoon (5 mL) salt

½ teaspoon (2 mL) fennel seeds

½ teaspoon (2 mL) anise seeds

½ teaspoon (2 mL) caraway seeds

Melted butter or margarine

Limpa is a light rye bread mildly flavored with orange peel, instant coffee, fennel, anise and caraway seeds. It's delicious while still warm from the oven.

1. Combine ¼ cup (60 mL) of the water, molasses and yeast. Stir to dissolve yeast and let stand until bubbly, about 5 minutes. Blend instant coffee into yeast mixture.

2. Fit processor with steel blade. Measure flours, butter, orange rind, salt, fennel, anise and caraway seeds into work bowl. Process until mixed, 5 seconds.

3. Add yeast mixture to flour mixture. Process until blended, about 10 seconds.

4. Turn on processor and very slowly drizzle just enough remaining water through feed tube into flour mixture so dough forms a ball that cleans the sides of the bowl. Process until ball turns around bowl about 25 times. Turn off processor and let dough stand 1 to 2 minutes.

5. Turn on processor and gradually drizzle in enough remaining water to make dough soft, smooth and satiny but not sticky.** Process until dough turns around bowl about 15 times.

6. Turn dough onto lightly floured surface. Shape into ball and place in lightly greased bowl, turning to grease all sides. Cover loosely with plastic wrap and let stand in warm place (85°F. or 30°C.) until doubled, about 1 hour.

7. Punch down dough. Shape into loaf and place in greased 8½x4½x2½-inch (21.5x11.5x6.5 cm) loaf pan. Cover loosely with plastic wrap and let stand in warm place until almost doubled, about 45 minutes.

8. Heat oven to 350°F. (180°C.). Bake until loaf sounds hollow when tapped, 35 to 40 minutes.

9. Remove immediately from pan and place on wire rack. Brush melted butter over crust, if desired. Cool.

Dutch Rye Bread

Makes 1 loaf

¾ cup (180 mL) water

¼ cup (60 mL) packed brown sugar

1 tablespoon (15 mL) butter or margarine

1 teaspoon (5 mL) salt

1 teaspoon (5 mL) anise seeds

2 to 2½ cups (500 to 625 mL) all-purpose flour*

½ cup (125 mL) rye flour

1 package (¼ oz. or 7 g) active dry yeast

Vegetable oil

The flavors of rye, anise and brown sugar predominate in this European bread that's good with just about any meal. Try it for sandwiches, too.

1. Combine water, sugar, butter, salt and anise seeds in small saucepan. Heat over high heat until boiling. Remove from heat and cool until 120° to 130°F. (49° to 54°C.).

2. Fit processor with steel blade. Measure 1 cup (250 mL) of the all-purpose flour, rye flour and yeast into work bowl. Process until mixed, about 5 seconds.

3. Turn on processor and gradually add cooled water mixture through feed tube to flour mixture. Process until smooth, about 30 seconds. Let stand 1 minute.

4. Turn on processor and add enough of the remaining flour through feed tube so dough forms a ball that cleans the sides of the bowl. Process until ball turns around bowl about 25 times. *continued*

---

*Spoon flour into dry measuring cup and level off. Do not scoop.

**If dough is too dry and stiff, too soft and sticky, or if the processor shuts off, correct problem according to directions on page 25.

Dutch Rye Bread *(continued)*

5. Turn dough onto lightly floured surface. Shape into ball and place in lightly greased bowl, turning to grease all sides. Cover loosely with plastic wrap and let stand in warm place (85°F. or 30°C.) until doubled, about 1 hour.

6. Punch down dough. Shape into a loaf and place in greased 8½x4½x2½-inch (21.5x11.5x6.5 cm) loaf pan. Brush with oil and let stand in warm place until doubled, about 45 minutes.

7. Heat oven to 375°F. (190°C.). Bake until loaf sounds hollow when tapped, 30 to 35 minutes.

8. Remove immediately from pan. Brush crust with oil, if desired. Cool on wire rack.

English Muffins

Makes 1 dozen muffins

¼ cup (60 mL) warm water (105° to 115°F. or 41° to 46°C.)

1 package (¼ oz. or 7 g) active dry yeast

1 tablespoon (15 mL) sugar

2½ cups (625 mL) all-purpose flour*

2 tablespoons (30 mL) butter or margarine

1 teaspoon (5 mL) salt

1 egg

¼ to ½ cup (60 to 125 mL) milk, at room temperature

Cornmeal

These muffins will disappear quickly. They're so much better than the store-bought variety, and they're really easy to make.

1. Combine water, yeast and sugar. Stir to dissolve yeast and let stand until bubbly, about 5 minutes.

2. Fit processor with steel blade. Measure flour, butter and salt into work bowl. Process until mixed, about 15 seconds.

3. Add yeast mixture and egg to flour mixture. Process until blended, about 10 seconds.

4. Turn on processor and very slowly drizzle just enough milk through feed tube into flour mixture so dough forms a ball that cleans the sides of the bowl. Process until ball turns around bowl about 25 times. Turn off processor and let dough stand 1 to 2 minutes.

5. Turn on processor and gradually drizzle in enough remaining milk to make dough soft, smooth and satiny but not sticky.** Process until dough turns around bowl about 15 times.

6. Turn dough onto lightly greased surface. Shape into ball and place in lightly greased bowl, turning to grease all sides. Cover loosely with plastic wrap and let stand in warm place (85°F. or 30°C.) until doubled, about 1 hour.

7. Punch down dough. Grease a cookie sheet and sprinkle generously with cornmeal. Roll out dough on lightly greased surface until about ⅜ inch (1 cm) thick. Cut with floured 3-inch (8 cm) round cookie or biscuit cutter. Place cutouts on prepared cookie sheet. Reroll and cut leftover dough. Sprinkle cutouts with cornmeal. Cover loosely with plastic wrap and let stand in warm place until doubled, about 45 minutes.

8. Heat a lightly greased, large fry pan over medium heat or an electric fry pan to 340°F. (170°C.). Cook muffins, uncovered, on each side until lightly browned, 5 to 6 minutes on each side.

9. Cool on wire rack. Split and toast muffins to serve.

---

*Spoon flour into dry measuring cup and level off. Do not scoop.

**If dough is too dry and stiff, too soft and sticky, or if the processor shuts off, correct problem according to directions on page 25.

Makes 1 bread

Zwiebel Kuchen (German Onion Bread)

¼ cup (60 mL) warm water (105° to 115°F or 41° to 46°C.)

1 package (¼ oz. or 7 g) active dry yeast

½ teaspoon (2 mL) sugar

2 cups (500 mL) all-purpose flour*

1 teaspoon (5 mL) salt

⅓ to ½ cup (80 to 125 mL) evaporated or fresh milk

Onion Topping (recipe follows)

Onion Bread is the German counterpart to Italy's pizza and France's quiche. It's simply a dough topped with a custardy mixture of onions, ham and sour cream. It's delicious hot for brunch, lunch or supper. Cold, it makes good snacking.

1. Combine water, yeast and sugar. Stir to dissolve yeast and let stand until bubbly, about 5 minutes.

2. Fit processor with steel blade. Measure flour and salt into work bowl. Process on/off to mix.

3. Add yeast mixture to flour mixture. Process until blended, about 10 seconds.

4. Turn on processor and very slowly drizzle just enough milk through feed tube into flour mixture so dough forms a ball that cleans the sides of the bowl. Process until ball turns around bowl about 25 times. Turn off processor and let dough stand 1 to 2 minutes.

5. Turn on processor and very slowly drizzle in just enough remaining milk to make dough soft, smooth and satiny but not sticky.** Process until dough turns around bowl about 15 times.

6. Turn dough onto lightly greased surface. Shape into ball and place in lightly greased bowl, turning to grease all sides. Cover loosely with plastic wrap and let stand in warm place (85°F. or 30°C.) until doubled, about 1 hour.

7. Prepare Onion Topping while dough is rising.

8. Punch down dough. Let dough stand 10 minutes. Grease a 9-inch (23 cm) square baking pan or a 10-inch (25 cm) round tart pan with removable bottom. Roll out dough on lightly floured surface to fit the pan. Place dough in pan and pat dough with fingers up sides of the pan about 1 inch (2.5 cm).

9. Spoon Onion Topping over dough. Let stand 20 to 30 minutes.

10. Heat oven to 375°F. (190°C.). Bake until wooden pick inserted in center comes out clean, about 30 minutes.

11. Cool 5 to 10 minutes on wire rack. Serve hot or cold.

Onion Topping

2 large onions (about 1 lb. or 450 g)

2 tablespoons (30 mL) butter or margarine

2 eggs

¼ cup (60 mL) dairy sour cream

2 tablespoons (30 mL) all-purpose flour

1 tablespoon (15 mL) caraway seeds

1 teaspoon (5 mL) salt

½ cup (125 mL) chopped, cooked ham

1. Fit processor with steel blade. Cut each onion in about 8 pieces and place in work bowl. Process on/off 3 or 4 times to coarsely chop onions.

2. Melt butter in saucepan. Add onions to the butter. Cook over low heat, uncovered, until very soft but not brown, about 30 minutes.

3. Beat eggs with whisk or fork in medium bowl. Mix in sour cream, flour, caraway seeds, salt, ham and cooked onions.

---

*Spoon flour into dry measuring cup and level off. Do not scoop.

**If dough is too dry and stiff, too soft and sticky, or if the processor shuts off, correct problem according to directions on page 25.

Quick Danish Pastry

3¼ cups (810 mL) all-purpose flour*

1¼ cups (310 mL) cold unsalted butter, cut in ¼-inch (0.5 cm) slices

¼ cup (60 mL) warm water (105° to 115°F. or 41° to 46°C.)

2 packages (¼ oz. or 7 g each) active dry yeast

½ cup (125 mL) evaporated milk, at room temperature

¼ cup (60 mL) sugar

2 eggs, at room temperature

1 teaspoon (5 mL) salt

½ teaspoon (2 mL) ground cardamom, optional

Buttery, flaky Danish pastries surely will become favorites in the culinary repertoire of anyone with a food processor. The dough, mixed quickly with the processor, can be shaped and filled in a variety of delicious ways.

1. Fit processor with steel blade. Measure 2 cups (500 mL) of the flour and butter into work bowl. Process on/off 6 to 10 times or just until butter is no smaller than kidney beans.

2. Transfer flour-butter mixture to a large mixing bowl. Stir in remaining 1¼ cups (310 mL) of the flour.

3. Refit processor with steel blade. Measure water and yeast into work bowl. Process until yeast is dissolved.

4. Blend milk, sugar, eggs, salt and cardamom, if desired, into yeast mixture. Let stand until bubbly, about 5 minutes.

5. Add milk mixture to flour mixture. Stir just enough to moisten flour (dough should be crumbly like a biscuit dough, not smooth and satiny like most yeast doughs.) Cover with plastic wrap and refrigerate 4 to 24 hours.

6. Shape, fill and bake pastry as directed in the following recipes.

Boston Cake

Makes 1 cake

Danish Pastry (see preceding recipe)

Buttercream Pastry Filling (recipe follows)

⅓ cup (80 mL) sugar

2 tablespoons (30 mL) ground cinnamon

Sugar Icing (see Index for page number)

This beautiful cake is prepared from the basic Danish pastry dough. The dough is rolled around cinnamon sugar, cut into thick slices and baked in a tube pan.

1. Prepare Danish Pastry as directed and refrigerate 4 to 24 hours.

2. Roll out pastry dough on floured surface into a rectangle 36x20 inches (90x50 cm), adding more flour as necessary to keep dough from sticking to surface or rolling pin. For easier shaping, let dough rest frequently for about 10 seconds, then continue rolling.

3. Prepare Buttercream Pastry Filling and spread over dough to within 1 inch (2.5 cm) of the edges.

4. Mix sugar and cinnamon. Sprinkle mixture evenly over Buttercream. Roll up dough jelly roll fashion. Pinch seam to seal. Cut into 3-inch (8 cm) wide slices and place slices cut side down around greased 2½ or 3 quart (2.5 or 3 L) ring mold or tube pan. Let stand at room temperature until doubled, about 1 hour.

5. Heat oven to 350°F. (180°C.). Bake until golden, 45 to 55 minutes.

6. Cool 5 minutes in pan. Transfer to serving plate. Drizzle Sugar Icing over cake. Cool.

Buttercream Pastry Filling

1 cup (250 mL) powdered sugar

½ cup (125 mL) cold butter or margarine, cut into ¼-inch (0.5 cm) slices

½ teaspoon (2 mL) vanilla

1. Fit processor with steel blade. Measure all ingredients into work bowl. Process until smooth and creamy (do not overprocess). Stop food processor and scrape sides of bowl during processing, if necessary. Makes about 1 cup (250 mL).

*Spoon flour into dry measuring cup and level off. Do not scoop.

Birthday Sugar Pretzel (Fodselsdagskringle)

Makes 1 pretzel

Danish Pastry (see Index
  for page number)
Buttercream Pastry Filling
  (see Index for page
  number)
Almond Buttercream,
  Vanilla or Lemon
  Custard Pastry Filling
  (recipes follow)
Candied Fruit Pastry
  Filling (recipe follows)
1 egg, beaten
Crushed sugar cubes, pearl
  sugar or granulated
  sugar, optional
Chopped almonds, optional
Almond Icing (see Index
  for page number)

Danish pastry shaped into a large pretzel is the traditional birthday cake in Denmark. It is usually served on a large wooden plate with holes drilled in the rim to hold candles.

1. Prepare Danish Pastry as directed and refrigerate 4 to 24 hours. Prepare fillings.

2. Roll out pastry dough on lightly floured surface into a rectangle 36x6 inches (90x15 cm). Spread Buttercream Filling lengthwise down center third of dough. Spread Almond Buttercream or Custard Filling evenly over Buttercream. Spread Candied Fruit Filling evenly over Almond or Custard Filling. Fold one third of the dough lengthwise over fillings. Fold remaining third of dough lengthwise over other dough. Pinch to seal well.

3. Turn dough over and place on ungreased cookie sheet in the shape of a large pretzel. Brush beaten egg over dough. Sprinkle sugar and almonds over dough, if desired. Cover loosely with plastic wrap and let stand at room temperature until doubled, 45 to 60 minutes.

4. Heat oven to 400°F. (200°C.). Uncover dough and bake until golden, about 15 minutes.

5. Prepare Almond Icing while pretzel is baking.

6. Remove pretzel from cookie sheet and place on wire rack. Drizzle Almond Icing over pretzel. Cool.

Almond Buttercream Pastry Filling

1 cup (250 mL) powdered
     sugar
½ cup (125 mL) cold butter,
     cut into ¼-inch (0.5 cm)
     slices
½ cup (125 mL) almond paste

1. Fit processor with steel blade. Measure all ingredients into work bowl. Process until smooth and creamy (do not overprocess). Stop food processor and scrape sides of bowl during processing, if necessary. Makes about 1½ cups (375 mL).

Vanilla Custard Pastry Filling

1 cup (250 mL) whipping
     cream
3 tablespoons (45 mL) sugar
2 tablespoons (30 mL) all-
     purpose flour
2 egg yolks
1 teaspoon (5 mL) vanilla

1. Combine cream, sugar, flour and egg yolks in small saucepan. Cook over medium heat, beating constantly with a whisk, until mixture boils. Continue cooking and beating until mixture thickens, 1 to 2 minutes.

2. Remove mixture from heat. Beat in vanilla. Cool. Makes about 1 cup (250 mL).

Lemon Custard Pastry Filling

1 cup (250 mL) whipping
     cream
¼ cup (60 mL) sugar
2 tablespoons (30 mL) all-
     purpose flour
2 egg yolks
Grated rind and juice of
  1 lemon

1. Combine cream, sugar, flour, and egg yolks in small saucepan. Cook over medium heat, beating constantly with a whisk, until mixture boils. Continue cooking and beating until mixture thickens, 1 or 2 minutes.

2. Remove mixture from heat. Beat in lemon rind and juice. Cool. Makes about 1 cup (250 mL).

Candied Fruit Pastry Filling

1   **cup (250 mL) mixed candied fruit (citron, cherries, pineapple)**

⅓   **cup (80 mL) chopped almonds**

1. Fit processor with steel blade. Add fruit and almonds to work bowl. Process on/off 3 or 4 times until combined. Makes about 1⅓ cups (330 mL).

Makes 2 dozen pastries

Combs or Bear Claws

   Danish Pastry (see Index for page number)
   Buttercream Pastry Filling (see Index for page number)
   Almond Buttercream Pastry Filling (see Index for page number)

1   **cup (250 mL) crushed sugar cubes or pearl sugar**

1   **cup (250 mL) sliced almonds**
   Water
   Almond Icing, optional (see Index for Page number)

Combs are considered tarts in the Scandinavian countries and are what most Americans think of as Danish pastry.

1. Prepare Danish Pastry as directed and refrigerate 4 to 24 hours. Prepare fillings.

2. Divide Pastry into 4 equal parts. Roll out each part, one at a time, into a 12-inch (30 cm) square. Spread ¼ cup (60 mL) of the Buttercream across center third of the dough. Spread about ⅓ cup (80 mL) of the Almond Buttercream evenly over Buttercream. Fold one unfilled third of dough over fillings, then fold other unfilled third of dough over it. Pinch to seal well. Flatten slightly with hands.

3. Combine sugar and almonds. Cut dough crosswise into 2-inch (5 cm) slices. Dip slices in water, then coat with sugar-almond mixture and place flat on ungreased cookie sheets. Cut 4 parallel 1-inch (2.5 cm) cuts along one long edge of each slice. Curve slice slightly to spread the cuts. Cover loosely with plastic wrap and let stand at room temperature until doubled, 45 to 60 minutes.

4. Heat oven to 400°F. (200°C.). Uncover dough and bake until golden, 12 to 15 minutes.

5. Remove pastries from cookie sheets and place on wire rack. Prepare Almond Icing, if desired, and drizzle over pastries.

Makes 32 pastries

Snails

   Danish Pastry (see Index for page number)
   Buttercream Pastry Filling (see Index for page number)
   Hazelnut (recipe follows) or Candied Fruit Pastry Filling (see Index for page number)

1   **egg, beaten**
   Sugar Icing (see Index for page number)

These round spirals of Danish pastry dough are wrapped around buttercream and hazelnut fillings. Baking them in paper cupcake liners helps them keep their shape and prevents them from sticking on the cookie sheet.

1. Prepare Danish Pastry as directed and refrigerate 4 to 24 hours. Prepare fillings.

2. Divide pastry in half. Roll out each half on lightly floured surface into a 16x8-inch (40x20 cm) rectangle. Spread half of Buttercream evenly over each rectangle. Spread half of Hazelnut Filling over Buttercream. Roll up dough jelly-roll fashion beginning on long side. Cut crosswise into 1-inch (2.5 cm) slices. Fit each slice, cut side up, into a paper cupcake liner and place on ungreased cookie sheet. Let stand at room temperature until doubled, 30 to 45 minutes.

3. Heat oven to 400°F. (200°C.). Brush beaten egg over each slice. Bake until golden, 12 to 15 minutes.

4. Prepare Sugar Icing and brush or drizzle over hot Snails. Cool.

Hazelnut (or Filbert) Pastry Filling

1 cup (250 mL) hazelnuts or filberts
1 cup (250 mL) granulated sugar
2 tablespoons (30 mL) butter or margarine
1 egg

1. Heat oven to 300°F. (150°C.). Arrange nuts in single layer on cookie sheet (with sides) or in 13x9x2-inch (33x23x5 cm) baking pan. Bake until nuts begin to brown, about 10 minutes.

2. Fit processor with steel blade. Add nuts to work bowl and process until nuts resemble cornmeal.

3. Add remaining ingredients to nuts. Process until a smooth paste is formed, 10 to 15 seconds. Makes about 2 cups (500 mL).

Pumpernickel

Makes 1 loaf

¼ cup (60 mL) warm water (105° to 115°F. or 41° to 46°C.)
1 package (¼ oz. or 7 g) active dry yeast
1 tablespoon (15 mL) sugar
1½ cups (375 mL) whole wheat flour
½ cup (125 mL) rye flour
½ cup (125 mL) all-purpose flour*
1 tablespoon (15 mL) caraway seeds
1 tablespoon (15 mL) butter or margarine
1 teaspoon (5 mL) salt
½ to ¾ cup (125 to 180 mL) evaporated or fresh milk, at room temperature
Cold water
Melted butter or margarine, optional

This is a German bread that's moist, dark, rather compact and full of flavor. It's shaped into a long narrow loaf, similar to French bread and is best sliced thin. It's very good for making cheese, ham or roast beef sandwiches.

1. Combine warm water, yeast and sugar. Stir to dissolve yeast and let stand until bubbly, about 5 minutes.

2. Fit processor with steel blade. Measure flours, caraway seeds, butter and salt into work bowl. Process until mixed, about 10 seconds.

3. Add yeast mixture to flour mixture. Process until blended, about 10 seconds.

4. Turn on processor and very slowly drizzle just enough milk through feed tube into flour mixture so dough forms a ball that cleans the sides of the bowl. Process until ball turns around bowl about 25 times. Turn off processor and let dough stand 1 to 2 minutes.

5. Turn on processor and gradually drizzle in enough remaining milk to make dough soft but not sticky.** Process until dough turns around bowl about 15 times.

6. Turn dough onto lightly greased surface. Shape into ball and place in lightly greased bowl, turning to grease all sides. Cover with inverted bowl or plastic wrap and let stand 15 minutes. Shape into a strand about 15 inches (37.5 cm) long and place diagonally on a large greased cookie sheet. Cover loosely with plastic wrap and let stand in warm place (85°F. or 30°C.) until doubled, about 1 hour.

7. Heat oven to 350°F. (180°C.). Brush cold water over loaf. Bake until loaf sounds hollow when tapped, 35 to 40 minutes.

8. Remove from cookie sheet and place on wire rack. Brush melted butter over loaf, if desired. Cool.

Norwegian Rye Flatbread

Makes 1 loaf

¼ cup (60 mL) warm water (105° to 115°F. or 41° to 46°C.)
1 package (¼ oz. or 7 g) active dry yeast
1 teaspoon (5 mL) sugar
continued

Flat is the right word for this chewy rye bread. After baking, it's only about ¾-inch (2 cm) thick. It's very good with soups, stews or salads and makes a delicious base for thinly sliced meats or cheese.

1. Combine water, yeast and sugar. Stir to dissolve yeast and let stand until bubbly, about 5 minutes.

---

*Spoon flour into dry measuring cup and level off. Do not scoop.

**If dough is too dry and stiff, too soft and sticky, or if the processor shuts off, correct problem according to directions on page 25.

Norwegian Rye Flatbread *(continued)*

½   cup (125 mL) milk

2   tablespoons (30 mL) lard or vegetable shortening

2   tablespoons (30 mL) light molasses

1   teaspoon (5 mL) salt

½   teaspoon (2 mL) fennel seeds

½   teaspoon (2 mL) anise seeds

2   cups (500 mL) rye flour

¾   to 1 cup (180 to 250 mL) all-purpose flour*
    Vegetable oil

2. Combine milk, lard, molasses, salt, fennel and anise seeds in small saucepan. Heat mixture over low heat until 110° to 115°F. (43° to 46°C.).

3. Fit processor with steel blade. Measure 1 cup (250 mL) of the rye flour and ¾ cup (180 mL) of the all-purpose flour into work bowl. Process until mixed, about 5 seconds.

4. Add yeast mixture and milk mixture to flour mixture. Process until smooth, about 30 seconds.

5. Turn on processor and add remaining 1 cup (250 mL) of the rye flour and enough of the remaining ¼ cup (60 mL) all-purpose flour through feed tube so dough forms a ball that cleans the sides of the bowl. Process until ball turns around bowl about 25 times. Turn off processor and let dough stand 1 to 2 minutes.

6. Turn dough onto lightly floured surface. Shape into ball and place on greased cookie sheet. Roll out dough into a circle 12 inches (30 cm) in diameter. Cover loosely with plastic wrap and let stand in warm place (85°F. or 30°C.) until doubled, about 45 minutes.

7. Heat oven to 425°F. (220°C.). Pierce top of loaf all over with tines of a fork. Brush with oil. Bake until evenly browned, 15 to 20 minutes.

8. Remove immediately from cookie sheet. Cool on wire rack.

Makes 1 loaf

English Currant Bread

¼   cup (60 mL) warm water (105° to 115°F. or 41° to 46°C.)

4   tablespoons (60 mL) sugar

1   package (¼ oz. or 7 g) active dry yeast

2¾   cups (680 mL) all-purpose flour*

¼   cup (60 mL) cold butter or margarine, cut into 4 pieces

1   teaspoon (5 mL) salt

½   teaspoon (2 mL) ground cinnamon

½   teaspoon (2 mL) ground mace, optional

1   egg, beaten

¼   to ½ cup (60 to 125 mL) milk, at room temperature

1   cup (250 mL) currants or dark raisins
    Vegetable oil
    Sugar Icing (see Index for page number)

The English love currants and add them to many foods including this popular bread.

1. Combine warm water, 1 tablespoon (15 mL) of the sugar and yeast. Stir to dissolve yeast and let stand until bubbly, about 5 minutes.

2. Fit processor with steel blade. Measure flour, butter, salt, cinnamon and mace, if desired, into work bowl. Process until mixed, about 15 seconds.

3. Add yeast mixture and egg to flour mixture. Process until blended, about 10 seconds.

4. Turn on processor and very slowly drizzle just enough milk through feed tube into flour mixture so dough forms a ball that cleans the sides of the bowl. Process until ball turns around bowl about 25 times. Turn off processor and let dough stand 1 to 2 minutes.

5. Turn on processor and gradually drizzle in enough remaining milk to make dough soft, smooth and satiny but not sticky.** Process until dough turns around bowl about 15 times.

6. Turn dough onto lightly floured surface. Knead currants into dough. Shape dough into ball and place in lightly greased bowl, turning to grease all sides. Cover loosely with plastic wrap and let stand in warm place (85°F. or 30°C.) until doubled, about 1 hour.

7. Punch down dough. Shape dough into loaf (see Shaping in Index) and place in greased 9x5x3-inch (23x13x8 cm) loaf pan. Brush with oil and let stand in warm place until almost doubled, 45 to 50 minutes.

8. Heat oven to 375°F. (190°C.). Bake until golden and loaf sounds hollow when tapped, 25 to 30 minutes.

9. Remove loaf immediately from pan. Spread Sugar Icing over top crust. Cool on wire rack.

---

*Spoon flour into dry measuring cup and level off. Do not scoop.

**If dough is too dry and stiff, too soft and sticky, or if the processor shuts off, correct problem according to directions on page 25.

Swedish Beer Bread

Makes 1 loaf

2   tablespoons (30 mL) warm water (105° to 115°F. or 41° to 46°C.)
1   package (¼ oz. or 7 g) active dry yeast
2   tablespoons (30 mL) molasses
2   cups (500 mL) all-purpose flour*
½   cup (125 mL) rye flour
2   tablespoons (30 mL) butter or margarine
1   tablespoon (15 mL) grated orange rind, optional
1   teaspoon (5 mL) anise seeds
½   teaspoon (2 mL) salt
½   to ¾ cup (125 to 180 mL) beer, at room temperature
1   tablespoon (15 mL) cold water
     Sugar, optional

This version of a popular Scandinavian rye bread is flavored with beer, molasses, orange and anise. Bake it in a round shape and cut it in wedges or slices to serve.

1. Combine warm water, yeast and 1 tablespoon (15 mL) of the molasses. Stir to dissolve yeast and let stand until bubbly, about 5 minutes.

2. Fit processor with steel blade. Measure flours, butter, orange rind, if desired, anise and salt into work bowl. Process until mixed, 5 seconds.

3. Add yeast mixture to flour mixture. Process until blended, about 10 seconds.

4. Turn on processor and very slowly drizzle just enough beer through feed tube into flour mixture so dough forms a ball that cleans the sides of the bowl. Process until ball turns around bowl about 25 times. Turn off processor and let dough stand 1 to 2 minutes.

5. Turn on processor and gradually drizzle in enough remaining beer to make dough soft, smooth and satiny but not sticky.** Process until dough turns around bowl about 15 times.

6. Turn dough onto lightly floured surface. Shape into ball and place in lightly greased bowl, turning to grease all sides. Cover loosely with plastic wrap and let stand in warm place (85°F. or 30°C.) until doubled, about 1 hour.

7. Punch down dough. Shape into a ball and place on greased cookie sheet. Roll or pat into circle 7 inches (18 cm) in diameter. Cover loosely with plastic wrap and let stand in warm place until doubled, about 1 hour.

8. Heat oven to 350°F. (180°C.). Mix remaining 1 tablespoon (15 mL) of the molasses with cold water. Brush mixture over loaf. Sprinkle with sugar, if desired. Bake until loaf sounds hollow when tapped, 25 to 30 minutes.

9. Remove from cookie sheet. Cool on wire rack.

Swiss Twist

Makes 1 loaf

¾   to 1 cup (180 to 250 mL) warm water (105° to 115°F. or 41° to 46°C.)
3   tablespoons (45 mL) sugar or honey
1   package (¼ oz. or 7 g) active dry yeast
2¾   cups (680 mL) all-purpose flour*
¼   cup (60 mL) instant nonfat dry milk solids
2   tablespoons (30 mL) vegetable oil
1   teaspoon (5 mL) salt
1   egg, beaten
1   tablespoon (15 mL) cold water

This handsome European bread is made of a simple dough that's shaped into a three stranded braid and topped with a two stranded twist.

1. Combine ¼ cup (60 mL) of the warm water, 1 tablespoon (15 mL) of the sugar and yeast. Stir to dissolve yeast and let stand until bubbly, about 5 minutes.

2. Fit processor with steel blade. Measure flour, dry milk, oil, remaining 2 tablespoons (30 mL) of the sugar and salt into work bowl. Process until mixed, about 10 seconds.

3. Add yeast mixture to flour mixture. Process until blended, about 10 seconds.

4. Turn on processor and slowly drizzle just enough remaining water through feed tube into flour mixture so dough forms a ball that cleans the sides of the bowl. Process until ball turns around bowl about 25 times. Turn off processor and let dough stand 1 to 2 minutes.

5. Turn on processor and gradually drizzle in enough remaining water to make dough soft, smooth and satiny but not sticky.** Process until dough turns around bowl about 15 times.

*Spoon flour into dry measuring cup and level off. Do not scoop.

**If dough is too dry and stiff, too soft and sticky, or if the processor shuts off, correct problem according to directions on page 25.

Swiss Twist (continued)

6. Turn dough onto lightly floured surface. Shape into ball and place in lightly greased bowl, turning to grease all sides. Cover loosely with plastic wrap and let stand in warm place (85°F. or 30°C.) until doubled, about 1 hour.

7. Punch down dough. Cut off about ½ cup (125 mL) of the dough and reserve. Divide remaining dough into 3 equal parts. Shape each part into strand 25 inches (63 cm) long. Braid the strands together and place on greased cookie sheet. Tuck ends under and pinch to seal.

8. Divide reserved dough into 2 equal parts. Shape each part into strand 25 inches (63 cm) long. Twist the 2 strands together.

9. Beat egg and cold water. Brush mixture over braided strands. Place twisted strands on top of braided strands. Tuck ends under and pinch to seal. Brush egg mixture over twisted strands.

10. Heat oven to 375°F. (190°C.). Bake until golden and loaf sounds hollow when tapped, 20 to 25 minutes.

11. Remove from cookie sheet. Cool on wire rack.

Makes 2 loaves

Potica

The secret to perfect Potica (pronounced "po-teet'-sa") is to stretch the dough as thinly as posible before rolling it around a sweet walnut filling.

3   **tablespoons (45 mL) warm water (105° to 115°F. or 41° to 46°C.)**

1   **package (¼ oz. or 7 g) active dry yeast**

2   **eggs, beaten**

¼   **cup (60 mL) sugar**

3   **cups (750 mL) all-purpose flour***

¼   **cup (60 mL) cold butter or margarine, cut into 4 pieces**

¾   **teaspoon (4 mL) salt**

2   **to 5 tablespoons (30 to 75 mL) milk**

   Walnut Filling (recipe follows)

4   **to 6 tablespoons (60 to 90 mL) melted butter or margarine**

   Powdered sugar

1. Combine warm water and yeast. Stir to dissolve yeast. Blend in eggs and sugar and let stand until bubbly, about 5 minutes.

2. Fit processor with steel blade. Measure flour, cold butter and salt into work bowl. Process until mixed, about 10 seconds.

3. Turn on processor and very slowly drizzle yeast mixture and just enough milk through the feed tube into flour mixture so dough forms a ball that cleans the sides of the bowl. Process until ball turns around bowl about 25 times. Turn off processor and let dough stand 1 to 2 minutes. (Dough should be slightly sticky.)

4. Place dough in lightly greased bowl. Cover loosely with plastic wrap and let stand in warm place (85°F. or 30°C.) until doubled, about 1 hour.

5. Prepare Walnut Filling while dough is rising.

6. Punch down dough. Divide dough in half. Turn one half of dough onto well floured countertop or table cloth. Roll out to make as large a circle as possible (add more flour, if necessary, to keep dough from sticking to surface or rolling pin). Let dough rest 10 minutes. Roll dough out as thinly as posible (gently pull edges with fingers to stretch). Let dough rest 10 minutes. Continue rolling and stretching until circle of dough is 18 to 24 inches (45 to 60 cm) in diameter. Trim off any thick edges.

7. Brush melted butter evenly over dough. Spread half of Walnut Filling evenly over dough. Gently roll dough up jelly-roll fashion. Place in a "U" shape, seam side down, on greased cookie sheet. Repeat rolling, filling and shaping with remaining half of dough.

8. Let dough stand in warm place until doubled, about 1 hour.

9. Heat oven to 350°F. (180°C.). Bake until evenly brown, 30 to 35 minutes.

10. Remove from cookie sheets and place on wire racks. Brush crust of loaves with melted butter. Sprinkle powdered sugar over loaves. Cool.

---

*Spoon flour into dry measuring cup and level off. Do not scoop.

FOREIGN BREADS

Walnut Filling

8   ounces (225 g) walnuts
½   cup (125 mL) evaporated milk
½   cup (125 mL) sugar
¼   cup (60 mL) honey
1   teaspoon (5 mL) vanilla

1. Fit processor with steel blade. Add walnuts to work bowl. Process until nuts resemble cornmeal.

2. Transfer nuts to small saucepan. Blend in milk, sugar and honey. Cook over medium heat until mixture bubbles. Reduce heat and simmer until mixture is thick, 2 to 3 minutes.

3. Remove from heat. Stir in vanilla. Cool.

Crete Bread

Makes 1 loaf

½   to ¾ cup (125 to 180 mL) warm water (105° to 115°F. or 41° to 46°C.)
1   package (¼ oz. or 7 g) active dry yeast
1   tablespoon (15 mL) honey
2½ cups (625 mL) all-purpose flour*
⅓   cup (80 mL) instant nonfat dry milk solids
2   tablespoons (30 mL) butter or margarine
1   teaspoon (5 mL) salt
1   egg, beaten
    Crunchy Cheese Topping (recipe follows)

This interesting bread comes from Crete, an island in the Mediterranean, where it's a mealtime accompaniment. It's a simple round loaf topped with a crunchy mixture of Parmesan cheese, walnuts, sesame and anise seeds.

1. Combine ¼ cup (60 mL) water, yeast and honey. Stir to dissolve yeast and let stand until bubbly, about 5 minutes.

2. Fit processor with steel blade. Measure flour, dry milk, butter and salt into work bowl. Process until mixed, about 15 seconds.

3. Add yeast mixture and egg to flour mixture. Process until blended, about 10 seconds.

4. Turn on processor and very slowly drizzle just enough remaining water through feed tube into flour mixture so dough forms a ball that cleans the sides of the bowl. Process until ball turns around bowl about 25 times. Turn off processor and let dough stand 1 to 2 minutes.

5. Turn on processor and gradually drizzle in enough remaining water to make dough soft, smooth and satiny but not sticky.** Process until dough turns around bowl about 15 times.

6. Turn dough onto lightly floured surface. Shape into ball and place in lightly greased bowl, turning to grease all sides. Cover loosely with plastic wrap and let stand in warm place (85°F. or 30°C.) until doubled, about 1 hour.

7. Punch down dough. Shape into smooth ball and place on greased cookie sheet. Roll or pat dough into circle 8 inches (20 cm) in diameter.

8. Prepare Crunchy Cheese Topping and spread evenly over dough. Let dough stand in warm place until almost doubled, about 45 minutes.

9. Heat oven to 375°F. (190°C.). Bake until evenly brown, 25 to 30 minutes.

10. Remove from cookie sheet. Cool on wire rack.

Crunchy Cheese Topping

¼   cup (60 mL) grated Parmesan cheese
¼   cup (60 mL) finely chopped walnuts
2   tablespoons (30 mL) sesame seeds, toasted
1   teaspoon (5 mL) anise seeds
¼   teaspoon (1 mL) ground ginger
1   egg, beaten

1. Combine all ingredients.

*Spoon flour into dry measuring cup and level off. Do not scoop.

**If dough is too dry and stiff, too soft and sticky, or if the processor shuts off, correct problem according to directions on page 25.

Clockwise: Challah,
Swedish Limpa, Gannat
(French Cheese Bread)

Pizza

Clockwise: Moravian Sugar Cake,
Crumb Coffee Cake, Sour Cream
Coffee Ring

Clockwise: Pecan Raisin Coffee Cake, Pecan Coffee Cake, Honey Pecan Coffee Cake

FUN AND NOVELTY BREADS

Pizza

Makes 1 pizza (about 6 servings)

½ to ¾ cup (125 to 180 mL) warm water (105° to 115°F. or 41° to 46°C.)

1 package (¼ oz. or 7 g) active dry yeast

1 teaspoon (5 mL) sugar

2 cups (500 mL) all-purpose flour*

1 tablespoon (15 mL) olive or vegetable oil

½ teaspoon (2 mL) salt
  Pizza Sauce (recipe follows)

4 ounces (115 g) sliced pepperoni (about 1 cup or 250 mL)

1 small green pepper, seeded and sliced

1 small onion, peeled and sliced

8 ounces (225 g) shredded Mozarella cheese (about 2 cups or 500 mL)

1 ounce (30 g) grated Parmesan cheese (about ⅓ cup or 80 mL)

Who can turn down pizza, especially when it's homemade? With the food processor, the dough is a snap to prepare. Use it, too, for quickly mixing a "from scratch" pizza sauce and for shredding and slicing ingredients for the topping.

1. Combine ¼ cup (60 mL) of the water, yeast and sugar. Stir to dissolve yeast and let stand until bubbly, about 5 minutes.

2. Fit processor with steel blade. Measure flour, oil and salt into work bowl. Process until mixed, about 5 seconds.

3. Add yeast mixture to flour mixture. Process until blended, about 10 seconds.

4. Turn on processor and very slowly drizzle just enough remaining water through feed tube into flour mixture so dough forms a ball that cleans the sides of the bowl. Process until ball turns around bowl about 25 times. Turn off processor and let dough stand 1 to 2 minutes.

5. Turn on processor and gradually drizzle in enough remaining water to make dough soft, smooth and satiny but not sticky.** Process until dough turns around bowl about 15 times.

6. Turn dough onto greased pizza pan 14 inches (35 cm) in diameter or large cookie sheet. Shape dough into ball. Cover with inverted bowl or plastic wrap and let stand 10 minutes.

7. Prepare Pizza Sauce while dough is resting.

8. Roll or pat dough out to cover pan, making a slight ridge around outside edge. Spread Pizza Sauce evenly over dough. Top with pepperoni, green pepper, onion and cheeses.

9. Heat oven to 425°F. (220°C.). Bake until crust is golden and cheese is bubbly, 15 to 20 minutes. Serve hot.

Pizza Sauce

3 tomatoes, peeled, seeded and quartered

1 can (8 oz. or 225 g) tomato sauce

1 to 2 teaspoons (5 to 10 mL) Italian herb seasoning or leaf oregano

½ teaspoon (2 mL) salt

¼ teaspoon (1 mL) sugar

⅛ teaspoon (0.5 mL) pepper

1. Fit processor with steel blade. Place tomatoes in work bowl. Process on/off 3 or 4 times to coarsely chop tomatoes.

2. Add tomato sauce and seasonings to chopped tomato. Process on/off to mix.

*Spoon flour into dry measuring cup and level off. Do not scoop.

**If dough is too dry and stiff, too soft and sticky, or if the processor shuts off, correct problem according to directions on page 25.

FUN AND NOVELTY BREADS

Egg Bagels

Makes 1 dozen bagels

½ to ¾ cup (125 to 180 mL) warm water (105° to 115°F. or 41° to 46°C.)

1 package (¼ oz. or 7 g) active dry yeast

1 teaspoon (5 mL) sugar

2½ cups (625 mL) all-purpose flour*

1 tablespoon (15 mL) vegetable oil

1 teaspoon (5 mL) salt

2 eggs

2 quarts (2 L) water

2 tablespoons (30 mL) sugar

2 tablespoons (30 mL) cold water

Boiling the dough before baking is what makes a bagel a bagel. That's how it gets its shiny appearance and its marvelous chewy texture.

1. Combine ¼ cup (60 mL) of the warm water, yeast and 1 teaspoon (5 mL) of the sugar. Stir to dissolve yeast and let stand until bubbly, about 5 minutes.

2. Fit processor with steel blade. Measure flour, oil and salt into work bowl. Process until mixed, about 5 seconds.

3. Add yeast mixture and 1 of the eggs to flour mixture. Process until blended, about 10 seconds.

4. Turn on processor and very slowly drizzle just enough remaining warm water through feed tube into flour mixture so dough forms a ball that cleans the sides of the bowl. Process until ball turns around bowl about 25 times. Turn off processor and let dough stand 1 to 2 minutes.

5. Turn on processor and gradually drizzle in enough remaining warm water to make dough soft, smooth and satiny but not sticky.** Process until dough turns around bowl about 15 times.

6. Turn dough onto lightly greased surface. Shape into ball and cover with plastic wrap. Let stand about 15 minutes.

7. Divide dough into 12 equal pieces. Shape each piece into a strand about 6 inches (15 cm) long. Bring both ends of each strand together to form a doughnut shape. Moisten ends and pinch together to seal. Place bagels on greased cookie sheet and let stand at room temperature about 15 minutes.

8. Combine 2 quarts (2 L) of water and 2 tablespoons (30 mL) of sugar in Dutch oven or stock pot. Bring water to a boil. Gently place bagels in boiling water. Cook 3 or 4 bagels at a time. When they rise to the surface, turn them over and cook until puffy, 1½ to 2 minutes longer. Remove bagels from water with a slotted spoon and place on greased cookie sheet.

9. Heat oven to 425°F. (220°C.). Beat remaining egg and 2 tablespoons (30 mL) cold water with a fork. Brush mixture over bagels. Bake until crusts are golden and crisp, 20 to 25 minutes.

10. Remove from cookie sheet. Cool on wire rack.

Raisin Spice Bagels Prepare dough as directed for Egg Bagels, adding 1½ tablespoons (22 mL) sugar, 1 teaspoon (5 mL) ground cinnamon and ¼ teaspoon (1 mL) ground nutmeg to work bowl with flour, oil and salt. Continue preparing dough as directed. Turn dough onto lightly greased surface and knead in ½ cup (125 mL) dark raisins. Continue shaping, cooking and baking as directed for Egg Bagels.

Pita (Pocket Bread)

Makes 8 pitas

¾ to 1 cup (180 to 250 mL) warm water (105° to 115°F. or 41° to 46°C.)

1 package (¼ oz. or 7 g) active dry yeast

1 tablespoon (15 mL) sugar

2¾ cups (680 mL) all-purpose flour*
continued

Pita bread is common in Middle Eastern cultures and can be found in the cuisines of several countries. These small round breads puff during baking and form pockets. Split in half, they hold a variety of fillings, from the traditional Falafel or meat fillings and yogurt to tuna or egg salad or even taco fixings.

1. Combine ¼ cup (60 mL) of the water, yeast and sugar. Stir to dissolve yeast and let stand until bubbly, about 5 minutes.

---

*Spoon flour into dry measuring cup and level off. Do not scoop.

**If dough is too dry and stiff, too soft and sticky, or if the processor shuts off, correct problem according to directions on page 25.

Pita (Pocket Bread) *(continued)*

1 teaspoon (5 mL) salt
1 teaspoon (5 mL) vegetable
oil

2. Fit processor with steel blade. Measure flour, salt and oil into work bowl. Process on/off to mix.

3. Add yeast mixture to flour mixture. Process until blended, about 10 seconds.

4. Turn on processor and very slowly drizzle just enough remaining water through feed tube into flour mixture so dough forms a ball that cleans the sides of the bowl. Process until ball turns around bowl about 25 times. Turn off processor and let dough stand 1 to 2 minutes.

5. Turn on processor and gradually drizzle in enough remaining water to make dough soft, smooth and satiny but not sticky.** Process until dough turns around bowl about 15 times.

6. Let dough stand, covered, in work bowl at room temperature until almost doubled, 45 to 60 minutes. Process on/off to punch down dough.

7. Turn dough onto lightly floured surface. Divide dough into 8 equal parts. Shape each part into a ball. Roll out each part into circle 6 inches (15 cm) in diameter and place on ungreased, floured cookie sheet. Cover loosely with plastic wrap and let stand in warm place (85°F. or 30°C.) until almost doubled, about 45 minutes.

8. Heat oven to 500°F. (260°C.). Bake until lightly browned and puffy, 5 to 7 minutes.

9. Remove from cookie sheet and place on paper toweling. Cool.

Makes 3 dozen

Dutch Rusks

¼ cup (60 mL) warm water
(105° to 115°F. or 41° to
46°C.)
4 tablespoons (60 mL) sugar
1 package (¼ oz. or 7 g)
active dry yeast
¼ cup (60 mL) cream, half
and half or evaporated
milk
¼ cup (60 mL) butter or
margarine, melted and
cooled
½ teaspoon (2 mL) salt
1 egg, beaten
2 to 2½ cups (500 to 625
mL) all-purpose flour*

Dutch Rusks are crispy rounds of bread that are baked twice. They're very good as a base for Eggs Benedict, creamed meat, seafood or vegetable dishes, or simply spread with butter and eaten as bread.

1. Combine water, 1 tablespoon (15 mL) of the sugar and yeast. Stir to dissolve yeast and let stand until bubbly, about 5 minutes. Blend remaining 3 tablespoons (45 mL) of the sugar, cream, melted butter, salt and egg into yeast mixture.

2. Fit processor with steel blade. Measure 2 cups (500 mL) of the flour into work bowl. Turn on processor and slowly drizzle yeast mixture through feed tube into flour. Add remaining flour 1 tablespoon (15 mL) at a time, if necessary, to make a dough that cleans the sides of the bowl. Process until dough turns around bowl about 25 times.**

3. Let dough stand, covered, in work bowl at room temperature until doubled, 45 to 60 minutes.

4. Process on/off to punch down dough. Turn dough onto lightly floured surface and roll out to about ½ inch (1.5 cm) thick. Cut into circles about 4 inches (10 cm) in diameter using floured cookie cutter, glass or can. Place rounds 1½ inches (4 cm) apart on greased cookie sheets. Cover loosely with plastic wrap and let stand in warm place (85°F. or 30°C.) until doubled, about 30 minutes.

7. Heat oven to 400°F. (200°C.). Bake until golden, about 7 minutes. Reduce oven temperature to 200°F. (95°C.).

8. Remove rounds from cookie sheets. Cool on wire rack.

9. Cut rounds in half horizontally using sharp knife. Arrange halves on cookie sheets in one layer. Bake at 200°F. (95°C.) until crisp and dry, about 1½ hours.

10. Remove from cookie sheets. Cool on wire rack.

---

*Spoon flour into dry measuring cup and level off. Do not scoop.

**If dough is too dry and stiff, too soft and sticky, or if the processor shuts off, correct problem according to directions on page 25.

FUN AND NOVELTY BREADS

Onion Bagels

Makes 12 bagels

¾ to 1 cup (180 to 250 mL) warm water (105° to 115°F. or 41° to 46°C.)

1 package (¼ oz. or 7 g) active dry yeast

1 teaspoon (5 mL) sugar

2¾ cups (680 mL) all-purpose flour*

2 tablespoons (30 mL) instant minced onions

1 tablespoon (15 mL) vegetable oil

1 teaspoon (5 mL) salt

2 quarts (2 L) water

2 tablespoons (30 mL) sugar

1 egg

2 tablespoons (30 mL) cold water

Poppy seeds, optional

It's hard to resist bagels, especially when they're fresh from the oven. These classics are excellent split in half, toasted and spread with butter. Serving them with cream cheese and lox is traditional, of course, and unbeatable.

1. Combine ¼ cup (60 mL) of the warm water, yeast and 1 teaspoon (5 mL) of the sugar. Stir to dissolve yeast and let stand until bubbly, about 5 minutes.

2. Fit processor with steel blade. Measure flour, onions, oil and salt into work bowl. Process until mixed, about 5 seconds.

3. Add yeast mixture to flour mixture. Process until blended, about 10 seconds.

4. Turn on processor and very slowly drizzle just enough remaining water through feed tube into flour mixture so dough forms a ball that cleans the sides of the bowl. Process until ball turns around bowl about 25 times. Turn off processor and let dough stand 1 to 2 minutes.

5. Turn on processor and gradually drizzle in enough remaining water to make dough soft, smooth and satiny but not sticky.** Process until dough turns around bowl about 15 times.

6. Turn dough onto lightly greased surface. Shape into ball and cover with plastic wrap. Let stand about 15 minutes.

7. Divide dough into 12 equal pieces. Shape each piece into a strand about 6 inches long. Bring both ends of each strand together to form a doughnut shape. Moisten ends and pinch together to seal. Place bagels on greased cookie sheet and let stand at room temperature about 15 minutes.

8. Combine 2 quarts (2 L) of water and 2 tablespoons (30 mL) of the sugar in Dutch oven or stock pot. Bring water to a boil. Gently place bagels in boiling water. Cook 3 or 4 bagels at a time. When they rise to the surface, turn them over and cook until puffy, 1½ to 2 minutes longer. Remove bagels from water with slotted spoon and place on greased cookie sheet.

9. Heat oven to 425°F. (220°C.). Beat egg and 2 tablespoons (30 mL) cold water with a fork. Brush mixture over bagels. Bake until crusts are golden and crisp, 20 to 25 minutes.

10. Remove from cookie sheet. Cool on wire rack.

Lavash

Makes 2 flat breads

½ to ¾ cup (125 to 180 mL) warm water (105° to 115°F. or 41° to 46°C.)

1 package (¼ oz. or 7 g) active dry yeast

1 teaspoon (5 mL) sugar

2 cups (500 mL) all-purpose flour*

1 tablespoon (15 mL) butter or margarine

1 teaspoon (5 mL) salt

All-purpose flour

This Armenian flat bread can be either soft or crisp, depending upon how long it's in the oven. Soft, it's used to wrap around different kinds of fillings. Crisp, it can be used in place of crackers with cheeses, dips and spreads.

1. Combine ¼ cup (60 mL) of the water, yeast and sugar. Stir to dissolve yeast and let stand until bubbly, about 5 minutes.

2. Fit processor with steel blade. Measure flour, butter and salt into work bowl. Process until mixed, about 5 seconds.

3. Add yeast mixture to flour mixture. Process until blended, about 10 seconds. *continued*

---

*Spoon flour into dry measuring cup and level off. Do not scoop.

**If dough is too dry and stiff, too soft and sticky, or if the processor shuts off, correct problem according to directions on page 25.

Lavash *(continued)*

4. Turn on processor and very slowly drizzle just enough remaining water through feed tube into flour mixture so dough forms a ball that cleans the sides of the bowl. Process until ball turns around bowl about 25 times. Turn off processor and let dough stand 1 to 2 minutes.

5. Turn on processor and gradually drizzle in enough remaining water to make dough soft, smooth and satiny but not sticky.** Process until dough turns around bowl about 15 times.

6. Turn dough onto lightly greased surface. Shape into a ball and cover with an inverted bowl or plastic wrap, then with a towel to keep dough warm. Let stand at room temperature until doubled, about 1 hour.

7. Uncover dough and knead 4 or 5 times to remove air bubbles. Divide dough in half. Shape each half into a ball and coat lightly with flour. Let stand 10 minutes.

8. Roll out each half of dough on lightly floured surface into a circle about 15 inches (38 cm) in diameter. Pierce dough all over with tines of a fork. Place dough on large greased cookie sheets.

9. Heat oven to 375°F. (190°C.). Bake until lightly browned and bubbles appear on top surface, about 10 minutes for soft Lavash or 15 to 20 minutes for crisp Lavash.

10. Remove from cookie sheets. Cool on wire rack.

Peppered Cheese Bread

Makes 2 loaves

¾ to 1 cup (180 to 250 mL) warm water (105° to 115°F. or 41° to 46°C.)
1 package (¼ oz. or 7 g) active dry yeast
1 tablespoon (15 mL) sugar
2¾ cups (680 mL) all-purpose flour*
⅓ cup (80 mL) shredded Swiss cheese
2 tablespoons (30 mL) grated Parmesan cheese
2 tablespoons (30 mL) butter or margarine, at room temperature
1½ teaspoons (7 mL) salt
½ teaspoon (2 mL) red pepper sauce
¼ teaspoon (1 mL) ground pepper
   Vegetable oil

Shape this flavorful bread into long narrow loaves, then slice the baked bread crosswise for snack sized pieces. It's super for hors d'oeurves topped with spreads or small pieces of meat and cheese.

1. Combine ¼ cup (60 mL) of the water, yeast and sugar. Stir to dissolve yeast and let stand until bubbly, about 5 minutes.

2. Fit processor with steel blade. Measure flour, cheeses, butter, salt, red pepper sauce and ground pepper into work bowl. Process until mixed, about 10 seconds.

3. Add yeast mixture to flour mixture. Process until blended, about 10 seconds.

4. Turn on processor and very slowly drizzle just enough remaining water through feed tube into flour mixture so dough forms a ball that cleans the sides of the bowl. Process until ball turns around bowl about 25 times. Turn off processor and let dough stand 1 to 2 minutes.

5. Turn on processor and gradually drizzle in enough remaining water to make dough soft, smooth and satiny but not sticky.** Process until dough turns around bowl about 15 times.

6. Turn dough onto lightly greased surface. Shape dough into ball. Cover with inverted bowl or plastic wrap and let stand 10 minutes.

7. Divide dough in half. Shape each half into a strand 12 to 15 inches (30 to 38 cm) long, depending on size of available cookie sheet. Place strands about 4 inches (10 cm) apart on greased cookie sheet. Brush with oil and let stand in warm place (85°F. or 30°C.) until almost doubled, about 45 minutes.

8. Heat oven to 375°F. (190°C.). Bake until golden and loaves sound hollow when tapped, 20 to 25 minutes.

9. Remove from cookie sheet. Cool on wire rack.

---

*Spoon flour into dry measuring cup and level off. Do not scoop.

**If dough is too dry and stiff, too soft and sticky, or if the processor shuts off, correct problem according to directions on page 25.

FUN AND NOVELTY BREADS

Diamond Crisps

Makes 4 dozen

¼ cup (60 mL) warm water (105° to 115°F. or 41° to 46°C.)

1 package (¼ oz. or 7 g) active dry yeast

½ cup (125 mL) sweetened, condensed milk

3 cups (750 mL) all-purpose flour*

1 cup (250 mL) cold butter or margarine, cut into ½-inch (1.5 cm) slices

½ teaspoon (2 mL) ground cardamom

1 egg, white, slightly beaten
   Sugar

Sweet, rich, and very tasty, Diamond Crisps are sort of a cross between a pastry and a cookie. They're made from an easy yeast raised dough that's shaped into small diamonds.

1. Combine water and yeast. Stir to dissolve yeast. Blend in condensed milk and let stand until bubbly, about 5 minutes.

2. Fit processor with steel blade. Measure 2 cups (500 mL) of the flour, butter and cardamom into work bowl. Process on/off 12 to 15 times until mixture resembles cornmeal.

3. Transfer flour-butter mixture to a large mixing bowl. Stir in remaining 1 cup (250 mL) of the flour.

4. Add yeast mixture to flour mixture. Stir just enough to moisten flour. (Dough should be crumbly like a biscuit dough, not smooth and satiny like most yeast doughs.) Cover with plastic wrap and refrigerate 8 to 24 hours.

5. Divide dough in half. Roll out each half on a well floured surface into a 10x18-inch (25x45 cm) rectangle. Cut into diamond shapes by making parallel cuts diagonally across dough 2 inches (5 cm) apart.

6. Place diamonds about 1 inch (2.5 cm) apart on greased cookie sheets. Brush with beaten egg white and sprinkle generously with sugar. Let stand at room temperature about 15 minutes.

7. Heat oven to 350°F. (180°C.). Bake until golden and crisp, about 15 minutes. Cool on cookie sheets on wire rack.

Italian Pine Nut Sticks

Makes 40 bread sticks

½ to ¾ cup (125 to 180 mL) warm water (105° to 115°F. or 41° to 46°C.)

1 package (¼ oz. or 7 g) active dry yeast

1 tablespoon (15 mL) sugar

½ teaspoon (2 mL) anise seeds, crushed

2¼ cups (560 mL) all-purpose flour*

⅔ cup (160 mL) pine nuts (pignola nuts) or slivered almonds

¼ cup (60 mL) olive or vegetable oil

1 teaspoon (5 mL) salt

1 egg, beaten

2 tablespoons (30 mL) coarse salt

Pine nuts, anise seeds and olive oil add their distinctive flavors to these intriguing bread sticks.

1. Combine ¼ cup (60 mL) of the water, yeast, sugar and anise. Stir to dissolve yeast and let stand until bubbly, about 5 minutes.

2. Fit processor with steel blade. Measure flour, nuts, oil and 1 teaspoon (5 mL) salt into work bowl. Process until mixed, about 15 seconds.

3. Add yeast mixture to flour mixture. Process until blended, about 10 seconds.

4. Turn on processor and very slowly drizzle just enough remaining water through feed tube into flour mixture so dough forms a ball that cleans the sides of the bowl. Process until ball turns around bowl about 25 times. Turn off processor and let dough stand 1 to 2 minutes.

5. Turn on processor and gradually drizzle in enough remaining water to make dough soft, smooth and satiny but not sticky.** Process until dough turns around bowl about 15 times.

6. Let dough stand, covered, in work bowl at room temperature about 30 minutes. Process on/off to punch down dough.

7. Divide dough in half. Divide each half into 20 equal parts. Shape each part into a strand about 6 inches (15 cm) long. Place strands about 1 inch (2.5 cm) apart on greased cookie sheets. Cover loosely with plastic wrap and let stand in warm place (85°F. or 30°C.) until doubled, about 30 minutes.

8. Heat oven to 300°F. (150°C.). Brush strands with beaten egg and sprinkle with coarse salt. Bake until crisp, 25 to 30 minutes.

9. Remove from cookie sheets and cool on wire rack.

*Spoon flour into dry measuring cup and level off. Do not scoop.

**If dough is too dry and stiff, too soft and sticky, or if the processor shuts off, correct problem according to directions on page 25.

Makes 1 dozen pretzels

Soft Pretzels

¾ to 1 cup (180 to 250 mL)
    warm water (105° to
    115°F. or 41° to 46°C.)
1   package (¼ oz. or 7 g)
    active dry yeast
1   tablespoon (15 mL) sugar
2¾ cups (680 mL) all-purpose
    flour*
1   teaspoon (5 mL) salt
6   cups (1.5 L) water
¼   cup (60 mL) baking soda
1   egg white
    Coarse salt

Preparing these fresh, chewy pretzels is fun and satisfying. It's easy, too. The only thing to watch for is to be careful when lifting the pretzels into the boiling water—they can easily lose their shape.

1. Combine ¼ cup (60 mL) of the warm water, yeast and sugar. Stir to dissolve yeast and let stand until bubbly, about 5 minutes.

2. Fit processor with steel blade. Measure flour and salt into work bowl. Process on/off to mix.

3. Add yeast mixture to flour mixture. Process until blended, about 10 seconds.

4. Turn on processor and very slowly drizzle just enough remaining warm water through feed tube into flour mixture so dough forms a ball that cleans the sides of the bowl. Process until ball turns around bowl about 25 times. Turn off processor and let dough stand 1 to 2 minutes.

5. Turn on processor and gradually drizzle in enough remaining warm water to make dough soft, smooth and satiny but not sticky.** Process until dough turns around bowl about 15 times.

6. Turn dough onto lightly greased surface. Shape into a ball. Cover with inverted bowl or plastic wrap and let stand about 10 minutes.

7. Divide dough into 12 equal parts. Shape each part into a strand about 20 inches (50 cm) long. Shape each strand into a pretzel and place on well greased cookie sheet. Let pretzels stand at room temperature until almost doubled, about 30 minutes.

8. Combine 6 cups (1.5 L) water and baking soda in large stainless steel or enamel (aluminum will discolor) saucepan or Dutch oven. Bring water to boil.

9. Carefully lift pretzels one at a time off cookie sheet using a large pancake turner and lower into boiling water. Cook until pretzels are puffy, about 15 seconds. Remove pretzels from water using a slotted spoon and place ½ inch (1.5 cm) apart on greased cookie sheet. Brush pretzels with egg white and sprinkle lightly with coarse salt.

10. Heat oven to 400°F. (200°C.). Bake until golden, about 20 minutes.

11. Remove from cookie sheet. Cool on wire rack.

Soft Rye Pretzels
Prepare dough as directed for Soft Pretzels substituting ½ cup (125 mL) rye flour for ½ cup (125 mL) of the all-purpose flour and adding 1 tablespoon (15 mL) caraway seeds. Continue mixing, shaping and baking as directed for Soft Pretzels.

Hard Pretzels
Prepare dough as directed for Soft Pretzels, adding ¼ cup (60 mL) vegetable oil to work bowl with flour and salt. Turn dough onto lightly greased surface. Shape into a ball and divide into 32 equal parts (divide ball into quarters, divide each quarter into quarters, then divide each quarter in half). Shape each part into a thin strand about 10 inches (25 cm) long. Shape each strand into a pretzel and place on well greased cookie sheet. Let pretzels stand at room temperature until almost doubled, about 30 minutes. Cook in boiling water as directed for Soft Pretzels and place on greased cookie sheet. Brush with egg white and sprinkle with coarse salt. Heat oven to 300°F. (150°C.). Bake until crisp, 30 to 40 minutes. Remove from cookie sheet and cool on wire rack. Makes 32 pretzels.

---

*Spoon flour into dry measuring cup and level off. Do not scoop.

**If dough is too dry and stiff, too soft and sticky, or if the processor shuts off, correct problem according to directions on page 25.

FUN AND NOVELTY BREADS

Crunchy Bread Sticks

Makes 16 sticks

¾ to 1 cup (180 to 250 mL) warm water (105° to 115°F. or 41° to 46°C.)

1 package (¼ oz. or 7 g) active dry yeast

1 tablespoon (15 mL) sugar

2¾ cups (680 mL) all-purpose flour*

2 tablespoons (30 mL) vegetable oil

2 teaspoons (10 mL) salt
Vegetable oil

1 egg white
Coarse salt, sesame or poppy seeds

Everybody in the family, especially the kids, will love homemade bread sticks. With a food processor, they're quite simple to make and fun, too.

1. Combine ¼ cup (60 mL) of the water, yeast and sugar. Stir to dissolve yeast and let stand until bubbly, about 5 minutes.

2. Fit processor with steel blade. Measure flour, 2 tablespoons (30 mL) of the oil and salt into work bowl. Process until mixed, about 5 seconds.

3. Add yeast mixture to flour mixture. Process until blended, about 10 seconds.

4. Turn on processor and very slowly drizzle just enough remaining water through feed tube into flour mixture so dough forms a ball that cleans the sides of the bowl. Process until ball turns around bowl about 25 times. Turn off processor and let dough stand 1 to 2 minutes.

5. Turn on processor and gradually drizzle in enough remaining water to make dough soft, smooth and satiny but not sticky.** Process until dough turns around bowl about 15 times.

6. Turn dough onto lightly greased surface. Shape into ball. Cover with inverted bowl or plastic wrap and let stand 10 minutes. Divide dough into 16 equal parts. Shape each part into a strand 12 to 14 inches (30 to 35 cm) long, depending on size of available cookie sheets. Dip strands in oil and place on ungreased cookie sheet about 3-inches (8 cm) apart.

7. Brush strands with unbeaten egg white. Sprinkle coarse salt, sesame or poppy seeds over strands. Let stand at room temperature until almost doubled, about 30 minutes.

8. Heat oven to 300°F. (150°C.). Bake until golden and dry, 30 to 40 minutes.

9. Remove from cookie sheets and cool on wire rack.

Cheese Bread Sticks Prepare dough as directed for Crunchy Bread Sticks. Add ¼ cup (60 mL) grated Parmesan or Romano cheese or ½ cup (125 mL) finely shredded Cheddar or Swiss cheese to work bowl with flour, oil and salt. Continue mixing, shaping and baking as directed for Crunchy Bread Sticks.

Cheddar Snack Loaves

Makes 2 loaves

¾ to 1 cup (180 to 250 mL) warm water (105° to 115°F. or 41° to 46°C.)

2 tablespoons (30 mL) sugar

1 package (¼ oz. or 7 g) active dry yeast

2 ounces (60 g) Cheddar cheese, in one piece

2¾ cups (680 mL) all-purpose flour*

2 tablespoons (30 mL) butter or margarine, at room temperature

¾ teaspoon (4 mL) salt

continued

These long, narrow loaves with a zesty Cheddar cheese flavor look like little French breads. They're ideal as a cocktail bread topped with cheeses, meat, spreads or fresh butter. They can be made and shaped the day ahead, then refrigerated until time to go in the oven.

1. Combine ¼ cup (60 mL) of the water, sugar and yeast. Stir to dissolve yeast and let stand until bubbly, about 5 minutes.

2. Fit processor with shredding disc. Fit cheese into feed tube, cutting it if necessary. Process until all cheese is shredded.

3. Remove shredding disc and fit processor with steel blade. Add flour, butter and salt to cheese in work bowl. Process on/off 3 or 4 times to blend butter into mixture.

4. Add yeast mixture and 1 egg to flour mixture. Process until blended, about 10 seconds.

---

*Spoon flour into dry measuring cup and level off. Do not scoop.

**If dough is too dry and stiff, too soft and sticky, or if the processor shuts off, correct problem according to directions on page 25.

Cheddar Snack Loaves *(continued)*

1 egg
Vegetable oil
1 egg white
Sesame seeds, optional

5. Turn on processor and very slowly drizzle just enough remaining water through feed tube into flour mixture so dough forms a ball that cleans the sides of the bowl. Process until ball turns around bowl about 25 times. Turn off processor and let dough stand 1 to 2 minutes.

6. Turn on processor and gradually drizzle in enough remaining water to make dough soft, smooth and satiny but not sticky.** Process until dough turns around bowl about 15 times.

7. Turn dough onto lightly greased surface. Divide into 2 equal parts. Shape each part into a strand 12 to 15 inches (30 to 38 cm) long, depending on size of available cookie sheet. Place strands about 4 inches (10 cm) apart on greased cookie sheet. Brush with oil and let stand in warm place (85°F. or 30°C.) until almost doubled, about 45 minutes.

8. Heat oven to 350°F. (180°C.). Brush loaves with unbeaten egg white and sprinkle with sesame seeds, if desired. Bake until loaves are golden and sound hollow when tapped, 20 to 25 minutes.

9. Remove from cookie sheet. Cool on wire rack.

Refrigerator Cheddar Snack Loaves
Prepare and shape loaves as directed for Cheddar Snack Loaves. Place on greased cookie sheet, brush with oil and cover tightly with plastic wrap. Refrigerate 4 to 24 hours. Uncover loaves and let stand at room temperature while preheating oven. Bake as directed for Cheddar Snack Loaves.

Makes about 4 dozen pieces

Cinnamon Zwieback

¼ cup (60 mL) warm water (105° to 115°F. or 41° to 46°C.)
8 tablespoons (120 mL) sugar
1 package (¼ oz. or 7 g) active dry yeast
2½ cups (625 mL) all-purpose flour*
½ teaspoon (2 mL) salt
½ teaspoon (2 mL) ground nutmeg
2 eggs
¼ to ½ cup (60 to 125 mL) evaporated or fresh milk, at room temperature
2 tablespoons (30 mL) cold milk
1 teaspoon (5 mL) ground cinnamon

Everyone from youngsters to oldsters like this age-old toast. This homemade version is delicious and quite easy to make with a food processor.

1. Combine water, 1 tablespoon (15 mL) of the sugar and yeast. Stir to dissolve yeast and let stand until bubbly, about 5 minutes.

2. Fit processor with steel blade. Measure flour, 3 tablespoons (45 mL) of the remaining sugar, salt and nutmeg into work bowl. Process on/off to mix.

3. Add yeast mixture and 1 of the eggs to flour mixture. Process until blended, about 10 seconds.

4. Turn on processor and very slowly drizzle just enough milk through feed tube into flour mixture so dough forms a ball that cleans the sides of the bowl. Process until ball turns around bowl about 25 times. Turn off processor and let dough stand 1 to 2 minutes.

5. Turn on processor and gradually drizzle in enough remaining milk to make dough soft, smooth and satiny but not sticky.** Process until dough turns around bowl about 15 times.

6. Turn dough onto lightly greased surface. Shape into ball and place in lightly greased bowl, turning to grease all sides. Cover loosely with plastic wrap and let stand in warm place (85°F. or 30°C.) until doubled, about 1 hour.

7. Punch down dough. Divide dough in half. Shape each half into strand 12 inches (30 cm) long and about 2 inches (5 cm) wide. Place strands about 4 inches (10 cm) apart on greased cookie sheet. Cover loosely with plastic wrap and let stand in warm place until almost doubled, about 30 minutes. *continued*

---

*Spoon flour into dry measuring cup and level off. Do not scoop.

**If dough is too dry and stiff, too soft and sticky, or if the processor shuts off, correct problem according to directions on page 25.

8. Heat oven to 375°F. (190°C.). Beat remaining egg and 2 tablespoons (30 mL) of the cold milk with a fork. Brush mixture over loaves. Combine remaining 4 tablespoons (60 mL) of the sugar and cinnamon. Sprinkle generously over loaves. Bake until golden, about 20 minutes.

9. Remove loaves from cookie sheet. Cool on wire rack. Reduce oven temperature to 200°F. (95°C.).

10. Cut cooled loaves into ½ inch (1.5 cm) thick slices. Arrange slices in single layer on cookie sheets. Bake at 200°F. (95°C.) until crisp and dry, about 1½ hours.

11. Remove from cookie sheets. Cool on wire rack.

Kifles (Kipfels)

Makes 3 dozen

2 tablespoons (30 mL) warm water (105° to 115°F. or 41° to 46°C.)

8 tablespoons (120 mL) granulated sugar

1 package (¼ oz. or 7 g) active dry yeast

½ cup (125 mL) dairy sour cream

2 eggs, separated

2¼ to 2½ cups (560 to 625 mL) all-purpose flour *

½ cup (125 mL) butter or margarine, at room temperature

¼ teaspoon (1 mL) cream of tartar

1 cup (250 mL) walnut pieces

1 teaspoon (5 mL) vanilla Powdered sugar

These little cookie-like crescents of meringue-filled bread reportedly were created by bakers in Vienna 300 years ago and were eventually discovered by Marie Antoinette. She took the recipe back to France where chefs turned it into a delicious pastry, the croissant.

1. Combine water, 1 tablespoon (15 mL) of the sugar and yeast. Stir to dissolve yeast and let stand until bubbly, about 5 minutes. Blend sour cream and egg yolks into yeast mixture.

2. Fit processor with steel blade. Measure 1½ cups (375 mL) of the flour and butter into work bowl. Process until mixed, about 15 seconds.

3. Turn on processor and slowly add yeast mixture through feed tube to flour mixture. Add enough of the remaining flour through feed tube to make a dough that cleans the sides of the bowl. Process until dough turns around bowl about 25 times.

4. Turn dough onto lightly floured surface. Shape into ball and place in lightly greased bowl, turning to grease all sides. Cover tightly and refrigerate until thoroughly chilled, at least 4 hours. (Dough will keep up to 5 days tightly wrapped in refrigerator.)

5. Just before shaping dough, beat egg whites and cream of tartar with electric mixer at high speed until stiff but not dry, just until whites no longer slip when bowl is tilted. Reserve.

6. Fit processor with steel blade. Measure nuts, remaining 7 tablespoons (105 mL) of the granulated sugar and vanilla into work bowl. Process just until nuts are finely chopped. Fold nut mixture gently but thoroughly into egg whites. Reserve.

7. Turn dough onto lightly floured surface and knead 3 or 4 times. Divide dough into 3 equal parts. Roll out each part into a circle about 10 inches (25 cm) in diameter. Spread ⅓ of the meringue-nut mixture evenly over outer 4 inches of the circle (do not spread mixture in center of circle). Cut circle into 12 wedges. Roll up each wedge, starting at wide end and rolling toward point. Place on greased cookie sheets about 1 inch (2.5 cm) apart. Curve ends of each roll to form crescent shapes.

8. Heat oven to 375°F. (190°C.). Bake until golden, 15 to 20 minutes.

9. Remove from cookie sheet. Cool on wire rack. Sprinkle powdered sugar over Kifles.

*Spoon flour into dry measuring cup and level off. Do not scoop.

Mexican Turtle Bread

Makes 1 loaf

¼ cup (60 mL) warm water (105° to 115°F. or 41° to 46°C.)

1 package (¼ oz. or 7 g) active dry yeast

1 tablespoon (15 mL) sugar

2¾ cups (680 mL) all-purpose flour*

1¼ teaspoons (6 mL) salt

3 tablespoons (45 mL) lard, butter or margarine, melted and cooled

½ to ¾ cup (125 to 180 mL) milk, at room temperature

2 tablespoons (30 mL) all-purpose flour

Melted lard, butter or margarine

Mexicans love to make breads in all sorts of fanciful animal shapes. A Mexican bakery can sport everything from turtles to aligators, to fish, to birds. Here are the directions for producing a delicious bread shaped like a turtle.

1. Combine water, yeast and sugar. Stir to dissolve yeast and let stand until bubbly, about 5 minutes.

2. Fit processor with steel blade. Measure 2¾ cups (680 mL) of the flour and 1 teaspoon (5 mL) of the salt into work bowl. Process on/off to mix.

3. Add yeast mixture and 3 tablespoons (45 mL) of the melted lard to flour mixture. Process until blended, about 10 seconds.

4. Turn on processor and very slowly drizzle just enough milk through feed tube into flour mixture so dough forms a ball that cleans the sides of the bowl. Process until ball turns around bowl about 25 times. Turn off processor and let dough stand 1 to 2 minutes.

5. Turn on processor and gradually drizzle in enough remaining milk to make dough soft, smooth and satiny but not sticky.** Process until dough turns around bowl about 15 times.

6. Turn dough onto lightly greased surface. Shape into ball and place in lightly greased bowl, turning to grease all sides. Cover loosely with plastic wrap and let stand in warm place (85°F. or 30°C.) until doubled, about 1 hour.

7. Punch down dough. Cover with plastic wrap and let stand 10 minutes. Roll dough into a 12x6-inch (30x15 cm) oval. Brush with melted lard. Fold 6-inch (15 cm) side over as for Parkerhouse Roll, allowing bottom 6-inch (15 cm) edge to extend about ½ inch (1.5 cm). Place on greased cookie sheet. Gently squeeze the extended portion together and shape into the turtle's head. Gently twist about 1 tablespoon (15 mL) of dough at each of the four corners to form the turtle's legs. Press a ridge with sides of hands around the outside of the dough and gently push dough together to form a slightly dome-shaped shell.

8. Cover dough loosely with plastic wrap and let stand in warm place until almost doubled, about 45 minutes.

9. Heat oven to 375°F. (190°C.). Score top of the turtle's shell into 1-inch (2.5 cm) squares about ¼ inch (0.5 cm) deep, using the processor's steel blade, sharp knife or razor blade. Brush dough with melted lard. Combine remaining 2 tablespoons (30 mL) of the flour and ¼ teaspoon (1 mL) of the salt. Sprinkle mixture over dough. Bake until golden, 30 to 35 minutes. (Cover legs and head with small pieces of aluminum foil if they brown too quickly.)

10. Remove from cookie sheet. Cool on wire rack.

---

*Spoon flour into dry measuring cup and level off. Do not scoop.

**If dough is too dry and stiff, too soft and sticky, or if the processor shuts off, correct problem according to directions on page 25.

FUN AND NOVELTY BREADS

Corn Tortillas

Makes 1 dozen tortillas

2   cups (500 mL) masa harina
    (dehydrated masa flour)
1¼ to 1½ cups (310 to 375
    mL) warm water (105° to
    115°F. or 41° to 46°C.)

These unleavened, thin rounds of bread are the traditional bread of Mexico. They are extremely versatile: they can be rolled, folded, stacked, torn or cut and paired with numerous varieties of fillings. They can be cooked so they are soft and chewy or crisp and crunchy. To make them, you need a special corn flour called masa harina that's available in many supermarkets, Mexican groceries or specialty shops.

1. Fit processor with steel blade. Measure masa harina into work bowl.

2. Turn on processor and slowly add water through feed tube into masa harina until dough forms a ball that cleans the sides of the bowl. Process until dough turns around bowl about 10 times. (Dough will not look like a yeast dough, but should be similar to pastry dough.)

3. Turn dough onto lightly greased surface. Divide dough into 12 equal parts. Shape each part into smooth ball.

4. Place each ball between 2 pieces of waxed paper, flatten slightly and roll into a circle about 6 inches (15 cm) in diameter, or place in tortilla press and press down firmly.

5. Heat an ungreased electric griddle to 350°F. (180°C.) or heat an ungreased fry pan over medium heat until hot enough to sizzle a drop of water. Remove top piece of waxed paper from tortilla and invert tortilla, waxed paper side up, onto griddle. Peel away waxed paper carefully as the tortilla cooks. Cook tortilla, turning frequently, until it's dry and flecked with brown specks, about 2 minutes. Stack on plate.

Flour (Wheat) Tortillas

Makes 1 dozen tortillas

2   cups (500 mL) all-purpose
    flour*
¼   cup (60 mL) lard, butter,
    margarine, or shortening
1   teaspoon (5 mL) salt
½   to ¾ cup (125 to 180 mL)
    warm water (105° to
    115°F. or 41° to 46°C.)

These flour tortillas are easy to make in any kitchen because they are made from all-purpose flour. Like their counterparts made of corn flour, they can be enjoyed in a variety of Mexican dishes or simply eaten plain, spread with butter while still warm.

1. Fit processor with steel blade. Measure flour, lard and salt into work bowl. Process until mixed, about 15 seconds.

2. Turn on processor and slowly add enough water through feed tube into flour mixture until dough forms a ball that cleans the sides of the bowl. Process until dough turns around bowl about 10 times. (Dough will not look like a yeast dough, but should be similar to pastry dough.)

3. Turn dough onto lightly greased surface. Divide dough into 12 equal parts. Shape each part into smooth ball.

4. Roll out each ball of dough on lightly floured surface to a circle about 8 inches (20 cm) in diameter.

5. Heat an ungreased electric griddle to 350°F. (180°C.) or heat an ungreased fry pan over medium heat until hot enough to sizzle a drop of water. Cook tortillas on each side until dry and flecked with brown specks, about 30 seconds on each side. Stack on plate.

*Spoon flour into dry measuring cup and level off. Do not scoop.

COFFEE CAKES

Date Pecan Crescent

Makes 2 coffee cakes

½ cup (125 mL) warm water (105° to 115°F. or 41° to 46°C.)

¾ cup (180 mL) sugar

2 packages (¼ oz. or 7 g each) active dry yeast

¼ teaspoon (1 mL) salt

3 eggs, separated

2½ to 2¾ cups (625 to 680 mL) all-purpose flour*

¾ cup (180 mL) butter or margarine, at room temperature

1½ cups (375 mL) chopped pecans

1 package (8 oz. or 225 g) pitted dates, chopped

Prepare the dough for this rich tasting bread one day, then shape and bake it the next day. It's great for brunches and special occasions.

1. Combine water, ¼ cup (60 mL) of the sugar, yeast and salt in small bowl. Let stand until bubbly, about 5 minutes. Stir in egg yolks.

2. Fit processor with steel blade. Measure 1 cup (250 mL) of the flour and the butter into work bowl. Process until well blended, about 10 seconds.

3. Turn on processor and slowly drizzle yeast mixture through feed tube into flour-butter mixture.

4. Add 1½ cups (375 mL) of the remaining flour to flour-yeast mixture. Process until well blended, stopping processor once or twice, if necessary, to scrape sides of the bowl.

5. Add remaining flour 1 tablespoon (15 mL) at a time, if necessary, to make a dough that cleans sides of the bowl. Process until dough turns around bowl about 25 times.**

6. Turn dough onto lightly floured surface. Shape into ball and place in lightly greased bowl, turning to grease all sides. Cover tightly and refrigerate until thoroughly chilled, 4 to 24 hours.

7. Just before shaping dough beat egg whites with electric mixer until foamy. Add remaining ½ cup (125 mL) of the sugar, 1 tablespoon at a time, beating constantly until sugar is dissolved and whites are glossy and stand in soft peaks.

8. Turn dough onto lightly floured surface and knead 3 or 4 times. Divide dough in half. Roll each half into a 10x12-inch (25x30 cm) rectangle. Reserve ½ cup (125 mL) of the meringue. Spread each rectangle of dough with half of remaining meringue. Sprinkle half of pecans and dates over meringue on each rectangle. Roll up dough jelly-roll fashion. Pinch seam and ends to seal. Place each roll on greased cookie sheet. Curve ends of dough to form crescent. Cover loosely with plastic wrap and let stand in warm place (85°F. or 30°C.) until doubled, 1 to 1¼ hours.

9. Heat oven to 350°F. (180°C.). Bake crescents for 20 minutes. Spread each crescent with ¼ cup (60 mL) of the reserved meringue and sprinkle each with 2 tablespoons (30 mL) chopped pecans. Bake until done, about 10 minutes longer.

10. Remove crescents immediately from cookie sheets and cool on wire racks.

---

*Spoon flour into dry measuring cup and level off. Do not scoop.

**If dough is too dry and stiff, too soft and sticky, or if the processor shuts off, correct problem according to directions on page 25.

COFFEE CAKES

Makes 1 coffee cake

Pecan Coffee Cake

2   to 2½ cups (500 to 625 mL)
    all-purpose flour*
3   tablespoons (45 mL) sugar
2   tablespoons (30 mL) butter
    or margarine
1   package (¼ oz. or 7 g)
    active dry yeast
¼   teaspoon (1 mL) salt
¼   cup (60 mL) hot water
    (120° to 130°F. or 49° to
    54°C.)
¼   cup (60 mL) evaporated or
    fresh milk, at room
    temperature
1   egg, beaten
    Vegetable oil
    Pecan Topping (recipe
    follows)

This delicious coffee cake is topped with a cinnamon spiced, streusel-like mixture that gets crunchy during baking.

1. Fit processor with steel blade. Measure 1 cup (250 mL) of the flour, sugar, butter, yeast, and salt into work bowl. Process until mixed, about 5 seconds.

2. Combine water, milk and egg. Turn on processor and gradually add water-egg mixture through feed tube to flour mixture. Process until smooth, about 30 seconds. Let stand 2 to 3 minutes.

3. Turn on processor and add enough of the remaining flour through feed tube so dough forms a ball that cleans the sides of the bowl. Process until ball turns around bowl about 25 times. Let dough stand in work bowl about 10 minutes.

4. Turn dough onto lightly floured surface. Roll into a 13x9-inch (33x23 cm) rectangle. Fit dough into greased 13x9x2-inch (33x23x5 cm) baking pan. Brush with oil. Let stand in warm place (85°F. or 30°C.) until doubled, about 45 minutes.

5. Prepare Pecan Topping while dough is rising.

6. Heat oven to 375°F. (190°C.). Sprinkle Pecan Topping over dough. Press topping into dough using back of spoon. Bake until wooden pick inserted in center comes out clean, 20 to 25 minutes. Cool in pan on wire rack.

Pecan Topping

½   cup (125 mL) sugar
½   cup (125 mL) all-purpose
    flour*
½   cup (125 mL) chopped
    pecans
½   cup (125 mL) butter or
    margarine, at room
    temperature
1   teaspoon (5 mL) ground
    cinnamon

1. Combine all ingredients in small mixing bowl.

Makes 1 coffee cake

Overnight Walnut Ring

¼   cup (60 mL) warm water
    (105° to 115°F. or 41° to
    46°C.)
2   tablespoons (30 mL)
    granulated sugar
1   package (¼ oz. or 7 g)
    active dry yeast
⅓   to ½ cup (80 to 125 mL)
    milk
4   tablespoons (60 mL) butter
    or margarine, at room
    temperature

This pretty bread, sweetly flavored with a cinnamon-nut filling, is shaped into a ring and then sliced. The slices are fanned out on the cookie sheet to form an attractive "wreath" of dough.

1. Combine water, granulated sugar and yeast. Stir to dissolve yeast and let stand until bubbly, about 5 minutes.

2. Combine ⅓ cup (80 mL) milk, 2 tablespoons (30 mL) of the butter and salt in small saucepan. Heat over low heat just until warm (105° to 115°F. or 41° to 46°C.). Butter may not melt completely. Remove from heat.

3. Fit processor with steel blade. Measure flour into work bowl. Add yeast mixture. Process on/off until mixed, about 5 seconds.   *continued*

*Spoon flour into dry measuring cup and level off. Do not scoop.

½ teaspoon (2 mL) salt
2 cups (500 mL) all-purpose flour*
½ cup (125 mL) chopped walnuts
2 tablespoons (30 mL) brown sugar
1 teaspoon (5 mL) ground cinammon
Vegetable oil
Powdered sugar

4. Turn on processor. Add milk mixture through feed tube to flour mixture. Process until mixed, about 30 seconds. If necessary, add more of the remaining milk to make a very soft dough. Cover processor and let dough stand in work bowl at room temperature 15 minutes.

5. Mix walnuts, remaining 2 tablespoons (30 mL) butter, brown sugar and cinnamon.

6. Turn out dough onto lightly floured surface. Roll out dough into an 8-inch (20 cm) square. Spread walnut mixture over dough. Roll up dough jelly-roll fashion. Pinch seam to seal. Arrange in circle on large greased cookie sheet. Pinch ends of dough together to seal. With scissors, cut ⅔ of the way through ring at ¾-inch (2 cm) intervals, leaving center of ring intact. Gently lay each section on its side, cut side up to show walnut filling. Brush with oil. Cover with plastic wrap and refrigerate overnight.

7. Let ring stand at room temperature 15 minutes before baking.

8. Heat oven to 375°F. (190°C.). Bake until golden, 20 to 25 minutes. Remove from cookie sheet and place on wire rack. Sprinkle generously with powdered sugar. Cool.

Quick Marmalade Coffee Cake

Makes 1 coffee cake

Marmalade Topping (recipe follows)
¾ cup (180 mL) granulated sugar
¼ cup (60 mL) butter, margarine or vegetable shortening, at room temperature
1 egg
½ cup (125 mL) milk
2 teaspoons (10 mL) baking powder
½ teaspoon (2 mL) salt
1⅔ cups (410 mL) all-purpose flour*

Quick is the right word for this coffee cake. The easy batter is whipped together in just seconds with a food processor. Top it with sweet orange marmalade topping.

1. Prepare Marmalade Topping. Reserve.

2. Fit processor with steel blade. Measure sugar and butter into work bowl. Process until creamy, about 15 seconds.

3. Add egg to sugar mixture. Process until blended, about 5 seconds.

4. Turn on processor and add milk through feed tube to sugar mixture. Process just until mixed, about 5 seconds.

5. Add baking powder and salt. Process on/off once to mix. Add flour. Process on/off 5 or 6 times just until it is blended into sugar mixture. Do not overprocess.

6. Spread batter evenly over bottom of greased 11x7x1½-inch (28x18x4 cm) or 9-inch (23 cm) square baking pan. Spread Marmalade Topping over batter.

7. Heat oven to 375°F. (190°C.). Bake until wooden pick inserted in center comes out clean, 30 to 35 minutes. Cool cake in pan on wire rack.

Marmalade Topping

½ cup (125 mL) all-purpose flour*
½ cup (125 mL) packed brown sugar
½ cup (125 mL) orange marmalade
2 tablespoons (30 mL) butter or margarine
1 tablespoon (15 mL) milk

1. Fit processor with steel blade. Measure all ingredients into work bowl. Process on/off 5 or 6 times until mixture is blended. Remove from work bowl.

*Spoon flour into dry measuring cup and level off. Do not scoop.

Raisin Nut Round

¼ cup (60 mL) water

¼ cup (60 mL) evaporated milk

6 tablespoons (90 mL) butter or margarine, at room temperature

1 egg, at room temperature

1 teaspoon (5 mL) vanilla

2 to 2¼ cups (500 to 560 mL) all-purpose flour*

¼ cup (60 mL) granulated sugar

1 package (¼ oz. or 7 g) active dry yeast

½ teaspoon (2 mL) salt

½ cup (125 mL) graham cracker crumbs

½ cup (125 mL) chopped pecans

½ cup (125 mL) dark raisins

⅓ cup (80 mL) packed brown sugar

1 cup (250 mL) powdered sugar

¼ teaspoon (1 mL) almond extract

2 to 3 tablespoons (30 to 45 mL) milk

The dough for this coffee cake is rolled jelly-roll fashion around a luscious pecan-raisin filling. The handsome loaf is quickly shaped by simply winding the dough into a loose coil.

1. Combine water, evaporated milk and 4 tablespoons (60 mL) of the butter in small saucepan. Heat over low heat until very warm (120° to 130°F. or 49° to 54°C.). Blend egg and vanilla into milk mixture.

2. Fit processor with steel blade. Measure 1 cup (250 mL) of the flour, granulated sugar, yeast and salt into work bowl. Process on/off 2 or 3 times to mix.

3. Turn on processor and add milk mixture through feed tube to flour mixture. Process until smooth, about 20 seconds.

4. Turn on processor and add enough of the remaining flour through feed tube so dough forms a ball that cleans the sides of the bowl. Process until ball turns around bowl about 25 times. Cover work bowl and let dough stand in work bowl in warm place (85°F. or 30°C.) until doubled, about 1 hour.

5. Turn dough onto lightly floured surface. Roll into a 10x20-inch (25x50 cm) rectangle. Spread dough with remaining 2 tablespoons (30 mL) butter. Combine graham crumbs, pecans, raisins and brown sugar. Sprinkle mixture over buttered dough. Roll up dough jelly-roll fashion beginning with 20-inch (50 cm) side. Pinch seam to seal. Arrange dough in a loose spiral on large greased cookie sheet. Brush with oil. Let stand in warm place until doubled, about 1 hour.

6. Heat oven to 350°F. (180°C.). Bake until evenly brown, 30 to 35 minutes. Remove from cookie sheet and cool on wire rack.

7. Blend powdered sugar, almond extract and enough milk to make smooth mixture thick enough to spread. Spread over cooled cake.

Honey Pecan Coffee Cake

½ to ¾ cup (125 to 180 mL) warm water (105° to 115°F. or 41° to 46°C.)

4 tablespoons (60 mL) sugar

1 package (¼ oz. or 7 g) active dry yeast

2¾ cups (680 mL) all-purpose flour*

2 tablespoons (30 mL) butter or margarine

¾ teaspoon (4 mL) salt

1 egg, beaten

½ cup (125 mL) chopped pecans

¼ cup (60 mL) honey

This beautiful coffee cake tastes as good as it looks. It's easily shaped by winding strips of dough into a sprial. A generous sprinkling of pecans and a drizzling of honey add a delicious finishing touch.

1. Combine ¼ cup (60 mL) of the water, 1 tablespoon (15 mL) of the sugar and yeast. Stir to dissolve yeast and let stand until bubbly, about 5 minutes.

2. Fit processor with steel blade. Measure flour, butter, remaining 3 tablespoons (45 mL) of the sugar and salt into work bowl. Process until mixed, about 15 seconds.

3. Add yeast mixture and egg to flour mixture. Process until blended, about 10 seconds.

4. Turn on processor and very slowly drizzle just enough remaining water through feed tube into flour mixture so dough forms a ball that cleans the sides of the bowl. Process until ball turns around bowl about 25 times. Turn off processor and let dough stand 1 to 2 minutes.

5. Turn on processor and gradually drizzle in enough remaining water to make dough soft, smooth and satiny but not sticky.** Process until dough turns around bowl about 15 times. *continued*

---

*Spoon flour into dry measuring cup and level off. Do not scoop.

**If dough is too dry and stiff, too soft and sticky, or if the processor shuts off, correct problem according to directions on page 25.

6. Turn dough onto lightly floured surface. Shape into ball. Cover with inverted bowl or plastic wrap and let stand 20 to 30 minutes.

7. Uncover dough. Roll into a 6x20-inch (15x50 cm) rectangle. Cut lengthwise into 5 equal strips. Arrange strips in greased 9-inch (23 cm) round cake pan or on greased cookie sheet by winding, cut edges down, into a loose spiral. Pinch ends of dough together to form a continuous strip of dough. Sprinkle pecans over dough. Cover loosely with plastic wrap and let stand in warm place (85°F. or 30°C.) until doubled, about 1¼ hours.

8. Heat oven to 375°F. (190°C.). Drizzle honey over dough. Bake until evenly brown, 25 to 30 minutes.

9. Remove from pan or cookie sheet immediately and cool on wire rack.

Crumb Coffee Cake

Makes 2 coffee cakes

Crumb Topping (recipe
   follows)
2¼ cups (560 mL) all-purpose
   flour*
⅓   cup (80 mL) sugar
1   package (¼ oz. or 7 g)
   active dry yeast
1   teaspoon (5 mL) salt
⅓   cup (80 mL) milk
¼   cup (60 mL) water
¼   cup (60 mL) butter or
   margarine
1   egg
1   egg white

This classic is easy to make with a food processor. It's simply a basic sweet yeast dough that's covered with a thick layer of cinnamon spiced crumb topping.

1. Prepare Crumb Topping. Reserve.

2. Fit processor with steel blade. Measure 1 cup (250 mL) of the flour, sugar, yeast and salt into work bowl. Process on/off 2 or 3 times to mix.

3. Combine milk, water and butter in small saucepan. Heat over low heat until very warm (120° to 130°F. or 49° to 54°C.). Blend egg and egg white into milk mixture with a fork.

4. Turn on processor and add milk mixture through feed tube to flour mixture. Process until smooth, about 20 seconds.

5. Add remaining flour to mixture in work bowl. Process until well blended, about 30 seconds.

6. Divide dough between two greased 8-inch (20 cm) round cake pans. Spread or pat dough with hands to completely cover bottoms of pans.

7. Sprinkle about 2 cups (500 mL) Crumb Topping over dough in each pan. Let stand in warm place (85°F. or 30°C.) until doubled, about 1½ hours.

8. Heat oven to 375°F. (190°C.). Bake cakes until wooden pick inserted in center comes out clean, about 30 minutes.

9. Cool cakes in pans on wire rack.

Crumb Topping

½   cup (125 mL) cold butter
   or margarine, cut into 4
   pieces
2   cups (500 mL) all-purpose
   flour*
½   cup (125 mL) sugar
2   tablespoons (30 mL) water
1   tablespoon (15 mL) ground
   cinnamon
1   egg yolk

1. Fit processor with steel blade. Measure all ingredients into work bowl. Process until mixture resembles corn meal, about 15 seconds.

*Spoon flour into dry measuring cup and level off. Do not scoop.

COFFEE CAKES

Sour Cream Coffee Ring

Makes 1 coffee cake

1 cup (250 mL) walnuts
2 tablespoons (30 mL) brown sugar
1 teaspoon (5 mL) ground cinnamon
1¼ cups (310 mL) granulated sugar
¾ cup (180 mL) cold butter or margarine, cut in ½-inch (1.5 cm) wide pieces
2 eggs, beaten
1 cup (250 mL) dairy sour cream
1½ teaspoons (7 mL) baking powder
1 teaspoon (5 mL) vanilla
½ teaspoon (2 mL) baking soda
2 cups (500 mL) all-purpose flour*

This attractive coffee cake is speedy to prepare since it doesn't need any rising time. It's simply a sour cream flavored cake batter with a tasty layer of walnut filling, that's baked in a bundt or tube pan.

1. Fit processor with steel blade. Add nuts, brown sugar and cinnamon to work bowl. Process on/off 2 or 3 times or until nuts are finely chopped. Remove from work bowl and reserve.

2. Refit processor with steel blade. Place granulated sugar and butter in work bowl. Process until mixture is creamed, about 20 seconds.

3. Turn on processor and slowly add eggs through feed tube to sugar mixture. Process until mixture is well blended, about 10 seconds.

4. Spoon sour cream over sugar mixture. Add baking powder, vanilla and soda. Process until blended, about 10 seconds.

5. Add flour to sour cream mixture. Process until well blended, 15 to 20 seconds. Stop processor and scrape sides of bowl, if necessary.

6. Heat oven to 350°F. (180°C.). Butter and flour inside of a 9-inch (23 cm) tube or bundt pan. Spoon half of the batter into pan. Sprinkle half of the nut mixture over batter in pan. Spoon remaining batter into pan. Top with remaining nut mixture.

7. Bake until wooden pick or cake tester inserted in center of cake comes out clean, 45 to 55 minutes. Cool 10 minutes in pan. Invert onto wire rack or serving plate.

Moravian Sugar Cake

Makes 1 coffee cake

¼ cup (60 mL) packed brown sugar
¼ cup (60 mL) walnut pieces
2 tablespoons (30 mL) cold butter or margarine
2 teaspoons (10 mL) ground cinnamon
¼ to ½ cup (60 to 125 mL) warm water (105° to 115°F. or 41° to 46°C.)
4 tablespoons (60 mL) granulated sugar
1 package (¼ oz. or 7 g) active dry yeast
2¾ cups (680 mL) all-purpose flour*
2 tablespoons (30 mL) instant nonfat dry milk solids
1 teaspoon (5 mL) salt
¼ cup (60 mL) butter or margarine, melted and cooled
2 eggs, beaten

This is an easy cake to make and a grand one to eat. Rich, cinnamon spiced dough is shaped into strands that are wound into a spiral for baking. The cake is covered with a delicious brown sugar-nut topping. For Christmas you can knead ½ cup each golden raisins and slivered almonds into the dough after processing and before shaping.

1. Fit processor with steel blade. Measure brown sugar, walnuts, 2 tablespoons (30 mL) cold butter and ½ teaspoon (2 mL) of the cinnamon into the work bowl. Process on/off 4 to 5 times until walnuts are finely chopped. Remove mixture from work bowl and reserve.

2. Combine ¼ cup (60 mL) of the water, 1 tablespoon (15 mL) of the granulated sugar and yeast. Stir to dissolve yeast and let stand until bubbly, about 5 minutes.

3. Refit processor with steel blade. Measure flour, remaining 3 tablespoons (45 mL) granulated sugar, dry milk, remaining 1½ teaspoons (7 mL) cinnamon and salt into work bowl. Process until mixed, about 5 seconds.

4. Add yeast mixture, melted butter and eggs to flour mixture. Process until blended, about 10 seconds.

5. Turn on processor and very slowly drizzle just enough remaining water through feed tube into flour mixture so dough forms a ball that cleans the sides of the bowl. Process until ball turns around bowl about 25 times. Turn off processor and let dough stand 1 to 2 minutes.   *continued*

*Spoon flour into dry measuring cup and level off. Do not scoop.

6. Turn on processor and gradually drizzle in enough remaining water to make dough soft, smooth and satiny but not sticky.** Process until dough turns around bowl about 15 times.

7. Turn dough onto lightly floured surface. Shape into ball and cover with inverted bowl or plastic wrap. Let stand 20 minutes.

8. Uncover dough and divide in half. Shape each half into a 36-inch (90 cm) long strand. Arrange both strands in a loose spiral in a greased 8- or 9-inch (20 or 23 cm) round or square cake pan. Sprinkle with reserved walnut mixture. Let stand in warm place (85°F. or 30°C.) until doubled, about 1 hour.

9. Heat oven to 350°F. (180°C.). Bake cake until evenly brown, 30 to 35 minutes. Remove immediately from pan and cool on wire rack.

Brown Sugar Nut Puffs and Apricot Coffee Cake

Makes 12 puffs and 1 coffee cake

½ cup (125 mL) pecan pieces
¼ cup (60 mL) packed brown sugar
½ cup (125 mL) butter or margarine, at room temperature
3 cups (750 mL) all-purpose flour*
½ cup (125 mL) granulated sugar
1 package (¼ oz. or 7 g) active dry yeast
1 teaspoon (5 mL) salt
1 cup (250 mL) hot water (120° to 130°F. or 49° to 54°C.)
2 eggs
⅓ cup (80 mL) apricot or peach preserves
¼ teaspoon (1 mL) ground cinnamon

Here's a handy recipe that's really two recipes in one: a dozen brown sugar-pecan sticky buns and a delicious coffee cake topped with apricot preserves and cinnamon sugar. Both the buns and the cake are prepared from the same easy batter.

1. Fit processor with steel blade. Measure pecans and brown sugar into work bowl. Process on/off 3 or 4 times until pecans are chopped. Add ¼ cup (60 mL) of the butter to pecan mixture. Process on/off 8 to 10 times just until mixed but still crumbly. Remove mixture from work bowl and reserve.

2. Refit processor with steel blade. Measure 2 cups (500 mL) of the flour, ¼ cup (60 mL) of the granulated sugar, remaining ¼ cup (60 mL) of the butter, yeast and salt into work bowl. Process until mixed, about 15 seconds.

3. Turn on processor and add the water through feed tube to flour mixture. Process until well blended, 2 minutes.

4. Add eggs to batter. Process until blended, about 10 seconds.

5. Add remaining 1 cup (250 mL) flour to batter. Process until blended, about 20 seconds. Cover processor and let batter stand at room temperature until doubled, about 1 hour.

6. Divide pecan mixture evenly between 12 greased muffin cups, placing 1 rounded teaspoon mixture in each cup.

7. Process on/off 2 or 3 times to stir down batter. Spoon half of batter into muffin cups, using 1 rounded tablespoon (15 mL) batter per cup.

8. Pour remaining half of batter into greased 8 or 9-inch (20 or 23 cm) round cake pan. Spoon apricot preserves over cake. Mix remaining ¼ cup (60 mL) of the sugar and cinnamon. Sprinkle sugar mixture over preserves on cake.

9. Let batters stand in warm place (85°F. or 30°C.) until doubled, 30 minutes for puffs and 45 minutes for coffee cake.

10. Heat oven to 375°F. (190°C.). Bake until golden, 18 to 20 minutes for puffs and 20 to 25 minutes for coffee cake. Loosen puffs and invert immediately onto serving plate. Cool cake in pan on wire rack.

---

*Spoon flour into dry measuring cup and level off. Do not scoop.

**If dough is too dry and stiff, too soft and sticky, or if the processor shuts off, correct problem according to directions on page 25.

COFFEE CAKES

German Butterkuchen

Makes 1 coffee cake

½ cup (125 mL) cold butter
  or margarine, cut into 8
  pieces
1½ cups (375 mL) sugar
½ to 1 teaspoon (2 to 5 mL)
  ground cinnamon
¼ cup (60 mL) warm water
  (105° to 115°F. or 41° to
  46°C.)
1 package (¼ oz. or 7 g)
  active dry yeast
1 cup (250 mL) milk
¼ cup (60 mL) butter or
  margarine
1 teaspoon (5 mL) salt
3 cups (750 mL) all-purpose
  flour*
2 eggs, beaten
⅓ cup (80 mL) sliced almonds

You'll love this simple coffee cake that's prepared from an easy yeast batter. It's topped with a buttery, cinnamon streusel and a sprinkling of sliced almonds. During baking the streusel drizzles down into the cake, flavoring it richly throughout.

1. Fit processor with steel blade. Measure ½ cup (125 mL) cold butter, 1 cup (250 mL) of the sugar and cinnamon into the work bowl. Process on/off 8 to 10 times until mixture is blended but still crumbly. Remove from work bowl and reserve.

2. Combine water and yeast. Stir to dissolve yeast and let stand until bubbly, about 5 minutes.

3. Combine milk, ¼ cup (60 mL) butter, remaining ½ cup (125 mL) sugar and salt in small saucepan. Heat over low heat just until warm (105° to 115°F. or 41° to 46°C.). Butter may not melt completely. Remove from heat.

4. Refit processor with steel blade. Measure 2 cups (500 mL) of the flour into work bowl. Turn on processor and add eggs and yeast mixture through feed tube. Process until mixed, about 10 seconds.

5. Turn on processor. Add milk mixture through feed tube to flour mixture. Process until blended, about 15 seconds. Add remaining flour, ¼ cup (60 mL) at a time, processing about 5 seconds after each addition. Process until smooth, about 10 seconds longer.

6. Pour batter into a greased 13x9x2-inch (33x23x5 cm) baking pan. Let stand in warm place (85°F. or 30°C.) until doubled, about 45 minutes.

7. Heat oven to 375°F. (190°C.). Sprinkle reserved sugar mixture evenly over batter in pan. Sprinkle almonds over sugar mixture. Bake until wooden pick inserted in center comes out clean, 25 to 30 minutes. Cool in pan on wire rack.

Pecan Raisin Coffee Cake

Makes 1 coffee cake

2 cups (500 mL) all-purpose
  flour*
1 cup (250 mL) sugar
½ cup (125 mL) cold butter or
  margarine, cut into 8
  pieces
1 teaspoon (5 mL) ground
  cinnamon
½ teaspoon (2 mL) ground
  ginger
¼ teaspoon (1 mL) ground
  nutmeg
½ cup (125 mL) dark raisins
½ cup (125 mL) chopped
  pecans
⅔ cup (160 mL) buttermilk
1 egg, beaten
1 teaspoon (5 mL) baking
  powder
½ teaspoon (2 mL) baking
  soda

This will be a big favorite with almost everyone. It's an old fashioned coffee cake with a wonderful spicy crumb topping that's mixed with raisins and pecans.

1. Fit processor with steel blade. Measure flour, sugar, butter, and spices into work bowl. Process until mixture resembles cornmeal, about 15 seconds.

2. Remove 1 cup (250 mL) of the flour mixture from the work bowl. Stir raisins and pecans into the 1 cup (250 mL) flour mixture. Reserve.

3. Blend buttermilk and egg in measuring cup. Measure baking powder and soda into flour mixture remaining in processor work bowl. Turn on processor and slowly add the buttermilk mixture through feed tube to flour mixture. Process until smooth, about 10 seconds. Stop processor and scrape sides of bowl, if necessary.

4. Sprinkle ¾ cup of the reserved raisin-flour mixture evenly over bottom of greased 9-inch (23 cm) square baking pan. Pour batter evenly over raisin mixture in pan. Sprinkle remaining raisin mixture over batter in pan.

5. Heat oven to 375°F. (190°C.). Bake until wooden pick inserted in center of cake comes out clean, 35 to 40 minutes. Cool cake in pan on wire rack.

*Spoon flour into dry measuring cup and level off. Do not scoop.

Danish Wales Bread

Makes 1 coffee cake

This outstanding bread is perfect for entertaining. It's actually two breads in one: a flaky butter pastry on the bottom and a puffy cream puff pastry on top. For a pretty finish, it's covered with a simple icing and toasted almond slices.

Butter Pastry (recipe
  follows)
Cream Puff Pastry (recipe
  follows)
1   egg, beaten
4   tablespoons (60 mL) milk
2   cups (500 mL) powdered
    sugar
½   teaspoon (2 mL) almond
    extract
½   cup (125 mL) toasted,
    sliced almonds

1. Prepare Butter Pastry. Divide pastry in half. Roll out each half into a 5x15-inch (13x38 cm) rectangle. Place pastry rectangles lengthwise on a 14x17-inch (35x48 cm) cookie sheet about 2 inches (5 cm) apart. Refrigerate while preparing Cream Puff Pastry.

2. Prepare Cream Puff Pastry batter and let cool 15 minutes.

3. Mix egg and 2 tablespoons (30 mL) of the milk with a fork. Brush mixture over pastry rectangles. Divide Cream Puff Pastry in half. Spread each half evenly over a pastry rectangle. Brush with egg mixture.

4. Heat oven to 375°F. (190°C.). Bake until pastry is golden and puffy, 35 to 45 minutes.

5. Remove from cookie sheet. Cool on wire rack 10 minutes. Blend powdered sugar, remaining 2 tablespoons (30 mL) milk and almond extract. Drizzle over pastry. Sprinkle with almonds.

Butter Pastry

1½ cups (375 mL) all-purpose
    flour*
½   cup (125 mL) cold butter,
    cut into ¼-inch (0.5 cm)
    thick slices
2   tablespoons (30 mL) sugar
½   teaspoon (2 mL) salt
1   egg, beaten
1   tablespoon (15 mL) ice-cold
    water
1   tablespoon (15 mL)
    vegetable oil
1   teaspoon (5 mL) lemon
    juice

1. Fit processor with steel blade. Measure flour, butter, sugar and salt into work bowl. Process on/off twice to mix.

2. Mix egg, water, oil and lemon juice with fork. Turn on processor and pour egg mixture through feed tube into flour mixture. Process just until pastry forms a crumbly ball that cleans sides of the bowl, not more than 15 seconds.

Cream Puff Pastry

1   cup (250 mL) warm water
½   cup (125 mL) butter or
    margarine
1   teaspoon (5 mL) sugar
½   teaspoon (2 mL) salt
1   cup (250 mL) all-purpose
    flour*
4   eggs

1. Combine water, butter, sugar and salt in medium saucepan. Bring to boil over medium-high heat, stirring until butter melts. Add flour all at once. Stir vigorously until mixture is smooth and forms soft ball.

2. Fit processor with steel blade. Transfer flour mixture to work bowl.

3. Turn on processor. Add eggs, one at a time, through feed tube to flour mixture. Process until eggs are thoroughly blended into flour mixture, about 15 seconds. Let mixture stand in work bowl at room temperature at least 15 minutes to cool. (It should be stiff enough to hold its shape on a spoon.)

Cream Puffs Prepare Cream Puff Pastry batter. Drop batter by rounded tablespoonsful onto greased cookie sheet. Heat oven to 400°F. (200°C.). Bake until golden and puffy, 35 to 45 minutes. Cool. Makes 12 cream puffs.

*Spoon flour into dry measuring cup and level off. Do not scoop.

SOURDOUGH BREADS

Sourdough Starter

1 cup (250 mL) warm water (105° to 115°F. or 41° to 46°C.)
1 package (¼ oz. or 7 g) active dry yeast
½ cup (125 mL) instant nonfat dry milk solids
½ cup (125 mL) unflavored natural yogurt
1½ cups (375 mL) all-purpose flour*

We often associate sourdough breads with the Old West because of the prospectors and pioneers who carried sourdough starters with them wherever they went. But sourdoughs are probably the world's oldest bread and may date back as far as 4,000 B.C. The starter, which is a sour, fermented flour mixture, acts as the leavening in bread. The sourdough starter recipe that follows will serve you as well as the ones the Old West depended on. To keep the starter going, remember to replenish it at least once every two weeks.

1. Combine water and yeast in large glass bowl, crock or other nonmetallic container. Stir to dissolve yeast.

2. Add dry milk and yogurt to yeast mixture. Beat with whisk until blended. Add flour and beat until smooth.

3. Cover bowl tightly. Let stand in warm place (85°F. or 30°C.) until starter has developed a sour aroma and is bubbly, 24 to 36 hours. Stir occasionally.

4. Keep Starter tightly covered in refrigerator.

5. To use, stir and pour off as much as recipe requires. Replenish remaining starter by blending in equal parts of flour and milk. Cover tightly and let stand at room temperature until bubbly. Refrigerate.

Note: Starter should be used and replenished every two weeks.

Sourdough French Bread

Makes 2 loaves

½ to ¾ cup (125 to 180 mL) warm water (105° to 115°F. or 41° to 46°C.)
1 package (¼ oz. or 7 g) active dry yeast
1 tablespoon (15 mL) sugar
2¼ cups (560 mL) all-purpose flour*
1 cup (250 mL) Sourdough Starter, at room temperature
1 teaspoon (5 mL) salt
Cornmeal

This chewy bread gets its typical, slightly sour flavor from the starter. Yeast is also added to speed up the time it takes for the bread to rise. From this basic French bread, you can make a variety of breads with different shapes and flavors.

1. Combine ¼ cup (60 mL) of the warm water, yeast and sugar. Stir to dissolve yeast and let stand until bubbly, about 5 minutes.

2. Fit processor with steel blade. Measure flour, starter and salt into work bowl. Add yeast mixture and process until well blended, about 15 seconds.

3. Turn on processor and very slowly drizzle just enough remaining warm water through feed tube into flour mixture so dough forms a ball that cleans the sides of the bowl. Process until ball turns around bowl about 25 times. Turn off processor and let dough stand 1 to 2 minutes.

4. Turn on processor and gradually drizzle in enough remaining warm water to make dough soft, smooth and satiny but not sticky.** Process until dough turns around bowl about 15 times.

*Spoon flour into dry measuring cup and level off. Do not scoop.

**If dough is too dry and stiff, too soft and sticky, or if the processor shuts off, correct problem according to directions on page 25.

5. Turn dough onto lightly greased surface. Divide dough in half. Shape each half into a strand 12 to 14 inches (30 to 35 cm) long.

6. Grease a large cookie sheet and sprinkle cornmeal over it. Place strands of dough about 4 inches (10 cm) apart on cookie sheet. Cover loosely with plastic wrap and let stand in warm place (85°F. or 30°C.) 30 minutes. Uncover dough and brush water over each loaf. Let stand in warm place until doubled, 30 to 45 minutes longer.

7. Heat oven to 425°F. (220°C.). Cut 3 or 4 slashes, each about 2 inches (5 cm) long and ¼ inch (0.5 cm) deep, in top of each loaf using the processor's steel blade, sharp knife or razor blade. Brush loaves with water.

8. Bake until golden, 25 to 35 minutes. Brush or spray loaves with water 3 or 4 times during baking. (For a crisper crust, place a shallow pan of boiling water on bottom shelf of oven to create steam during baking.)

9. Remove from cookie sheet. Cool on wire rack.

Sourdough Dinner Rolls
Prepare dough as directed for Sourdough French Bread. Shape dough into strand 16 inches (40 cm) long. Cut strand into 1 inch (2.5 cm) slices. Place slices on greased cookie sheet. Brush with water. Let stand in warm place until doubled, about 45 minutes. Heat oven to 400°F. (200°C.). Cut a slash 1 inch (2.5 cm) long and ¼ (0.5 cm) deep in top of each roll. Bake until golden, 15 to 20 minutes. Brush or spray rolls with water 2 or 3 times during baking. Remove from cookie sheet. Cool on wire rack.

Sourdough Hamburger Buns
Prepare dough as directed for Sourdough French Bread. Divide dough into 8 equal parts. Shape each part into a smooth ball and place on greased cookie sheet. Flatten balls using palm of hand. Brush with water. Let stand in warm place until doubled, about 1 hour. Heat oven to 375°F. (190°C.). Brush buns with water. Bake until golden, 20 to 25 minutes. Remove from cookie sheet. Cool on wire rack.

Sourdough Bread Sticks
Prepare dough as directed for Sourdough French Bread. Divide dough in half. Divide each half into 20 equal parts. Shape each part into a strand about 6 inches (15 cm) long. Place strands about 1 inch (2.5 cm) apart on greased cookie sheets. Cover loosely with plastic wrap and let stand in warm place until doubled, about 30 minutes. Heat oven to 300°F. (150°C.). Brush strands with 1 beaten egg and sprinkle with coarse salt. Bake until crisp, 25 to 30 minutes.

Sourdough Whole Wheat Bread
Prepare dough as directed for Sourdough French Bread substituting 1 cup (250 mL) whole wheat flour for 1 cup (250 mL) of the all-purpose flour. Divide dough in half. Shape each half into smooth ball and place on greased cookie sheet. Roll or pat into circle about 6 inches (15 cm) in diameter. Cut a large cross about ¼ inch (0.5 cm) deep in top of loaf using the processor's steel blade, sharp knife or razor blade. Let rise and bake as directed for Sourdough French Bread.

Sourdough Rye Bread
Prepare dough as directed for Sourdough French Bread substituting ½ cup (125 mL) rye flour for ½ cup (125 mL) of the all-purpose flour. Shape dough into smooth ball and place on large greased cookie sheet. Roll dough out into circle 14 inches (35 cm) in diameter. Poke a hole in the center and stretch so hole is about 2 inches (5 cm) in diameter. Brush loaf with water. Let stand in warm place until doubled, about 1 hour. Heat oven to 400°F. (200°C.). Pierce loaf all over with tines of a fork. Bake until golden, 25 to 30 minutes. Remove from cookie sheet. Cool on wire rack.

SOURDOUGH BREADS

Sourdough English Muffins

Makes 1 dozen muffins

¼ cup (60 mL) warm water (105° to 115°F. or 41° to 46°C.)
1 package (¼ oz. or 7 g) active dry yeast
½ cup (125 mL) milk, at room temperature
½ cup (125 mL) Sourdough Starter, at room temperature (see Index for page number)
2 teaspoons (10 mL) sugar
½ teaspoon (2 mL) salt
2½ to 3 cups (625 to 750 mL) all-purpose flour*
Cornmeal

It's hard to resist the temptation of these fresh, hot English Muffins, split toasted and spread with melting butter. They're easy to make with a food processor, and like other sourdough breads, have just a hint of sour flavor.

1. Combine water and yeast in 2 or 3 cup (500 or 750 mL) bowl. Stir to dissolve yeast. Blend in milk, Starter, sugar and salt. Let stand until bubbly, about 5 minutes.

2. Fit processor with steel blade. Measure 1½ cups (375 mL) of the flour into work bowl. Turn on processor and add yeast mixture through feed tube to flour. Process until blended, about 15 seconds.

3. Turn on processor and add enough of the remaining flour through feed tube so dough forms a ball that cleans the sides of the bowl. Process until ball turns around bowl about 25 times.

4. Turn dough onto lightly greased surface. Shape dough into ball and place in lightly greased bowl, turning to grease all sides. Cover loosely with plastic wrap and let stand in warm place (85°F. or 30°C.) until doubled, about 1 hour.

5. Punch down dough. Grease a large cookie sheet and sprinkle generously with cornmeal. Roll out dough on lightly greased surface until about ⅜ inch (1 cm) thick. Cut with floured 3-inch (8 cm) round cookie or biscuit cutter. Place cutouts on prepared cookie sheet. Reroll and cut leftover dough. Sprinkle cutouts with cornmeal. Cover loosely with plastic wrap and let stand in warm place until doubled, about 45 minutes.

6. Heat a lightly greased, large fry pan over medium heat or an electric fry pan to 275°F. (140°C.). Cook muffins, uncovered, on each side until golden, about 10 minutes on each side.

7. Cool on wire rack. Split and toast muffins to serve.

Sourdough Pancakes

Makes 4 to 6 servings

1 cup (250 mL) all-purpose flour*
1 cup (250 mL) Sourdough Starter (see Index for page number)
1 cup (250 mL) evaporated or fresh milk
2 tablespoons (30 mL) vegetable oil or melted butter or margarine
1 tablespoon (15 mL) sugar
½ teaspoon (2 mL) baking soda
½ teaspoon (2 mL) salt
1 egg

Fresh pancakes, hot from the griddle, generously topped with melting butter and maple syrup are a great way to start any day. The batter for these sourdough cakes stands overnight to develop the flavor.

1. Fit processor with steel blade. Measure flour and starter into work bowl.

2. Turn on processor and add milk through feed tube to flour mixture. Process until smooth, about 30 seconds. Let batter stand, covered, in work bowl at room temperature 12 hours or overnight.

3. Add oil, sugar, soda, salt and egg to batter. Process until blended, about 10 seconds.

4. Heat lightly greased electric griddle to temperature specified for pancakes or heat lightly greased fry pan over medium heat until hot enough to sizzle a drop of water. Bake on both sides on hot griddle or pan using about ¼ cup (60 mL) batter for each pancake.

Sourdough Waffles Prepare batter as directed for Sourdough Pancakes. Heat electric waffle baker. Pour batter into baker. Bake until steaming stops and waffle is golden brown.

*Spoon flour into dry measuring cup and level off. Do not scoop.

Sourdough French Bread
(top), Sourdough Pancakes
(center), Sourdough
English Muffins (bottom)

Clockwise: Beer Batter Rye Bread, Honey Wheat Casserole Bread, Oatmeal Casserole Bread

Clockwise: Favorite
Bran Muffins, Banana
Nut Bread, Baking
Powder Biscuits

Clockwise: Popovers,
Raisin Bran Bread, Lemon
Nut Muffins

CASSEROLE BREADS

Quick White Casserole Bread

Makes 1 loaf

2¾ cups (680 mL) all-purpose flour*

3 tablespoons (45 mL) instant nonfat dry milk solids

2 tablespoons (30 mL) sugar

2 tablespoons (30 mL) vegetable oil

1 package (¼ oz. or 7 g) active dry yeast

1 teaspoon (5 mL) salt

1 cup (250 mL) hot water (120° to 130°F. or 49° to 54°C.)

1 tablespoon (15 mL) sesame or poppy seeds, optional

This is the fast, easy way to make tender, moist yeast bread. The ingredients are mixed into a thick batter which requires no kneading and just one rising period. When baked, the bread has a textured top crust and an interior that's a bit coarser than yeast bread made from a dough.

1. Fit processor with steel blade. Measure 1¾ cups (430 mL) of the flour, dry milk, sugar, oil, yeast and salt into work bowl. Process until mixed, about 5 seconds.

2. Turn on processor and add water all at once through feed tube to flour mixture. Process until blended, about 30 seconds.

3. Turn on processor and add remaining 1 cup (250 mL) flour, ¼ cup (60 mL) at a time. Process 5 to 10 seconds after each addition.†

4. Pour batter into greased 1½ quart (1.5 L) baking dish. Sprinkle sesame or poppy seeds over batter, if desired.

5. Let stand in warm place (85°F. or 30°C.) until almost doubled, 40 to 45 minutes.

6. Heat oven to 375°F. (190°C.). Bake until wooden pick inserted in center comes out clean, 25 to 30 minutes.

7. Cool 10 minutes. Remove from dish and cool on wire rack.

Casserole Cheese Bread Prepare batter as directed for Quick White Casserole Bread. Pour half of the batter into greased 1½ quart (1.5 L) baking dish. Sprinkle 1 cup (250 mL) cubed Cheddar or Swiss cheese over batter. Pour remaining batter over cheese. Stir to mix in cheese. Proceed with rising and baking the bread as directed for Quick White Casserole Bread.

Herbed Casserole Bread Prepare batter as directed for Quick White Casserole Bread. Add 1 tablespoon (15 mL) dried herbs such as fines herbes, Italian Herb Seasoning, oregano, basil, marjoram, parsley (or any combination) with first flour addition. Proceed with mixing, rising and baking the bread as directed for Quick White Casserole Bread.

Oatmeal Casserole Bread Prepare batter as directed for Quick White Casserole Bread, substituting 1 cup (250 mL) uncooked quick or old fashioned oats for 1 cup (250 mL) of the flour. Add oatmeal to work bowl with ¾ cup (180 mL) flour, dry milk, sugar, oil, yeast and salt. Proceed with mixing, rising and baking the bread as directed for Quick White Casserole Bread.

*Spoon flour into dry measuring cup and level off. Do not scoop.

†If food processor sounds strained and/or motor slows down or stops, turn off processor immediately and stir any remaining flour into batter by hand.

Raisin Casserole Bread

Makes 1 loaf

2 cups (500 mL) all-purpose flour*
5 tablespoons (75 mL) sugar
2 tablespoons (30 mL) butter or margarine, at room temperature
1 package (¼ oz. or 7 g) active dry yeast
1 teaspoon (5 mL) salt
⅔ cup (160 mL) milk
1 egg
½ cup (125 mL) dark raisins
¼ teaspoon (1 mL) ground cinnamon

Here's an easy way to turn out a fresh loaf of everybody's favorite bread. Topped with a sweet cinnamon crust, this tempting bread is wonderful while still warm from the oven or toasted and spread with lots of fresh butter.

1. Fit processor with steel blade. Measure 1 cup (250 mL) of the flour, 4 tablespoons (60 mL) of the sugar, butter, yeast and salt into work bowl. Process until mixed, about 10 seconds.

2. Heat milk in small saucepan over low heat until 120° to 130°F. (49° to 54°C.). Turn on processor and add milk all at once through feed tube to flour mixture. Process until blended, about 30 seconds.

3. Add egg to batter. Process until blended, about 10 seconds.

4. Add remaining 1 cup (250 mL) flour, ¼ cup (60 mL) at a time through feed tube. Process 5 to 10 seconds after each addition.†

5. Sprinkle raisins over batter in work bowl. Process just until raisins are mixed in, about 5 seconds.

6. Pour batter into greased 1½ quart (1.5 L) baking dish.

7. Combine remaining 1 tablespoon (15 mL) sugar and cinnamon. Sprinkle over batter in baking dish.

8. Let stand in warm place (85°F. or 30°C.) until doubled, 1 to 1¼ hours.

9. Heat oven to 350°F. (180°C.). Bake until wooden pick or cake tester inserted in center comes out clean, about 30 minutes.

10. Cool 10 minutes. Remove bread from baking dish and cool on wire rack.

Honey Wheat Casserole Bread

Makes 1 loaf

1½ cups (375 mL) all-purpose flour*
1 cup (250 mL) whole wheat flour
3 tablespoons (45 mL) instant nonfat dry milk solids
2 tablespoons (30 mL) honey
2 tablespoons (30 mL) vegetable oil
1 package (¼ oz. or 7 g) active dry yeast
1 teaspoon (5 mL) salt
1 cup (250 mL) hot water (120° to 130°F. or 49° to 54°C.)
1 tablespoon (15 mL) wheat germ, optional

Honey and whole wheat flour flavor this easy, tasty bread that can be prepared and served in about 90 minutes.

1. Fit processor with steel blade. Measure ½ cup (125 mL) of the all-purpose flour, whole wheat flour, dry milk, honey, oil, yeast and salt into work bowl. Process until mixed, about 5 seconds.

2. Turn on processor and add water all at once through feed tube to flour mixture. Process until blended, about 30 seconds.

3. Turn on processor and add remaining 1 cup (250 mL) flour, ¼ cup (60 mL) at a time through feed tube. Process 5 to 10 seconds after each addition.†

4. Pour batter into greased 1½ quart (1.5 L) baking dish. Sprinkle wheat germ over batter, if desired.

5. Let stand in warm place (85°F. or 30°C.) until almost doubled, about 45 minutes.

6. Heat oven to 375°F. (190°C.). Bake until wooden pick or cake tester inserted in center comes out clean, 25 to 30 minutes.

7. Cool 10 minutes. Remove bread from baking dish and cool on wire rack.

---

*Spoon flour into dry measuring cup and level off. Do not scoop.

†If food processor sounds strained and/or motor slows down or stops, turn off processor immediately and stir any remaining flour into batter by hand.

Sally Lunn Bread

Makes 1 loaf

½ cup (125 mL) milk
¼ cup (60 mL) butter or margarine, cut into 4 pieces
2 teaspoons (10 mL) vinegar
2½ cups (625 mL) all-purpose flour*
¼ cup (60 mL) packed light brown sugar
1 package (¼ oz. or 7 g) active dry yeast
1 teaspoon (5 mL) salt
2 eggs

Using a food processor is the modern way to prepare this English bread that's been popular for several hundred years.

1. Combine milk, butter and vinegar in small saucepan. Heat over low heat until 120° to 130°F. (49° to 54°C.). Butter may not melt completely. Reserve.

2. Fit processor with steel blade. Measure 1½ cups (375 mL) of the flour, brown sugar, yeast and salt into work bowl. Process until mixed, about 5 seconds.

3. Turn on processor. Add eggs and milk mixture all at once through feed tube to flour mixture. Process until blended, about 30 seconds.

4. Turn on processor and add remaining 1 cup (250 mL) flour, ¼ cup (60 mL) at a time through feed tube. Process 5 to 10 seconds after each addition.†

5. Pour batter into large lightly greased mixing bowl. Cover loosely with plastic wrap and let stand in warm place (85°F. or 30°C.) until doubled, about 2 hours.

6. Stir down batter and pour into greased 1½ quart (1.5 L) baking dish. Let stand in warm place until almost doubled, about 45 minutes.

7. Heat oven to 375°F. (190°C.). Bake until wooden pick or cake tester inserted in center comes out clean, 30 to 35 minutes.

8. Cool 10 minutes. Remove bread from baking dish and cool on wire rack.

Bacon Potato Casserole Bread

Makes 1 loaf

2¼ cups (560 mL) all-purpose flour*
3 tablespoons (45 mL) instant nonfat dry milk solids
3 tablespoons (45 mL) instant mashed potato flakes
3 tablespoons (45 mL) bacon flavored bits
1 tablespoon (15 mL) sugar
1 tablespoon (15 mL) instant minced onions
1 package (¼ oz. or 7 g) active dry yeast
1 teaspoon (5 mL) garlic salt
1 cup (250 mL) hot water (120° to 130°F. or 49° to 54°C.)

This tender bread is robustly flavored with potato, bacon flavored bits, onion and garlic salt. It's good as a soup or salad accompaniment or with most roasted meats and poultry.

1. Fit processor with steel blade. Measure 1¼ cups (310 mL) of the flour and all remaining ingredients except the water into work bowl. Process until mixed, about 5 seconds.

2. Turn on processor and add water all at once through feed tube to flour mixture. Process until blended, about 30 seconds.

3. Turn on processor and add remaining 1 cup (250 mL) flour, ¼ cup (60 mL) at a time through feed tube. Process 5 to 10 seconds after each addition.†

4. Pour batter into greased 1½ quart (1.5 L) baking dish.

5. Let stand in warm place (85°F. or 30°C.) until almost doubled, about 45 minutes.

6. Heat oven to 350°F. (180°C.). Bake until wooden pick or cake tester inserted in center comes out clean, about 30 minutes.

7. Cool 10 minutes. Remove bread from baking dish and cool on wire rack.

---

*Spoon flour into dry measuring cup and level off. Do not scoop.

†If food processor sounds strained and/or motor slows down or stops, turn off processor immediately and stir any remaining flour into batter by hand.

CASSEROLE BREADS

Beer Batter Rye Bread

Makes 1 loaf

2 cups (500 mL) all-purpose flour*

½ cup (125 mL) rye flour

2 tablespoons (30 mL) molasses or packed brown sugar

2 tablespoons (30 mL) vegetable oil

1 tablespoon (15 mL) caraway seeds

1 package (¼ oz. or 7 g) active dry yeast

1 teaspoon (5 mL) salt

1 cup (250 mL) beer

This hardy batter bread is prepared with beer, rye flour, molasses and caraway seeds. It's good with roasted or barbecued meats and is great for sandwich making.

1. Fit processor with steel blade. Measure 1 cup (250 mL) of the all-purpose flour, rye flour, molasses, oil, caraway seeds, yeast and salt into work bowl. Process until mixed, about 5 seconds.

2. Heat beer in small saucepan over low heat until 120° to 130°F. (49° to 54°C.). Turn on processor and add beer all at once through feed tube to flour mixture. Process until blended, about 30 seconds.

3. Turn on processor and add remaining 1 cup (250 mL) flour, ¼ cup (60 mL) at a time through feed tube. Process 5 to 10 seconds after each addition.†

4. Pour batter into greased 1½ quart (1.5 L) baking dish.

5. Let stand in warm place (85°F. or 30°C.) until almost doubled, about 45 minutes.

6. Heat oven to 350°F. (180°C.). Bake until wooden pick inserted in center comes out clean, about 30 minutes.

7. Cool 10 minutes. Remove bread from baking dish and cool on wire rack.

Dilly Casserole Bread

Makes 1 loaf

2½ cups (625 mL) all-purpose flour*

2 tablespoons (30 mL) sugar

1 tablespoon (15 mL) instant minced onions

1 tablespoon (15 mL) butter or margarine

1 package (¼ oz. or 7 g) active dry yeast

1 teaspoon (5 mL) salt

1 teaspoon (5 mL) dill weed

1 cup (250 mL) creamed cottage cheese

½ cup (125 mL) hot water (120° to 130°F. or 49° to 54°C.)

1 egg

Cottage cheese makes this yeast bread moist and creamy. Dill weed and onion provide pleasantly mild seasoning.

1. Fit processor with steel blade. Measure 1½ cups (375 mL) of the flour, sugar, onions, butter, yeast, salt and dill weed into work bowl. Process until mixed, about 5 seconds.

2. Add cottage cheese to flour mixture. Process until blended, about 10 seconds.

3. Turn on processor and add water all at once through feed tube to flour mixture. Process until blended, about 20 seconds.

4. Add egg to batter. Process until blended, about 10 seconds.

5. Turn on processor and add remaining 1 cup (250 mL) flour, ¼ cup (60 mL) at a time through feed tube. Process 5 to 10 seconds after each addition.†

6. Pour batter into greased 1½ quart (1.5 L) baking dish.

7. Let stand in warm place (85°F. or 30°C.) until almost doubled, about 1¼ hours.

8. Heat oven to 350°F. (180°C.). Bake until wooden pick or cake tester inserted in center comes out clean, 35 to 40 minutes.

9. Cool 10 minutes. Remove bread from baking dish and cool on wire rack.

*Spoon flour into dry measuring cup and level off. Do not scoop.

†If food processor sounds strained and/or motor slows down or stops, turn off processor immediately and stir any remaining flour into batter by hand.

Kugelhoff

Makes 1 loaf

¼ cup (60 mL) warm water (105° to 115°F. or 41° to 46°C.)

1 package (¼ oz. or 7 g) active dry yeast

½ cup (125 mL) milk, at room temperature

½ cup (125 mL) butter or margarine, melted and cooled

½ cup (125 mL) granulated sugar

2 pieces pared lemon rind (each 1½x¼ inches or 4x0.5 cm)

2½ cups (625 mL) all-purpose flour*

½ teaspoon (2 mL) salt

2 eggs

½ cup (125 mL) dark raisins or currants

⅓ cup (80 mL) dry cake or cookie crumbs, optional
Sliced almonds, optional
Powdered sugar

This European batter bread (also spelled Kugelhupf) is actually a sweet coffee cake. The batter, rich in butter, sugar and eggs, is baked in a molded or tubed pan for a pretty effect.

1. Combine water and yeast. Stir to dissolve yeast and let stand until bubbly, about 5 minutes. Blend milk and melted butter into yeast mixture.

2. Fit processor with steel blade. Add granulated sugar and lemon rind to work bowl. Process until rind is minced, about 1 minute.

3. Add 1½ cups (375 mL) of the flour and salt to lemon-sugar. Process until mixed, about 5 seconds.

4. Turn on processor and add yeast mixture all at once through feed tube to flour mixture. Process until blended, about 20 seconds.

5. Add eggs to batter. Process until blended, about 10 seconds.

6. Turn on processor and add remaining 1 cup (250 mL) of the flour, ¼ cup (60 mL) at a time to batter. Process 5 to 10 seconds after each addition. †

7. Sprinkle raisins over batter in work bowl. Process just until raisins are mixed in, about 5 seconds.

8. Cover processor and let batter stand at room temperature in work bowl until almost doubled, 1 to 1¼ hours. Process on/off once or twice to beat down batter.

9. Grease a 1-quart (1 L) mold or 7-inch (18 cm) diameter tube pan. Sprinkle crumbs into pan, if desired, and turn pan to coat evenly. Arrange sliced almonds in pan, if desired, in fancy pattern. Pour batter evenly into prepared pan. Cover and let stand in warm place (85°F. or 30°C.) until doubled, about 45 minutes.

10. Heat oven to 350°C. (180°C.). Bake until wooden pick or cake tester inserted in center comes out clean, 40 to 50 minutes. (If bread browns too quickly, cover loosely with aluminum foil.)

11. Remove immediately from pan and cool on wire rack. Sprinkle powdered sugar over bread.

Bean Pot Bread

Makes 1 loaf

½ cup (125 mL) warm water (105° to 115°F. or 41° to 46°C.)

2 tablespoons (30 mL) sugar

1 package (¼ oz. or 7 g) active dry yeast

2½ cups (625 mL) all-purpose flour*

1 tablespoon (15 mL) instant minced onions

1 tablespoon (15 mL) butter or margarine

1 can (11½ oz. or 326 g) condensed bean with bacon soup

1 egg

If you like bean soup, you'll love this bread. It's prepared with canned bean with bacon soup and that's what gives it its distinctive flavor.

1. Combine water, sugar and yeast. Stir to dissolve yeast and let stand until bubbly, about 5 minutes.

2. Fit processor with steel blade. Measure 1½ cups (375 mL) of the flour, onions and butter into work bowl. Process until mixed, about 5 seconds.

3. Add soup to flour mixture. Process until blended, about 10 seconds.

4. Turn on processor. Add egg and yeast mixture all at once through feed tube to flour mixture. Process until blended, about 30 seconds.

5. Turn on processor and add remaining 1 cup (250 mL) flour, ¼ cup (60 mL) at a time through feed tube. Process 5 to 10 seconds after each addition. †

6. Pour batter into greased 1½ quart (1.5 L) baking dish.   *continued*

*Spoon flour into dry measuring cup and level off. Do not scoop.

†If food processor sounds strained and/or motor slows down or stops, turn off processor immediately and stir any remaining flour into batter by hand.

7. Let stand in warm place (85°F. or 30°C.) until almost doubled, about 45 minutes.

8. Heat oven to 375°F (190°C.). Bake until wooden pick or cake tester inserted in center comes out clean, 25 to 30 minutes.

9. Cool 10 minutes. Remove bread from baking dish and cool on wire rack.

Savarin

Makes 1 loaf

¼	cup (60 mL) warm water (105° to 115°F. or 41° to 46°C.)
1	package (¼ oz. or 7 g) active dry yeast
½	cup (125 mL) sugar
2	tablespoons (30 mL) milk
1	tablespoon (15 mL) rum or 1 teaspoon (5 mL) rum extract
2	eggs, beaten
2	cups (500 mL) all-purpose flour*
¼	cup (60 mL) cold butter or margarine, cut into 4 pieces
1	teaspoon (5 mL) grated lemon rind
¼	teaspoon (1 mL) salt Savarin Syrup (recipe follows)

In France this cake-like bread is served as a fancy dessert. It's made from a sweet batter, rich in eggs and butter, and baked in a fancy mold or tube pan. Immediately after baking, it's drenched with a hot orange syrup that soaks into the bread. Change the shape of the bread and the flavor of the syrup and you have Rum Babas.

1. Combine water and yeast. Stir to dissolve yeast. Blend sugar, milk, rum and eggs into yeast mixture. Let stand 5 minutes.

2. Fit processor with steel blade. Measure 1 cup (250 mL) of the flour, butter, lemon rind and salt into work bowl. Process until mixed, about 15 seconds.

3. Turn on processor and pour yeast mixture through feed tube into flour mixture. Process until smooth, about 45 seconds.

4. Turn on processor and add remaining 1 cup (250 mL) of the flour, ¼ cup (60 mL) at a time to batter. Process 5 to 10 seconds after each addition. †

5. Pour batter into large bowl. Cover loosely with plastic wrap and let stand in warm place (85°F. or 30°C.) until doubled, 1 to 1¼ hours.

6. Stir down batter and spoon into a well greased 5-cup (1250 mL) tube-type mold. Cover loosely with plastic wrap and let stand in warm place until almost doubled, about 45 minutes.

7. Heat oven to 375°F. (190°C.). Bake until wooden pick or cake tester inserted in center comes out clean, 30 to 35 minutes.

8. Prepare Savarin Syrup while bread is baking.

9. Remove bread from oven and place pan on wire rack. Drizzle hot Savarin Syrup evenly over hot bread. Cool bread in pan on wire rack. Turn out of pan when cooled.

Rum Babas Prepare batter as directed for Savarin through first rising. Stir down batter and spoon into 12 small greased Rum Baba molds or 6 ounce (170 g) custard cups. Let stand in warm place until almost doubled, about 30 minutes. Heat oven to 375°F. (190°C.). Bake until golden, 15 to 20 minutes. Prepare Savarin Syrup while Babas are baking, omitting the orange rind and substituting dark rum for the orange flavored liqueur. Pour syrup over babas and let cool in molds. Remove from molds to serve.

Savarin Syrup

1	cup (250 mL) sugar Rind of ½ an orange, pared into 1 inch (2.5 cm) pieces
½	cup (125 mL) water
¼	cup (60 mL) orange flavored liqueur

1. Fit processor with steel blade. Place sugar and orange rind in work bowl. Process until rind is minced, about 1 minute.

2. Place orange mixture in small saucepan. Add water and bring to boil. Cook over medium heat until sugar is completely dissolved, 20 to 25 minutes.

3. Remove from heat. Blend in liqueur.

*Spoon flour into dry measuring cup and level off. Do not scoop.

†If food processor sounds strained and/or motor slows down or stops, turn off processor immediately and stir any remaining flour into batter by hand.

QUICK BREADS

Muffins

Makes 12 small or 9 large muffins

1¾ cups (430 mL) all-purpose flour*
⅓ cup (80 mL) sugar
2 teaspoons (10 mL) baking powder
½ teaspoon (2 mL) salt
¼ cup (60 mL) cold butter or margarine, cut into 4 pieces
½ cup (125 mL) milk
1 egg, beaten

Homemade muffins fresh from the oven are a treat with any meal. With a food processor, they take just seconds to prepare. Process only until flour is moistened and batter is lumpy, and your muffins will be rounded, tender and tunnel-free.

1. Heat oven to 400°F. (200°C.).

2. Fit processor with steel blade. Measure flour, sugar, baking powder and salt into work bowl. Process on/off to mix.

3. Add butter to flour mixture. Process on/off 8 to 10 times or until mixture resembles coarse crumbs.

4. Combine milk and egg. Pour mixture over flour mixture. Process on/off 5 or 6 times or just until flour is moistened. Do not overprocess. Batter should be lumpy.

5. Spoon batter into greased muffin cups, filling each about ⅔ full. Bake until golden, 20 to 25 minutes. Serve hot.

Blueberry Muffins Prepare batter as directed for Muffins, increasing sugar to ½ cup (125 mL). Gently fold 1 cup (250 mL) fresh or thawed frozen blueberries or ¾ cup (180 mL) well drained canned blueberries into batter just before spooning into muffin cups. Bake as directed for Muffins.

Date or Raisin Muffins Prepare batter as directed for Muffins, adding 1 cup (250 mL) chopped, pitted dates or dark raisins to flour mixture before adding milk and egg. Process on/off, then add milk and egg. Continue as directed for Muffins.

Lemon Nut Muffins Add 1 cup (250 mL) chopped nuts and 2 teaspoons (10 mL) grated lemon rind to flour mixture before adding milk and egg. Process on/off, then add milk and egg. Continue as directed for Muffins.

Cinnamon Surprise Muffins Prepare batter as directed, adding ¼ teaspoon (1 mL) ground cinnamon to work bowl with flour, sugar, baking powder and salt. Fill muffin cups half full of batter, then drop 1 teaspoon (5 mL) fruit jelly, jam or preserves in center of batter in each cup. Cover with remaining batter. Bake as directed for Muffins.

*Spoon flour into dry measuring cup and level off. Do not scoop.

QUICK BREADS

Favorite Bran Muffins

Makes 12 small or 9 large muffins

1½ cups (375 mL) whole bran cereal

1¼ cups (310 mL) milk

¼ cup (60 mL) cold butter or margarine, cut into 4 pieces

1 egg

1¼ cups (310 mL) all-purpose flour*

1 cup (250 mL) chopped nuts, dates or raisins, optional

½ cup (125 mL) sugar

1 tablespoon (15 mL) baking powder

½ teaspoon (2 mL) salt

These classic muffins have been a favorite on breakfast tables across the country for years. With a food processor, they're so easy to make that you will want to serve them often.

1. Heat oven to 400°F. (200°C.).

2. Fit processor with steel blade. Measure cereal, milk, butter and egg into work bowl. Process on/off 3 or 4 times to mix. Let stand 5 minutes.

3. Add flour, nuts, if desired, sugar, baking powder and salt to cereal mixture. Process on/off 2 or 3 times, or just until flour is moistened. Do not overprocess. Batter should be lumpy.

4. Spoon batter into greased muffin cups, filling each about ¾ full. Bake until golden, 20 to 25 minutes.

Whole Wheat Muffins

Makes 12 small or 9 large muffins

¾ cup (180 mL) all-purpose flour*

¾ cup (180 mL) whole wheat flour

2 teaspoons (10 mL) baking powder

½ teaspoon (2 mL) salt

1 egg

½ cup (125 mL) packed brown sugar

½ cup (125 mL) milk

¼ cup (60 mL) vegetable oil

Great for breakfast or brunch, these sweet muffins have a slightly nutty flavor from the whole wheat flour. Serve them hot with plenty of fresh butter.

1. Heat oven to 375°F. (190°C.).

2. Fit processor with steel blade. Measure flours, baking powder and salt into work bowl. Process on/off to mix.

3. Beat egg with fork in bowl. Blend sugar, milk and oil into egg.

4. Pour egg mixture over flour mixture. Process on/off 2 or 3 times, or just until flour is moistened. Do not overprocess. Batter should be lumpy.

5. Spoon batter into greased muffin cups, filling each about ⅔ full. Bake until golden, 20 to 25 minutes.

Scones

Makes 8 scones

2½ cups (625 mL) all-purpose flour*

5 tablespoons (75 mL) sugar

2 teaspoons (10 mL) baking powder

½ teaspoon (2 mL) salt

½ teaspoon (2 mL) baking soda

½ cup (125 mL) cold butter or margarine, cut into 8 pieces

⅓ cup (80 mL) milk

2 eggs, beaten

Scones are a variation of a biscuit. The addition of sugar and egg to the dough makes them sweeter, richer and more cake like. They're delicious hot with butter and jelly or jam for breakfast, brunch or a snack.

1. Heat oven to 400°F. (200°C.).

2. Fit processor with steel blade. Measure flour, 4 tablespoons (60 mL) of the sugar, baking powder, salt and baking soda into work bowl. Process on/off to mix.

3. Add butter to flour mixture. Process until mixture resembles coarse crumbs, about 10 seconds.

4. Combine milk and eggs. Remove 1 tablespoon (15 mL) of the mixture and reserve. Pour remaining milk mixture over flour mixture. Process on/off 6 to 8 times, or just until flour is blended in and dough is soft.

continued

*Spoon flour into dry measuring cup and level off. Do not scoop.

152

Scones (continued)

5. Turn dough onto lightly floured surface. Shape into ball and place on ungreased cookie sheet. Roll or pat into a circle 8 inches (20 cm) in diameter. Cut dough into 8 wedges, using long sharp knife. Leave wedges in place, keeping circle intact.

6. Brush reserved egg-milk mixture over dough. Sprinkle remaining 1 tablespoon (15 mL) of the sugar over dough.

7. Bake until golden, 20 to 25 minutes.

8. Remove from cookie sheet. Cool on wire rack. Pull wedges apart to serve.

Whole Wheat Scones Prepare dough as directed for Scones, replacing the all-purpose flour with 2¼ cups (560 mL) whole wheat flour. Continue mixing, shaping and baking as directed for Scones.

Makes 1 large or 3 small loaves

Quick Pumpkin Bread

1 cup (250 mL) granulated or packed light brown sugar

⅓ cup (80 mL) cold butter or margarine, cut into 5 pieces

2 eggs

1 cup (250 mL) canned pumpkin

1½ cups (375 mL) all-purpose flour*

½ cup (125 mL) whole wheat flour

1½ teaspoons (7 mL) pumpkin pie spice

1 teaspoon (5 mL) baking soda

¾ teaspoon (4 mL) salt

½ teaspoon (2 mL) baking powder

¼ teaspoon (1 mL) ground cardamom, optional

½ cup (125 mL) dark raisins or chopped, pitted dates

½ cup (125 mL) chopped pecans or walnuts

Sweet and spicy, this bread has all the old fashioned flavor of pumpkin pie. Chopped nuts and raisins or dates add more good taste and texture.

1. Heat oven to 350°F. (180°C.).

2. Fit processor with steel blade. Measure sugar and butter into work bowl. Process until smooth, about 10 seconds.

3. Turn on processor and add eggs one at a time through feed tube to sugar mixture.

4. Add pumpkin, flours, pie spice, soda, salt, baking powder and cardamom, if desired, to sugar mixture. Process just until flour is moistened, about 5 seconds.

5. Sprinkle raisins or dates and nuts over batter. Process on/off 2 or 3 times or just until raisins and nuts are mixed into batter.

6. Turn batter into greased 9x5x3-inch (23x13x8 cm) loaf pan or 3 greased 5¾x3¼x2-inch (15x8.5x5 cm) loaf pans. Bake until wooden pick or cake tester inserted in center comes out clean, about 1 hour for larger loaf or 30 to 35 minutes for smaller loaves.

7. Cool bread 15 minutes in pan. Remove from pan and cool on wire rack.

Note: Whole wheat flour may be omitted, if desired, and a total of 2 cups (250 mL) all-purpose flour used instead.

---

*Spoon flour into dry measuring cup and level off. Do not scoop.

QUICK BREADS

Date Nut Bread

Makes 1 loaf

1½ cups (375 mL) water
1½ cups (375 mL) coarsely chopped, pitted dates
½ cup (125 mL) packed light brown sugar
2 tablespoons (30 mL) butter or margarine, at room temperature
1 egg
2½ cups (625 mL) all-purpose flour*
1 cup (250 mL) chopped pecans or walnuts
1 teaspoon (5 mL) baking soda
½ teaspoon (2 mL) salt

Extra moist, this classic quick bread is a favorite all year around, especially during the holidays.

1. Bring water to a boil in small saucepan. Stir in dates. Remove from heat and cool until lukewarm (about 110°F. or 43°C.).

2. Heat oven to 350°F. (180°C.).

3. Fit processor with steel blade. Measure brown sugar and butter into work bowl. Process on/off 3 or 4 times to mix.

4. Add egg to sugar mixture. Process until smooth, about 10 seconds.

5. Add date mixture to sugar mixture. Process on/off 4 or 5 times.

6. Add flour, nuts, baking soda and salt to date mixture. Process on/off 8 to 10 times or just until flour is moistened. Do not overprocess. Batter should be lumpy.

7. Pour batter into greased 9x5x3-inch (23x13x8 cm) loaf pan. Bake until wooden pick or cake tester inserted in center comes out clean, about 1¼ hours. (If bread browns too quickly, cover loosely with aluminum foil during last 15 to 20 minutes of baking.)

8. Cool bread 15 minutes in pan. Remove from pan and cool on wire rack.

Banana Nut Bread

Makes 1 loaf

2 ripe medium-sized bananas, peeled and cut into 1 inch (2.5 cm) pieces
1 tablespoon (15 mL) lemon juice
½ cup (125 mL) chopped pecans or walnuts
1¾ cup (430 mL) all-purpose flour*
⅔ cup (160 mL) sugar
½ cup (125 mL) butter or margarine, at room temperature, cut into 8 pieces
⅓ cup (80 mL) milk
2 eggs
1 teaspoon (5 mL) baking soda
½ teaspoon (2 mL) salt

This classic quick bread is incredibly easy to prepare with a food processor. First mash the bananas for a few seconds, then add all the remaining ingredients, process a few seconds longer, then bake.

1. Heat oven to 350°F. (180°C.).

2. Fit processor with steel blade. Place bananas and lemon juice in work bowl. Process until bananas are mashed, about 5 seconds.

3. Add ¼ cup (60 mL) of the nuts and all remaining ingredients to banana mixture. Process on/off 10 to 12 times, or just until flour is moistened. Do not overprocess. Batter should be lumpy.

4. Pour batter into greased 8½x4½x2½-inch (21.5x11.5x6.5 cm) loaf pan. Sprinkle remaining ¼ cup (60 mL) of the nuts over batter. Bake until wooden pick or cake tester inserted in center comes out clean, 55 to 65 minutes.

5. Cool bread 15 minutes in pan. Remove from pan and cool on wire rack.

*Spoon flour into dry measuring cup and level off. Do not scoop.

Cranberry Nut Bread

Makes 1 loaf

1½ cups (375 mL) fresh whole cranberries

1 cup (250 mL) broken pecans or walnuts

1 cup (250 mL) sugar

6 pieces (each about 1x½ inch or 2.5x1.5 cm) pared orange rind

2 cups (500 mL) all-purpose flour*

¼ cup (60 mL) cold butter or margarine, cut into 4 pieces

1½ teaspoons (7 mL) baking powder

½ teaspoon (2 mL) salt

½ teaspoon (2 mL) baking soda

¾ cup (180 mL) orange juice

1 egg, beaten

Cranberries, orange and nuts flavor this holiday favorite. For easier slicing, bake the bread the day before serving..

1. Heat oven to 350°F. (180°C.).

2. Fit processor with steel blade. Place cranberries and nuts in the work bowl. Process on/off 12 to 14 times or until coarsely chopped. Remove from work bowl and reserve.

3. Refit processor with steel blade. Add sugar and orange rind to work bowl. Process until rind is minced, about 1 minute.

4. Add flour, butter, baking powder, salt and baking soda to sugar mixture. Process until mixed, about 15 seconds.

5. Combine orange juice and egg. Pour over flour mixture. Process on/off 3 times.

6. Add cranberry-nut mixture to batter. Process on/off 8 to 10 times, or just until cranberry mixture is blended into batter. Do not overprocess. Batter should be lumpy.

7. Pour batter into greased 9x5x3-inch (23x13x8 cm) loaf pan. Bake until wooden pick or cake tester inserted in center comes out clean, 60 to 70 minutes.

8. Cool bread 15 minutes in pan. Remove from pan and cool on wire rack.

Zucchini Nut Bread

Makes 1 large or 2 small loaves

2 eggs

½ cup (125 mL) vegetable oil

1½ cups (375 mL) all-purpose flour*

1 cup (250 mL) chopped nuts or ½ cup (125 mL) each raisins and nuts

1 cup (250 mL) shredded zucchini

¾ cup (180 mL) sugar

1½ teaspoons (7 mL) ground cinnamon

1 teaspoon (5 mL) baking soda

1 teaspoon (5 mL) vanilla

½ teaspoon (2 mL) salt

½ teaspoon (2 mL) baking powder

When zucchini is abundant, it finds its way into all kinds of foods, such as this delicious, moist nut bread. A bit of cinnamon adds just the right spiciness.

1. Heat oven to 375°F. (190°C.).

2. Fit processor with steel blade. Measure all ingredients into the work bowl. Process just until flour is moistened, 5 to 10 seconds. Do not overprocess. Batter should be lumpy.

3. Pour batter into greased 8½x4½x2½-inch (21.5x11.5x6.5 cm) loaf pan or 2 greased 5¾x3¼x2-inch (15x8.5x5 cm) loaf pans. Bake until wooden pick or cake tester inserted in center comes out clean, about 1 hour for larger loaf or 30 to 35 minutes for smaller loaves.

4. Cool bread 15 minutes in pan. Remove from pan and cool on wire rack.

*Spoon flour into dry measuring cup and level off. Do not scoop.

QUICK BREADS

Raisin Bran Bread

1	cup (250 mL) all-purpose flour*
1	cup (250 mL) whole wheat flour
½	cup (125 mL) packed brown sugar
¼	cup (60 mL) wheat germ
1	tablespoon (15 mL) baking powder
1	teaspoon (5 mL) ground cinnamon
½	teaspoon (2 mL) salt
2	eggs
1¼	cups (310 mL) milk
2	tablespoons (30 mL) light molasses
2	tablespoons (30 mL) butter or margarine, melted
1½	cups (375 mL) whole bran cereal
½	cup (125 mL) dark raisins

This delicious loaf is a favorite of many, especially those who are fond of health foods. It's made with many of the health food staples: whole wheat flour, wheat germ, whole bran cereal, raisins, brown sugar and molasses.

1. Heat oven to 350°F. (180°C.).

2. Fit processor with steel blade. Measure flours, sugar, wheat germ, baking powder, cinnamon and salt into work bowl. Process until mixed, about 5 seconds.

3. Beat eggs with fork or whisk in large bowl.

4. Blend milk, molasses and butter into eggs. Stir in cereal and let stand about 2 minutes.

5. Pour bran mixture over flour mixture. Process on/off 5 times. Sprinkle raisins over batter. Process on/off 5 more times, or just until flour is moistened. Do not overprocess. Batter should be lumpy.

6. Pour batter into greased 8½x4½x2½-inch (21.5x11.5x6.5 cm) loaf pan. Bake until wooden pick or cake tester inserted in center comes out clean, 60 to 70 minutes.

7. Cool bread 15 minutes in pan. Remove from pan and cool on wire rack.

Makes 1 loaf

Pineapple Bran Bread

⅔	cup (180 mL) whole bran cereal
1	can (8 oz. or 225 g) crushed pineapple in syrup
½	cup (125 mL) sugar
½	cup (125 mL) milk
1	egg
2¼	cups (560 mL) all-purpose flour*
½	cup (125 mL) chopped walnuts or pecans
3	tablespoons (45 mL) butter or margarine, at room temperature
2	teaspoons (10 mL) baking powder
1	teaspoon (5 mL) salt
½	teaspoon (2 mL) baking soda

Crushed pineapple, bran cereal and chopped nuts flavor this delicious quick bread. Serve it fresh or slice and toast it the next day.

1. Heat oven to 350°F. (180°C.).

2. Fit processor with steel blade. Place cereal and pineapple in work bowl. Process on/off to mix.

3. Add sugar, milk and egg to cereal mixture. Process on/off to mix.

4. Add all remaining ingredients to cereal mixture. Process on/off 8 to 10 times, or just until flour is moistened. Do not overprocess. Batter should be lumpy.

5. Pour batter into greased 9x5x3-inch (23x13x8 cm) loaf pan. Bake until wooden pick or cake tester inserted in center comes out clean, about 1¼ hours.

6. Cool bread 15 minutes in pan. Remove from pan and cool on wire rack.

---

*Spoon flour into dry measuring cup and level off. Do not scoop.

Baking Powder Biscuits

Makes 1 dozen biscuits

- 2¼ cups (560 mL) all-purpose flour*
- 1 tablespoon (15 mL) baking powder
- ½ teaspoon (2 mL) salt
- ¼ cup (60 mL) cold butter or margarine, cut into 4 pieces
- ¾ cup (180 mL) milk

These basic biscuits are best hot from the oven served with fresh butter, honey or jam. The secret to getting them tender, light and flaky is to process the dough just until the flour is moistened.

1. Heat oven to 450°F. (230°C.).

2. Fit processor with steel blade. Measure flour, baking powder and salt into work bowl. Process on/off to mix.

3. Add butter to flour mixture. Process until mixture resembles coarse crumbs, about 10 seconds.

4. Pour milk over flour mixture. Process on/off 6 to 8 times, or just until flour is blended in and dough is soft.

5. Turn dough onto lightly floured surface. Knead gently 6 to 8 times. Roll or pat dough out until ½ inch (1.5 cm) thick.

6. Cut dough into 2½-inch (6.5 cm) circles using floured cutter.

7. Place biscuits on ungreased cookie sheet. Bake until golden, 12 to 15 minutes.

Shortcake Biscuits Heat oven to 400°F. (200°C.). Prepare dough as directed for Baking Powder Biscuits, reducing milk to ¼ cup (60 mL) and adding 2 beaten eggs. Add ¼ cup (60 mL) sugar to flour mixture. Combine milk and eggs and pour over flour-butter mixture. Continue mixing, kneading, and cutting as directed for Baking Powder Biscuits. Brush tops of biscuits with egg white, then sprinkle with sugar. Bake 15 to 20 minutes.

Popovers

Makes 6 large or 12 small muffins

- 1 cup (250 mL) all-purpose flour*
- 1 cup (250 mL) milk
- 1 tablespoon (15 mL) butter or margarine, at room temperature
- ½ teaspoon (2 mL) salt
- 3 eggs

In just minutes you can make the batter for these crispy Popovers. They "pop" because of the eggs and high ratio of liquid which creates steam inside the little breads during baking.

1. Heat oven to 375°F. (190°C.). Grease and flour 12 muffin cups or six 6 ounce (170 g) custard cups.

2. Fit processor with steel blade. Add all ingredients to the work bowl. Process 2½ minutes continuously.

3. Pour batter into prepared muffin or custard cups, filling each about ¾ full. Bake until dark brown and crispy, 45 to 50 minutes. Serve immediately.

Cheese Popovers Prepare batter as directed for Popovers, substituting ½ teaspoon (2 mL) garlic salt for salt. After processing batter 2½ minutes, stop processor and add ½ cup (125 mL) shredded Cheddar or Swiss cheese to batter. Process on/off twice to mix. Pour batter into cups and bake as directed for Popovers.

*Spoon flour into dry measuring cup and level off. Do not scoop.

INDEX

INDEX